PSYCHOTHERAPY RESEARCH AND PRACTICE

PSYCHOTHERAPY RESEARCH AND PRACTICE

BRIDGING THE GAP

EDITED BY

P. Forrest Talley
Hans H. Strupp
Stephen F. Butler

BasicBooks
A Division of HarperCollins*Publishers*

Designed by Ellen Levine

Library of Congress Cataloging-in-Publication Data

Talley, P. Forrest, 1955–
    Psychotherapy research and practice : bridging the gap / P. Forrest Talley, Hans H. Strupp, Stephen F. Butler.
        p.   cm.
    Includes bibliographical references and index.
    ISBN 0-465-06755-7
    1. Psychodynamic psychotherapy—Research. 2. Psychotherapists—Attitudes. I. Strupp, Hans H. II. Butler, Stephen F., 1950– . III. Title
RC489.P72T35 1994
616.89'14—dc20   94-8322
                                                                    CIP

94 95 96 97 ◆/HC 9 8 7 6 5 4 3 2 1

With affection we dedicate this book to our wives:
Rosalina, Lottie, and Mary Jo.

Contents

Contributors

Stephen F. Butler, Ph.D.
Director of Psychology, Brookside Hospital, Nashua, NH

John F. Clarkin, Ph.D.
Professor, Department of Psychology, Cornell University Medical College

Marshall Edelson, M.D., Ph.D.
Professor, Department of Psychiatry, Yale University School of Medicine

Robert Elliott, Ph.D.
Professor, Department of Psychology
University of Toledo

Jay Greenberg, Ph.D.
Private Practice, New York, NY

Leslie Greenberg, Ph.D.
Professor, Department of Psychology, York University

Leston Havens, Ph.D.
Professor of Psychiatry
Harvard Medical School

Mardi J. Horowitz, M.D.
Professor, Langley Porter Psychiatric Institute, University of California, San Francisco; Director, Program on Conscious and Unconscious Mental Processes, John D. and Catherine T. MacArthur Foundation

Kenneth I. Howard, PH.D.
Northwestern University

Otto F. Kernberg, M.D.
Associate Chairman and Medical Director, The New York Hospital, Cornell
University Medical Center, Westchester Division

Donald J. Kiesler, PH.D.
Professor and Director of Clinical Psychology, Department of Psychology
Virginia Commonwealth University

Lester Luborsky, PH.D.
Professor, Center for Psychotherapy Research, Department of Psychiatry,
University of Pennsylvania

Michael S. Maling, PH.D.
Northwestern University

Karla Moras, PH.D.
Assistant Professor of Psychology in Psychiatry, Department of Psychiatry,
University of Pennsylvania School of Medicine

Cheryl Morrow-Bradley, PH.D.
Adjunct Professor, Department of Psychology, University of Toledo

J. Christopher Muran, PH.D.
Beth Israel Medical Center, Mount Sinai School of Medicine

David E. Orlinsky, PH.D.
Professor, Committee on Human Development, University of Chicago

Renee H. Rhodes, PH.D.
Associate Research Scientist, Department of Psychology, Yale University

Jeremy D. Safran, PH.D.
Derner Institute, Adelphi University

Donald P. Spence, PH.D.
Robert Wood Johnson Medical School

William B. Stiles, PH.D.
Professor of Psychology, Miami University

Hans H. Strupp, PH.D.
Distinguished Professor, Department of Psychology, Vanderbilt University

P. Forrest Talley, PH.D.
Private Practice, Nashville, TN

Preface

FOR SEVERAL YEARS in the middle and late 1980s the Vanderbilt psychotherapy research team* would once each week crowd into a small conference room on the first floor of Wesley Hall, an old YMCA building that had been purchased by Vanderbilt University and converted for use by the Psychology Department. The room was small, barely big enough to hold the long table that our group of graduate students, fellows, professors, and occasional visiting dignitaries would squeeze around. Those unfortunate enough to come late to the meetings were forced to lodge themselves at the far end of the table. In the winter this position placed an individual perilously close to a temperamental radiator that crouched low, only inches behind the chair, and instilled a practical motive to maintain good posture. In summer the air conditioner, also located behind this seat and at head level, roared loudly enough to effectively make the individual sitting in front of it both deaf and dumb. Some were tempted to circumvent this debilitation by crouching low in their seat, but this of course destroyed the good posture that they had developed during the preceding winter months.

As if to balance the physical limitations imposed by these quarters, our discussions ranged far and wide over the field of psychotherapy. No issue was too small nor too large. Yet no matter where the conversation began, the intellectual terrain that was covered invariably included the twin towers of our profession, psychotherapy research and practice. Jumping back and forth from each of these, we spent a good number of hours in heated debate.

---

*Strupp, with more than 40 years of research and clinical experience, was the paterfamilias; Butler had initially joined the Vanderbilt psychotherapy research team as a postdoctoral fellow and subsequently became a full-time staff member; Talley was a graduate student in the department's doctoral program, struggling to find a dissertation to complete.

Some of the questions that generated the most heat were those aimed at the research/practice chasm and in particular the difficulty of making meaningful scientific inquiry about clinical issues that are known more intuitively than intellectually. Most often such inquiry means transforming clinical knowledge into constructs that can be operationally defined and empirically measured. The disturbing aspect of this transformation, and that which precipitated many of our discussions, was its tendency to strip away much of the clinical meaning from the issues that first sparked the desire for inquiry. Examples of this dilemma are pervasive and include attempts to measure the "good hour", resistance, therapist skill, outcome, and so on. In our work we frequently questioned whether we would be able to scientifically investigate similar issues without bleeding away their clinical meaning. Moreover, we wondered how the results from our inquiries might best be expressed so as to meaningfully inform practice.

These concerns are not unique to the Vanderbilt II Project, but instead strike at the very heart of our profession. This is seen in the Boulder model (Lerner, 1952) that for over forty years has served as the basis for training clinical psychologists. The linchpin of this model is the idea that research and practice should be united, in both an individual's education and career. A similar model is implicit in the field of psychiatry, where it shares a history with the rest of medicine of trying to mold practice in accord with the findings from research. Despite the promise this model seems to hold, psychodynamic therapists have preferred to find practical guidance from sources other than the research literature. This has been so clear as to be almost axiomatic. It is generally received as an accepted, if not somewhat sad, state of affairs that we must live with for the indefinite future. How extraordinary! Surely, when one of the central tenets of the mental health profession (namely, the treatment of patients will be based on findings from science) is regularly abandoned upon completion of training, some protest is justified. But these protests are seldom heard.

This strikes us as peculiar, for clearly either researchers or practitioners should feel troubled. Researchers, who in psychology are usually the mentors of practitioners, find their protégés turning their back on a key aspect of their training. This seems reason enough for complaint. Practitioners, on the other hand, might protest that they have been hoodwinked: after devoting years of training in which the importance of research to practice was regularly emphasized, they find themselves deriving little guidance from the scientific literature and needing to acquaint themselves with a vast body of clinically derived knowledge in order to fill the void. More voices need to be raised in response to this situation, and more energies devoted to its resolution. We must become less complacent, even at the risk of becoming contentious.

In recognizing that the marriage of research and psychodynamic psychotherapy has not fulfilled its promise, we are led to ask why. Have researchers failed to ask meaningful questions? Are the answers that do emerge from scientific inquiry insignificant to the clinician? Is there perhaps something about the art of psychotherapy that precludes meaningful scientific inquiry? Conversely, is it simply that therapists naively trust their own observations and intuitions to such an extent that the results of research are considered to be of no consequence?

These questions and others were posed to the clinicians and researchers who contributed to this book. Authors were selected according to a number of criteria, the primary ones being that they held a theoretical perspective congruent with psychodynamic therapy, had shown themselves to be critical thinkers within their area of concern, and had an interest in the subject matter. We have been fortunate in having so many outstanding thinkers accept our invitation.

In developing the structure for the book we first had five well-known practitioners articulate their concerns with regard to these issues. We then asked psychotherapy researchers to review two chapters apiece and respond to the main issues each clinician had delineated. These range from Greenberg's analysis of the limitations imposed by differing contexts to Edelson's distinction between psychotherapy, which he calls a form of story telling, and research, or hypothesis testing. These exchanges often make for provocative reading and, we might add, definitely move the discussion of this subject forward. Even on those occasions when the discussion gets bogged down, the interchange often becomes absorbing for the very reasons that are causing it to stall. This happens, for instance, when clinical contributors complain that research has not addressed certain issues when in fact it has, or when researchers respond to comments in ways that entirely ignore the therapeutic import of the point clinicians are trying to make. (So as not to appear high-handed, we need to admit that we too would have committed these and other sins had we written one of the main chapters; on reflection, this is a good reason for not having written a main chapter). These problems of course, reflect the very difficulties that have created a gap between research and practice and that motivated us to edit this volume.

Finally, what became of the results of our early efforts, back in the days before Wesley Hall met the business end of a wrecking ball, to build conceptual bridges between research and practice? Unfortunately, we did not come up with a blueprint for connecting the two, but we did discover that in the process of wrestling with the issue through vigorous inquiry and debate each of us had become a better clinician (Strupp, 1989). We wish this—and more—for the readers of this book.

REFERENCES

Lerner, G. F. J. (1952). Defining psychotherapy. *American Psychologist, 7,* 547.

Strupp, H. H. (1989). Psychotherapy: Can the practitioner learn from the researcher? *American Psychologist, 4,* 717–724.

Acknowledgments

THE EFFORT culminating in the realization of this book extends well beyond that of the three editors. We would like to gratefully acknowledge the contributions of several individuals in particular. These include Charles Talley, Jr., who was instrumental in formulating many of the original questions that framed this discussion and that even earlier led to a panel discussion of this same topic at the Society for Psychotherapy Research in New Mexico. Deborah Trotter and Kay Houston are thanked for their tireless efforts to relay communications between us, and their unflagging good cheer in the process. We appreciate Tommie Slayden's critical reviews of several chapters: she brought to the task a fresh perspective that inevitably resulted in revisions with greater clarity. Thanks also go to Stephen Francoeur and Jo Ann Miller at Basic Books for their support and patience in seeing this project to completion. Lastly, we extend our gratitude to each of the contributors, who generously devoted both their time and energy to this volume.

28.2.1934

Dr. Saul Rosenzweig
64 Plympton Street
Cambridge, Mass.
U.S.A.

My dear Sir

I have examined your experimental studies for the verification of psychoanalytic propositions with interest. I cannot put much value on
such confirmation because the abundance of reliable observations on
which these propositions rest makes them independent of experimental verification. Still, it can do no harm.

Sincerely yours,

Freud

A letter from Sigmund Freud responding to Saul Rosenzweig, who had sent him
several reprints of experimental investigations of psychoanalytic propositions.
Quoted by permission of Saul Rosenzweig.

CHAPTER 1

Psychotherapy Research: A Clinician's View

Jay Greenberg

ALTHOUGH FREQUENTLY LAMENTED, the gap between psychotherapy researchers and clinicians resists closure and threatens to widen. The two groups are separated virtually from professional birth. Our training experiences start us out in opposite directions; the distance increases quickly as different institutional affiliations (the academy of the researcher, the training institute of the clinician) immerse us in alternative professional cultures. Our differences may even reflect the workings of nature as well as nurture. Clinicians (despite occasional protests to the contrary) are personally committed to creating a particular sort of intimate relationship within which their patients can change. Researchers are personally committed to asking hard, sometimes provocative questions about that relationship and about the change that putatively grows from it. These differences of personal proclivity (which are significant even though a few people combine the two roles) contribute to mutual skepticism and even distrust.

As a result of this gap, there is often a peevish tone to the exchanges between researchers and clinicians. Researchers feel unfairly ignored. Their findings—hard data, quantifiable for all to see and replicable by the open-minded—are wasted on those who could use them for the benefit of all but who just will not be confused by the facts. Clinicians feel misunderstood. Researchers working in the safety and sterility of their laboratories cannot possibly know what life is like in the trenches. Not only is it messy down here, it is *subtle.* The researchers' data reflect the artificial interplay of made-up, oversimplified forces. Those who do not do clinical work—at least those who do not do it full-time—cannot even ask the right questions.

Lost in these feelings of mutual disenfranchisement are some far-reaching conceptual problems that confound communications between the two groups. These problems are inherent in the kind of enterprise that psychotherapy (especially psychoanalytic or psychodynamically based psychotherapy) is, in the kind of data upon which it relies, and in the kind of hypotheses that get constructed. The problems do not arise only when the discussion is interdisciplinary; they are present in every clinical debate and in every case conference.

Let me illustrate the issues with a clinical example. It is taken from a paper that was presented as part of a symposium on the effects of theory on clinical practice. The paper includes verbatim transcripts of three sessions. I will be taking several liberties with the presentation and thus will refer to the analyst as "Dr. A." I do want to acknowledge, however, that the paper was written by Martin Silverman (1987), who has given a courageous and candid presentation. He has both my gratitude and my apologies.

Dr. A's patient is a young woman who sought treatment for sexual and social inhibitions, masochistic tendencies, and depression. The analyst reports a history of "pseudostupidity" enacted with her father, evidently from early in childhood to the present. I am going to focus my comments on a fantasy reported by the patient and on the analyst's interpretation of it. Leading up to the fantasy, the patient summarizes a number of situations she has described:

> I get intimidated with men. I always feel that they know they have the knowledge. They have the brains, and I'm dumb. . . . It's the same thing here. I keep feeling like asking you, "What does it mean?" I always feel like you know. . . . I feel you're always a step ahead of me. You *know,* because you're smarter than I am and all the training and experience you have. (p. 152, italics in original)

The analyst intervenes for the first time: "I don't think that's what it is. I think you feel I know *because I'm a man,* that as a woman you don't have any brains" (pp. 152–153, italics added). The patient responds with some more comments, including, "Men intimidate me. It's like with my father. It's a mixture of excitement and pain and hurt and fear" (p. 153). There are some further exchanges between the two, leading up to the patient's report of a masturbation fantasy:

> There's—a doctor—a mad scientist—and his nurse and—he ties me down to— do things to me. . . . The fantasy had to do with—something—it had to do with getting bigger breasts. It's foolish—I feel sheepish [pause]. It's so silly [pause]. (p. 154)

Patient and analyst continue to discuss the patient's feeling that she is intimidated by men, after which she returns to the fantasy. She becomes explicit about a "slave and master" theme, refers to pornographic elements of it, and mentions bondage. She feels that she has to submit masochistically to the powerful men who have something to offer her but who would enslave her in return. The analyst goes on to interpret the transferential meaning of the fantasy as he understands it, finally telling the patient, "You want *me* to be the mad scientist forcing and hurting you and making changes in you" (p. 155, italics in original).

Dr. A presents his interpretation as a simple statement of fact about something that the patient wants but is unaware of wanting. Conceptually, however, things are not so clear-cut. Because the patient is unaware of wanting Dr. A to be a mad scientist and has not been able to articulate her desire prior to the analyst's comment, the interpretation is a conditional statement; it may or may not be true. Thus, like all psychoanalytic interpretations, Dr. A's is a hypothesis. Sophisticated methodologists would consider it an example of a "particular clinical hypothesis," one that, presumably, is relatively uncontaminated by broad theoretical preconceptions (Rubinstein, 1980). These are generally thought to be the easiest kind of hypothesis to validate using purely psychological methods. Accordingly, the interpretation ought to be subject to the confirmation process, both clinically and within a research setting.

So what we have is just the sort of situation that should bring clinicians and researchers together: a hypothesis together with a complete, unedited transcript of the exchange on which it is based. The treating analyst will be able to document the data from which he derived the interpretation, and he can point to the evidence (in terms of subsequent events recorded in the transcript) that he considers confirming. Researchers, in turn, will have access to the data (pre- and postinterpretation), so they should be able to make informed judgments about the clinician's conclusions. Dialogue, if not consensus, is in the cards.

But things are not so simple. To show why, I will return to Silverman's presentation, departing from his text and getting fanciful with the material. Assume that immediately after the analyst's intervention there were a number of changes in the patient's psychological state. Let us say that her mood improves, her anxiety decreases, and she recalls a memory (perhaps a memory of coercing her father into taking over some project of hers in a way that felt humiliating but also exciting). In the next session she reports that for the first time in years she has been orgasmic with her husband. Further, let us stipulate that since there is a transcript of the sessions, outside observers can agree that the reported changes are genuine. As you can see, I am loading the deck: I am setting things up so that an interpretation is followed by just the sorts of events that both clinicians and methodologists use as validating criteria. Because the situation I have constructed is one in which there is agreement that constructive change has occurred, there will be no tension among different observers around issues of therapeutic efficacy.

All is well, and it appears that we have the evidence we need—except for one thing. In my hypothetical situation Dr. A happens to be in supervision. His supervisor may have a somewhat more relational approach to treatment than Dr. A does, but this isn't really essential to the way things unfold. In the course of describing the session Dr. A recounts his interpretation and suggests that his patient's response confirmed its validity. Listening to the description of the session, the supervisor has a very different impression. Dr. A, he believes, has overlooked the obvious: patient and analyst have collaborated in enacting an important component of the patient's internal world. She has brought him something that she claims not to understand, and he, somewhat roughly and arrogantly, has told her what it means. In support of his understanding of the situation, the supervisor finds several examples in the session of points at which Dr. A has contradicted the patient, imposing his ideas and more or less insisting that she accept them. (We have already encountered Dr. A's statement to the patient that she is wrong about how she understands herself. There are, in fact, several examples of such exchanges in the transcript.)

The supervisor tells Dr. A that his interpretation was off the mark. The patient didn't want him to be the mad scientist; she believed him to be the mad scientist. And she had good reason to think this in light of his behavior (see Gill, 1987; Levenson, 1987). It follows that the patient's improvement proves nothing about the validity of the interpretation; it is just the predictable next act in a continuing saga of the patient empowering men by her submissiveness. If the supervisor is so inclined, he might describe what has happened as a transference cure, but that would just be icing on the cake of a thorough discrediting of the analyst's formulation.

Dr. A's supervisor has given us another psychoanalytic hypothesis. He believes that the patient has responded to the analyst's tendency to take on the male role in her archaic, troublesome, but still exciting sadomasochistic relationship. Recognizing this tendency confirms her expectations of male behavior. This temporarily reestablished what Freud (1912/1958) called the "preconditions to falling in love" (p. 99), or, in Fairbairn's (1958) terms, it recreated a relationship with a male authority that is an important element of the patient's internal object world. The replay of an exciting (Freud) or familiar (Fairbairn) relationship enabled her both to improve her mood and to achieve sexual satisfaction with her husband. Please note that this hypothesis competes with the original; it offers a dichotomously alternative explanation of what has occurred and why it has occurred.

Let us continue this flight of fancy and assume that Dr. A is convinced by his supervisor. The two agree to reject the original psychoanalytic hypothesis in favor of the alternative. Dr. A goes away chastened but also determined that next time he is going to pay as much close attention to process as he has been paying to content. The supervisor feels pleased that he has intervened—in the nick of time, perhaps—to shake up the system and get the analysis back on the right track.

You may have a sense that things aren't going to stop here. It turns out that Dr. A's supervisor is himself getting a consult on his supervisory work. Listening to the supervisor pridefully reporting how he noticed the enactment that Dr. A had missed, the consultant is amazed. Here is a perfect example of the parallel process in action! Dr. A has enacted the role of the compliant, pseudostupid, masochistic patient, and the supervisor has played out, with elegant perfection, the role of mad scientist. The supervisor has run roughshod over Dr. A's interpretation, rejecting it in the same way that Dr. A rejected his patient's explanation of her experience. Also like the analyst, the supervisor has imposed a new way of looking at things. Dr. A submitted, leaving both himself and the supervisor convinced that, without the supervisor, the analysis would have been useless or worse. Just as the patient felt she needed the analyst to give her bigger breasts, the analyst has behaved as if he needed the supervisor to give him deeper insight (which, if any of the participants is so inclined, might be associated to one or another body part). The supervisory process elegantly re-created what went on in the analysis.

The consultant does not stop with explaining the supervisory relationship; he too has a theory about what happened within the analytic process itself. The occurrence of a parallel process suggests that the analyst is unconsciously identified with the patient's helplessness and inadequacy; perhaps the patient has, also unconsciously, sensed this. But the patient's belief about her own inadequacy was exaggerated by a relationship with a father who was convinced that women live in a world in which they are endangered by and subject to the sexual preoccupations of men. (There is evidence for this in the transcript.) In contrast, the analyst has a relationship with a strong, supportive father—the supervisor.

The consultant sees two interlocking triads: patient-father-analyst and patient-analyst-supervisor. Because the analyst has this connection with a strong father, when the patient projects her helplessness onto the analyst he reacts differently than she can. In contrast to her submissiveness he responds (in session) powerfully, taking command. The patient senses this and is able to forge an identification not just with the analyst but with the analyst in relation to the supervisor as an internal object (see Ogden, 1989, for an elegant discussion of this sort of process in normal oedipal development). It is as a result of the internalization of the total triangular experience that the patient becomes stronger and is emboldened to try out some new things.

By now we have three competing psychoanalytic hypotheses. Since each purports to explain why the patient's state improved, the fact of her improvement can be offered as evidence for any one of them. The incompatibility of the alternative explanations bears emphasis.[1] To illustrate, I will focus on two broad, if possibly implicit, areas of disagreement.

---

[1]The incompatibility is most striking when we move from the analyst's to the supervisor's hypotheses. This is because in doing so we have switched from a one-person to a two-person, or social explanatory, model, a switch that defines the major debate in contemporary psychoanalytic thinking (see Greenberg and Mitchell, 1983). The consultant's hypothesis does not require a similarly dramatic shift in paradigm but nevertheless involves an alternative dynamic formulation.

The first is the locus of the psychic event. The analyst locates the relevant event (the repressed transference wish) entirely within the patient. Although this wish, like all wishes, involves an external object, the occurrence of the wish implies nothing about the behavior or the experience of the object. The analyst's participation is inconsequential.

The supervisor, in contrast, sees a transference perception or conviction of which the patient is not fully conscious (Greenberg, 1991). Perceptions and convictions, for all but the most doctrinaire, are inherently dyadic; they are plausible inferences based upon the patient's observations of the analyst (Hoffman, 1983). Aware of this, the supervisor turns his attention to data about the patient–analyst interaction and to those aspects of the analyst's participation upon which the patient's convictions might be (at least partially) based.

The consultant notices a larger pattern. The supervisor is not simply an objective commentator on facts brought to him; he enacts a relationship with the analyst that reflects what has gone on in the analysis itself. This gives the consultant a different perspective not only on the supervisor's experience but on the analyst's and the patient's as well. The analyst is caught up in a relationship with the patient on one side and the supervisor on another. This affects both the events of the supervision and the analysis itself. Accordingly, the patient's experience is not simply interpersonally determined; it is triangular at its core.

The second area of disagreement is the nature of the clinical evidence. Dr. A, although he might not be aware of it, is relying on what the philosopher Adolf Grünbaum (1984) has characterized as Freud's "tally argument." Briefly, the tally argument suggests that interpretations will be therapeutically effective only if they "tally with what is real" in the patient (Freud, 1916–17/1963, p. 452). The tally argument gives Dr. A reason to believe in the validity of his psychoanalytic hypothesis, because the changes reported by the patient provide ample evidence that significant improvement occurred.

The supervisor's perspective brings the tally argument into question. According to the supervisor, the patient did not get better because she was told the truth; she got better because she had participated in a transference enactment that was gratifying for one reason or another. The analyst's countertransferential belief in his own correctness (his strength and potency) was an essential element of that enactment. Thus, therapeutic change does not depend on the patient recovering repressed mental contents (making the unconscious conscious). In fact, change proves nothing about the interpretation; the change reflects only the effects of an interaction of which the interpretation was one element.[2] The patient would have gotten better if the patient and the analyst had engaged in another, manifestly different, interaction that nonetheless contained the same "meta-communication" (Jacobs, 1991), a communication perhaps about his availability as a strong, somewhat intimidating, but ultimately supportive father.

The consultant, in turn, might say to the supervisor what the supervisor said to the analyst. That is, he would point to a supervisory effect that was determined interactively rather than by the supervisor's greater insight. With respect to the change in the patient's state of mind and behavior, he would address a triangular, rather than a dyadic, enactment. Change, he would say, does not emerge from the engagement of two people; it reflects the deeper involvement of each participant in a larger social network. Many of those who are most important in the network are not present in the room.

The example makes clear that as new observers address the clinical data, new interpretations emerge. But the implications go further, because if we were to probe the thought processes of each participant in our drama, we would encounter a surprising and potentially disturbing phenomenon. It would turn out not only that each observer has a new theory but that each adduces a unique set of data in support of it.

Consider: The analyst will describe observations of the patient as he or she can make them. These will include nuances of the atmosphere in the consulting room that evoke and reverberate with the analyst's private associations. These associations may involve memories of past sessions with the patient, or they may reflect the analyst's personal history. They may be verbal, visual, affective, or kinesthetic. Some will linger, others will be more transient and elusive. Asked to explain how a particular interpretation (that is, a particular hypothesis) was formulated, the analyst will be able to give only a more or less incomplete response. Some of the data on which the interpretation was based will no longer be available. The analyst is likely to fill the gaps in his or her memory with other data; the process (and sometimes even the motive) can approximate what goes into the construction of a rationalization. This is not meant to disparage the analyst's formulation; it is meant to emphasize that the data on which it is based are ephemeral and not amenable to public record and that they are easily lost. Neither the supervisor nor the consultant can gain access to these data, even if the analyst fol-

---

[2]The meaning and impact of these therapeutically effective interactions is construed differently by different theorists. Some see them as developmentally essential events that were missed during the patient's childhood (Kohut, 1977; Loewald, 1960; Winnicott, 1965); others view them as novel exchanges that interrupt pathological relational patterns (Fairbairn, 1958; Sullivan, 1954).

lows Spence's (1982) suggestion to "unpack" session transcripts by recording personal but unspoken thoughts.

But there are also data that will be unavailable to the analyst. Regardless of how sensitive to countertransference the analyst might be (by virtue of training and/or personal predilection), there are elements of his or her own participation that must remain hidden. The analyst views the patient and the analytic process through what Schafer (1983), in a different context, calls "the eye that sees everything according to its own structure and cannot see itself seeing" (p. 145). Analysts typically cannot attend to nuances of their own verbal or vocal style, postural changes, timing or phrasing of interventions, facial expression, and so on. These will be apparent to the patient, and some are likely to be noticed by the supervisor reviewing transcripts or recordings of the session. The supervisor may pick up some of these changes as he or she observes the analyst reporting on what has transpired.

Similar considerations apply to the perspective of the consultant. Twice removed from the analyst's private world and excluded from the supervisor's personal experience with the analyst, the consultant is cut off from much that matters greatly, but he or she does have access to new data about the interaction of the other two participants. This leads inevitably to new sorts of hypotheses. Explanations in terms of a parallel process between patient–analyst and analyst–supervisor relationships are most likely to occur to the consultant, because the consultant's vantage point provides just the sort of overview from which the two relationships can be observed and compared. The comparison is possible only when someone is looking in on both situations from outside.

Perhaps the most confounding effect of adding new perspectives is that at each level of the process *the new hypothesis takes the preceding hypotheses as data and explains their occurrence.* Dr. A's interpretation explains the patient's fantasy and significant aspects of the symptom picture. It also explains what we might consider a hypothesis of the patient's, namely, that she *feels* stupid because she *is* stupid. The supervisor's idea explains the fantasy, the improvement, and why Dr. A thought his interpretation worked (and thus that his hypothesis was correct). The consultant's hypothesis explains why the patient got better, why the analyst thought she did, and why the supervisor believed that he had helped Dr. A. The consultant, taking them as data, will compare the analyst's and the supervisor's hypotheses as part of his or her search for a pattern.

To put this generally: Each participant in the process constructs a hypothesis that he or she thinks explains the occurrence of various events. But as we move up the therapeutic/supervisory chain, these hypotheses are no longer seen simply as explanations. Rather, they are seen as events, as elements of an interaction, *that themselves require explanation.* This underscores why we cannot really say that the therapist, supervisor, and consultant are looking at the same data. The theory of each is built upon a different observational base; the theories will be difficult to compare because they will address different phenomena.

It is tempting to stop with the thought that ascending the supervisory chain moves us closer to the truth because it adds data to the observational base. Consider, though, that at each level something is lost as well. The situation can be compared to the differences between the accounts of an event that might appear in a daily newspaper, in a year-end review, and in a history written years later. As time passes and as the observer's scope broadens, new patterns emerge that could not have been anticipated. Certainly, these illuminate the place of the event in its historical context. But much that mattered most about the event to those who lived through it is irretrievably lost.

This leads to an unexpected and perhaps somewhat troubling conclusion. While we are used to the idea that the analyst, as observer of the patient, is going to be blind to certain aspects of his or her role in a dyadic interaction, we must also realize that the supervisor is equally constrained. *The supervisor cannot see just the patient.* He or she is as bound to observe the dyad as the analyst is to observe the individual and thus has as limited (although quite different) a perspective. When Winnicott said that there is no such thing as a baby but only a nursing couple, he was describing what he—as a pediatrician and an outside observer—was able to see. Both the baby and its mother would have other ideas. The same considerations, of course, apply to the consultant. Consultants cannot see only the patient or only the dyad; they are obliged to observe the reverberating interaction of all three participants.

It is not surprising, then, that the analyst formulates a one-person hypothesis ("The patient wants such and such"), the supervisor comes up with a two-person hypothesis ("The analyst and the patient enact such and such"), and the consultant arrives at a three-person hypothesis ("Patient, analyst, and supervisor interact in a way that leads to such and such"). The scope of the hypothesis is determined by the perspective of the observer.

The Challenge for Research

So far, I have built a story that stays within the clinical setting; the events I have described occur routinely in everyday practice. But the story contains a lesson that can illuminate the relationship between clinicians and researchers. Researchers, like supervisors and consultants, often find themselves at odds with clinicians. This is inherent in their observing things from a perspective that is different from the therapist's. It is neither inadvertent nor tendentious that a relationship develops in which therapists are "insiders" and researchers are skeptical "outsiders."

Ever since Freud tried to convince the Viennese medical establishment that he was onto something about the inner experience of hysterics (and thus about the etiology of their neurosis), psychoanalysts have been notoriously unsuccessful at persuading skeptical outsiders of the validity of their findings or even of the utility of their method. There are many reasons for this, and one of the most crucial emerges in the sequence that I have described. Let me state the problem starkly: *From the moment outsiders start looking at what goes on in psychotherapy, they are likely to see a great deal that the clinician overlooks and to miss a great deal of what the clinician sees.*

The upshot of this is that when hypotheses get formulated, the clinician is likely to stress the ways in which the patient's internal world (or wish, in Silverman's formulation; for a Kleinian analyst it could be a split-off internal object relationship) influenced the clinician's personal experience (cognitive or affective). The skeptical outsider, noticing from the outset that there are two people in the consulting room, is going to be impressed by how everything that went on in the treatment happened within a broader context. The tension between clinicians and outsiders can always be traced to their different emphases on the importance of context. Context is everything to the outsider (the hypotheses of supervisor and consultant were based on therapist–patient interaction), and much that is most salient about it inevitably eludes the therapist's notice. The therapist, however, is not simply blind. Context doesn't simply illuminate; it also hides a great deal about what goes on within it. It may be true, as the old proverb has it, that the fish will be the last one to discover water. But who knows better than a fish what it is like to live in the ocean!

Freud was aware of the problem of context from the beginning, but he was preoccupied with protecting psychoanalysis from the attacks (moral as well as intellectual) of outsiders. Because of this he adopted an unfortunate theoretical strategy: he attempted to trivialize context. In his writings on technique he tried mightily to purify the clinical setting. If analysis is conducted properly, he argued, context (especially, of course, interpersonal context) can be ignored. The blank screen, the reflecting mirror, and the attitude of surgical detachment embodied Freud's epistemological wishful thinking as well as his clinical preferences. If the analyst applies the method, he hoped and taught, we can think of psychoanalytic interpretations as hypotheses that are subject to routine scientific confirmation, because they can be conceptually separated from the interpretive interaction.

Many analysts continue to believe that context can be reduced to a vanishing point, leaving only their interpretations to be studied. Charles Brenner (1976) addresses the issue clinically, arguing against conducting analysis face-to-face because he believes that "for a patient to be in a position to watch his analyst is like introducing extraneous sights and sounds into one's office" (p. 183). Although few would put it so starkly, analysts of other persuasions tend to agree. Bion's (1967/1988) idea that analysts not only *ought to* but *can* come to the session without "memory and desire" has become a keystone of the "contemporary Kleinian" approach to treatment (Spillius, 1988). Working from a very different theoretical system, Sullivan (1954) suggested that the psychiatrist could function as an "expert," immune to the emotional storms that affect others in the patient's life.

The same assumption determines the epistemological stance of many analysts. Donald Spence (1986), for instance, writes that "psychoanalysts are particularly sensitized (in the course of their training) to the dangers of suggestion, and schooled in a tradition which places an emphasis on minimal comment" (p. 259). Spence, who despite his emphasis on the influence of the analyst's theoretical commitments ultimately assumes the reducibility of context much as Brenner does, believes that we can study the effects of the interpretation free from "contamination" by interaction. Marshall Edelson (1984) agrees:

> The disciplined use of psychoanalytic technique which focuses on interpreting defense, rather than providing the analysand with suggestions about what he is defending against, also might cast doubt on a claim that suggestion is a plausible alternative explanation for an outcome observed in particular single subject research (pp. 129–130).

Few skeptical outsiders have been impressed. They find it difficult to agree with Brenner that the patient's recumbency eliminates (or even reduces) the impact of the analyst's presence and thus the importance of context. Few accept Spence's or Edelson's argument that our training immunizes us to contamination by our hopes, fears, and even our theories.

The most recent to notice the problem, and to stir up the antipathy between analysts and outsiders, has been Adolf Grünbaum (1984). Because he is clinically naive—not aware, for example, that the tally argument is refuted by what goes on in clinical settings every day, as my fanciful play with Silverman's example suggests—Grünbaum (along with many other philosophers of science) tends to focus his notion of context narrowly on the workings of suggestion.

But what the methodologists call suggestion is just a subset of a much larger class; it is part of what I am calling *context* and what those familiar with the therapeutic process are increasingly calling *interaction*. One indirect result of the emerging emphasis on the importance of interaction is that clinicians view theory in a fundamentally different way than do methodologists. For instance, Grünbaum's critique rests on his belief that the tally argument was central to Freud's argument for the validity of psychoanalytic hypotheses. I believe it can be shown that this assertion seriously underestimates Freud's epistemological sophistication. Certainly, there are few clinicians today who take the tally argument seriously. Most of us believe that the relationship between what we say to our patients and changes in symptoms and/or states of mind depends upon a great deal more than whether the interpretation (the therapist's theory) is correct (tallies with the "facts," that is, with something "real" within the patient).

Early on, Freud (1910/1957) himself insisted that the truth of an interpretation, while necessary, was not a sufficient guarantee of therapeutic efficacy. The correct interpretation will be ineffective or even pathogenic unless the patient has formed a "sufficient attachment" to the analyst (p. 226). Today we go much further: we question the very possibility and, *a fortiori*, the necessity of any interpretation being "correct" *in the sense of excluding all possible alternative interpretations.* This is the only meaning of "correctness" that Grünbaum finds relevant; for sophisticated clinicians it is a chimera. Thus, we routinely (if implicitly) reject what Grünbaum bombastically calls Freud's "necessary condition thesis." In its place, we assert that any interpretation is part of a larger process, the therapist-patient interaction, that is at the root of all change. The role of the therapist's theory in that interaction—and the relative effectiveness of alternative theories as determinants of therapeutic outcome—is far more complex than Grünbaum imagines.

These considerations leave me content to say that Grünbaum is beating a dead horse, at best.[3] But this doesn't answer the charge that our claims to be able to isolate the interpretation from its context, and so to demonstrate the validity of our theories, are artificial and self-serving. If anything, the emerging emphasis on interactive models of the psychotherapeutic situation underscores the impossibility of doing so. The problem of alternative perspectives on the therapeutic process and the different sorts of hypotheses to which these perspectives give rise is even more vexing than the methodologists imagine.

The Problem of Adjudication

We are left with the problem of adjudicating among the competing interpretations. Appealing to some final ambiguity that is inherent in living processes is an extravagance of the intellectually arrogant, many people believe; neither good science nor exasperated third-party funders of psychotherapy will support our indulgence in it for long. But often the adjudication is based on political rather than conceptual considerations. Thus, the inclusiveness of their ex-

[3]Because clinicians tend to be intimidated by philosophers, they fail to realize that Grünbaum's approach to scientific method generally and to the problem of confirmation in particular is highly controversial among his own colleagues. It is well beyond the scope of this chapter to go into the philosophical shortcomings of his position. (See Laor, 1985, for a brief overview and the work of the philosopher Richard Rorty, 1991, for a powerfully stated alternative approach to the broadest issues.)

planations and the power structure of psychoanalysis give authority to consultants' (and secondarily to supervisors') hypotheses.

The same is true of the relationship between clinicians and researchers. Grünbaum and other philosophers of science—impressed enough by their critique and blind to its limitations—believe that the evaluation of psychoanalytic hypotheses must be carried out in the laboratory. The belief afflicts some psychoanalysts as well. Daniel Stern (1985), while recognizing that their different perspectives lead clinicians and researchers to construct very different visions of the human infant, nevertheless writes:

> The current scientific *Zeitgeist* has a certain persuasive and legitimizing force in determining what is a reasonable view of things. And at this moment the *Zeitgeist* favors observational methods. . . . As related fields, presumably about the same subject matter though from different perspectives, they [quantitative research and clinical observation] will not tolerate too much dissonance, and it currently appears that it is psychoanalysis that will have to give way. (pp. 16–17)

Thus begins the war. Told to "give way," most clinicians do not simply do so. Instead, they ignore research findings.

But the problem of multiple perspectives is not simply a source of tension between clinicians and researchers; it makes itself felt within the research setting as well. Like clinicians, researchers find what they look for. Crucial decisions are made from the moment a research question is drafted. What, for instance, should one look at in attempting to study the psychoanalytic situation? The flow of the patient's associations? The analyst's contribution? Case reports? Written transcripts? Audiotapes? Videotapes? Is it necessary to get into the analyst's private experience, and if so, how can this be done? Is it possible to "unpack" the transcript via annotation, as Spence suggests one can? What about the patient's private experience, that is, what he or she thought (even consciously) but could not or would not say? I believe that each of these is at least potentially illuminating but also that the sorts of hypotheses that will be tested and the resultant research findings will be startlingly different depending upon which are seen as essential and which are dismissed as contaminating "noise." Clinicians, of course, are aware of the different results that emerge from differently constructed research projects. As a result, even when they take the research literature seriously, they are likely to read selectively. Each clinician will embrace research data that support (within some limit) what he or she already believes; findings that diverge greatly from one's own clinical experience will be ignored. David Hume said the same thing about our attitude toward miracles: We reject reports of "fact" that are too discrepant from what we believe. Typically, research findings reinforce existing theoretical beliefs; they do not change minds.[4]

In contrast to many on both sides of the dispute, I believe that the situation I have described is healthy for the practice of psychotherapy. Although it would be more comfortable to think of ourselves as participating in a linear march toward uncovering the "truth" about the human condition, there is much to be said for keeping in mind the value of multiple perspectives on a single interaction.

To make this point, I will conclude with an example of a psychoanalytic vision that, although widely abandoned, was one of the most fruitful in the history of our discipline. Virtually from the beginning of his career, Freud was committed to the idea that all human experience originates in the perception of inner sensation. This had both theoretical and clinical ramifications. Theoretically, Freud (1923/1961) was bound to say that our inner experiences "are more primordial, more elementary, than perceptions arising externally ...[they have] greater economic significance" (p. 22). Clinically, interpersonal experience is secondary to, and built upon, what we sense within us. This tells us how we are to listen to our patients: "A string of reproaches against other people leads one to suspect the existence of a string of self-reproaches with the same content. All that need be done is to turn back each particular reproach on to the speaker himself" (Freud, 1905/1953, p. 35).

This is a formula for ignoring the interpersonal, and a great deal else. It led Freud to his first theory of anxiety, the so-called "toxic theory." According to this broad hypothesis, anxiety always follows the rejection of an unacceptable instinctual impulse; the energy that drove the impulse has been transformed as a consequence of repression. This theory has strong clinical implications or, to put things another way, it guarantees tunnel vision. Where there is anxiety, Freud told us, there is hidden sexuality, a forbidden desire that has been banished from awareness. Ignore everything else that we know about being anxious, he promised, and we will be rewarded with a vision of the inner world that will be unparalleled in its depth, richness, and ability to explain a vast range of human achievement and disability. Not only that, but we will be able to cure the incurable *if we focus narrowly on what has never been imagined before.*

Even though Freud eventually rejected this theory—even though, in

---

[4]I do not want to be too discouraging about the possibility of benign influence, even on those who see things quite differently. Consultants and supervisors, of course, routinely help those who consult them. But that does not come about simply because one person is more right than another. Rather, as in psychotherapy itself, it is only possible to be helpful within the context of a mutually respectful relationship that is willingly joined by all participants. Clinicians and researchers today are far from having that sort of relationship. Perhaps projects like the one envisioned by the editors of this volume will contribute to getting a dialogue under way.

methodologists' terms, the hypothesis was falsified—psychoanalysis flourished as a field of study and as a therapeutic modality because of what it allowed Freud and his early followers to do, what it revealed to them about being human. Viewed in these terms, the first anxiety theory may be stronger than the more ambiguous, Janus-faced "signal theory" (Freud, 1926/1959). The second theory does not guide us so clearly; it points us now to the impulse, now to the circumstances within which the impulse arises and to the dangers inherent in social living. It is, perhaps, a theory for a more mature stage in the development of psychoanalysis as a discipline, a stage in which we are able to integrate an established appreciation of the workings of desire with a more textured appreciation of the demands of the real world.

Nor is this the end of our story. The affect theory recently proposed by Otto Kernberg (1982) competes with both of Freud's approaches. Affects themselves are irreducible in Kernberg's system; they do not depend upon either impulses or interpersonal context. Indeed, they determine the characteristics of both. This theory may be fruitful for a time when analysts are investigating the relationships between endogenous and social determinants of experience in a new way. Needless to say, I don't think either that this theory is the last word on the subject or that the needs of our discipline simply change in some linear way over time. Alternative theories illuminate different aspects of the human condition at any moment.

The same healthy tension among competing psychoanalytic theories characterizes the divergent sensibilities of researchers and clinicians. Many clinicians, for example, organize their interpretive systems around Margaret Mahler's theory of a normal symbiotic stage of development that gives way to separate, individuated living. They do so even though there is now a substantial body of evidence that refutes Mahler's theory. Summarizing these findings, Daniel Stern (1985) believes the evidence is strong enough to justify the conclusion that "there is no symbiotic-like phase" (p. 10). Even during moments of intense relatedness, Stern insists, "the core sense of self is not breached: the other is still perceived as a separate core other" (p. 105).

Stern's analysis of the research findings suggests an alternative vision of the nature of human relatedness. If accepted, the findings point the way to a radically different psychoanalytic interpretive system, a system that some clinicians have embraced. This has not, however, squelched all interest in organizing clinical material in terms of the tension between symbiosis and separateness. After all, this is a tradition that dates back at least to Aristophanes, who said more than 2,000 years ago:

> There is not a man [who] would deny that this meeting and melting into one another, this becoming one instead of two, was the very expression of his ancient need. And the reason is that human nature was originally one and we were a whole, and the desire and pursuit of the whole is called love. (quoted by Plato in the *Symposium*, p. 33)

The tradition continues into the present. Within the last decade Martin Bergman (1987) wrote, "We idealize the symbiotic phase and we yearn to re-find it when we love" (p. 278). Neither Aristophanes nor Bergman is likely to surrender to the new data, however compelling some researchers believe they are. This is not to say that the research is inconsequential. The data are interesting and will add to the vitality of psychoanalytic discourse, but they are not decisive.

These considerations shape my thoughts about the desire of some to confirm psychoanalytic hypotheses. As a clinician, I do not think that theory is a solution; rather, I believe, it is a tool. When we theorize we apply what we have learned (in our professional and our personal lives) to our clinical observations. Our theories inevitably shape what we can see, but at their most vital they are reciprocally altered by the observations themselves. Theory provides the framework that makes observation possible, but all theories eventually yield in the face of the very data they generate (see Greenberg, 1991).

There will always be alternative approaches to the human condition, and the debate over which is the most useful will go on forever. Research, precisely because it approaches the issues from a novel perspective, will always be a part of the debate. But I don't think that its role is to confirm or to disconfirm hypotheses. In this sense, perhaps psychotherapy research is fundamentally different by design and in intent from research in the hard sciences, but I will leave that question to the professional researchers. It is not, however, either a pessimistic or a nihilistic question. Quite to the contrary, I see diversity as our best hope for continuing vitality. For me, participating in my own, self-conducted, "interminable analysis" is one of the fringe benefits of my profession; it makes possible thinking old thoughts in new ways and seeing the familiar from a novel perspective. Certainty—any notion of a final "truth" or even of validity in the methodologists' sense—is the enemy of surprise, and surprise is the stuff of personal growth. We expect an openness to surprise from analytic practitioners; we can expect no less from psychoanalysis as a discipline.

REFERENCES

Bergman, M. (1987). *The anatomy of loving: The story of man's quest to know what love is*. New York: Fawcett Columbine.

Bion, W. (1988). Notes on memory and desire. In E. Spillius (Ed.), *Melanie Klein today: Vol. 2. Mainly practice* (pp. 17–21). London: Routledge. (Original work published 1967)

Brenner, C. (1976). *Psychoanalytic technique and psychic conflict*. New York: International Universities Press.

Edelson, M. (1984). *Hypothesis and evidence in psychoanalysis.* Chicago: University of Chicago Press.

Fairbairn, W. R. D. (1958). The nature and aims of psychoanalytical treatment. *International Journal of Psychoanalysis, 39,* 374–385.

Freud, S. (1905). Fragment of an analysis of a case of hysteria. In J. Strachey (Ed. & Trans.), *The standard edition of the complete psychological works of Sigmund Freud* (Vol. 7, pp. 1–122). London: Hogarth Press, 1953.

Freud, S. (1957). "Wild" psycho-analysis. In J. Strachey (Ed. & Trans.), *The standard edition of the complete psychological works of Sigmund Freud* (Vol. 11, pp. 219–227). London: Hogarth Press. (Original work published 1910)

Freud, S. (1958). The dynamics of transference. In J. Strachey (Ed. & Trans.), *The standard edition of the complete psychological works of Sigmund Freud* (Vol. 12, pp. 97–108). London: Hogarth Press. (Original work published 1912)

Freud S. (1963). *Introductory lectures on psycho-analysis.* In J. Strachey (Ed. & Trans.), *The standard edition of the complete psychological works of Sigmund Freud* (Vols. 15 & 16). London: Hogarth Press. (Original work published 1916–17)

Freud, S. (1961). The ego and the id. In J. Strachey (Ed. & Trans.), *The standard edition of the complete psychological works of Sigmund Freud* (Vol. 19, pp. 1–66). London: Hogarth Press. (Original work published 1923)

Freud, S. (1959). Inhibitions, symptoms, and anxiety. In J. Strachey (Ed. & Trans.), *The standard edition of the complete psychological works of Sigmund Freud* (Vol. 20, pp. 75–175). London: Hogarth Press. (Original work published 1926)

Gill, M. (1987). The analyst as participant. *Psychoanalytic Inquiry, 7,* 249–259.

Greenberg, J. (1991). *Oedipus and beyond: A clinical theory.* Cambridge, MA: Harvard University Press.

Greenberg, J., & Mitchell, S. (1983). *Object relations in psychoanalytic theory.* Cambridge, MA: Harvard University Press.

Grünbaum, A. (1984). *The foundations of psychoanalysis.* Berkeley and Los Angeles: University of California Press.

Hoffman, I. (1983). The patient as interpreter of the analyst's experience. *Contemporary Psychoanalysis, 19,* 389–422.

Jacobs, T. (1991). *The use of the self.* New York: International Universities Press.

Kernberg, O. (1982). Self, ego, affects, and drives. *Journal of the American Psychoanalytic Association, 30,* 893–917.

Kohut, H. (1977). *The restoration of the self.* New York: International Universities Press.

Laor, N. (1985). Psychoanalysis as science: The inductivists resistance revisited. *Journal of the American Psychoanalytic Association, 33,* 149–166.

Levenson, E. (1987). An interpersonal perspective. *Psychoanalytic Inquiry, 7,* 207–214.

Loewald, H. (1960). On the therapeutic action of psychoanalysis. In *Papers on psychoanalysis.* (pp. 221–256). New Haven, CT: Yale University Press, 1980.

Ogden, T. (1989). *The primitive edge of experience.* New York: Aronson.

Plato. *Symposium* (B. Jowett, Trans.). New York: Liberal Arts Press, 1956.

Rorty, R. (1991). *Objectivity, relativism, and truth: Philosophical papers* (Vol. 1). Cambridge, UK: Cambridge University Press.

Rubinstein, B. (1980). The problem of confirmation in clinical psychoanalysis. *Journal of the American Psychoanalytic Association, 28,* 397–417.

Schafer, R. (1983). *The analytic attitude.* New York: Basic Books.

Silverman, M. (1987). Clinical material. *Psychoanalytic Inquiry, 7,* 147–165.

Spence, D. (1982). *Narrative truth and historical truth.* New York: Norton.

Spence, D. (1986). Are free associations necessarily contaminated? *Behavioral and Brain Sciences, 9,* 259.

Spillius, E. (Ed.). (1988). *Melanie Klein today: Vol. 2. Mainly practice.* London: Routledge.

Stern, D. (1985). *The interpersonal world of the infant.* New York: Basic Books.

Sullivan, H. S. (1954). *The psychiatric interview.* New York: Norton.

Winnicott, D. W. (1965). *The maturational process and the facilitating environment.* New York: International Universities Press.

CHAPTER 2

The Failure to Ask the Hard Questions

Donald P. Spence

S OME 100 YEARS AGO, not long after Freud published *The Interpretation of Dreams,* another pioneer was writing a landmark critique of American and Canadian medical education. Abraham Flexner's (1910) advice, despite its age, has a significant bearing on many of the issues discussed in this book:

> Medicine is a discipline in which the effort is made to use knowledge procured in various ways in order to effect certain practical ends. With abstract general principles [read metapsychology] it has nothing to do. It harbors no preconceptions as to diseases or their cure. Instead of starting with a finished and supposedly adequate dogma or principle, it has progressively become less cocksure and more modest. It distrusts general propositions, a priori explanations, grandiose and comforting generalizations [worth memorizing]. It needs theories only as convenient summaries in which a number of ascertained facts may be used tentatively to define a course of action. It makes no effort to use its discoveries to substantiate a principle formulated before the facts were even suspected [worth underlining]. For it has learned from a previous history of human thought that men possessed of vague preconceived ideas are strongly disposed to force facts to fit, defend, or explain them. And this tendency both interferes with the free search for truth and limits the good which can be extracted from such truth. (p. 156)

Many aspects of our current predicament can be found in Flexner's critique. Part of the reason research findings have not been more useful to clinicians is that they are attempts either to validate one or more "vague preconceived ideas" that can never be disconfirmed or to provide evidence in support of "grandiose and comforting generalizations." Of equal importance for our present plight is the fact that theory in psychoanalysis has almost never been constructed from the bottom up, that is, in response to specific observations. This state of affairs is related to the fact that our public data base is all but invisible to the naked eye; as a result, there has grown up, over time, a gradual decoupling of theory from data. Deprived of a common set of facts that might represent the gist of our collective wisdom, theory is free to tell whatever story it chooses.

For an example of how theory can be projected (and protected) in a way that is uncluttered by actual facts, consider the following well-known description of the "good hour" in psychoanalysis:

> Let me start with a schematic example. It concerns an experience which, though not frequent, is familiar to all analysts. And it is one welcome to all. I mean "the good analytic hour." Its course is varied, and I offer only an abstraction from experiences well advanced in analytic therapy. Many a time the "good hour" does not start propitiously. It may come gradually into its own, say after the first ten or fifteen minutes, when some recent experience has been recounted, which may or may not refer to yesterday's session. Then a dream may come, and associations, and all begins to make sense.
>
> In particularly fortunate instances a memory from the near or distant past, or suddenly one from the dark days may present itself with varying degrees of affective charge. At times new elements are introduced as if they had always been familiar, so well do they fit into the scheme of things. And when the analyst interprets, sometimes all he needs to say can be put into a question. The patient may well do the summing up by himself, and himself arrive at conclusions. (E. Kris, 1956, pp. 445–455)

This is a spellbinding narrative that manages, in the absence of a single clinical observation, to convince us of the possibility of the "good hour" and acquaint us with the conditions under which it comes into being. Kris has created a specimen out of words alone; it is neither fact nor fiction but has some of the attributes of both. He presents us with a fantasy we would all like to share and describes it in a way that makes it sound real. But a close inspection of his account shows us that the details will always remain just out of sight. The memory from the "near or distant past" is left vague and undescribed; the "affective charge" is left unstated; and the way in which all the pieces fit into the "scheme of things" is left to our imagination. Even the final interpretation—perhaps only a question—goes unstated, along with the final summing up by the patient.

The description casts a mythic spell because it is presented in the form of a coherent narrative with the classic bookends of an uneasy beginning (it "does not start propitiously") and a happy ending ("the patient may well do the summing up by himself"). It tells a tale we would all like to share; as a result, we tend to read it in a largely uncritical manner. In the short space of a well-constructed paragraph, the "good hour" has come into being, and so artful is the presentation that many analysts remember the passage as being about an actual clinical occurrence. But it should be noted that persuasion is brought about entirely by means of the rhetorical voice.

Many of our most cherished theoretical notions in psychoanalysis are grounded largely in make-believe—a scientifically appalling state of affairs. But standard theory continues to flourish, largely unchanged, because the available "data" are stored primarily as memories in the minds of practicing analysts. In this somewhat plastic and porous state, they constitute a shifting and unreliable corpus that is permanently lost with the death of each practitioner. Even when the host is living, his memory is not open to public inspection or consensual validation, or available for the confirmation or disconfirmation of theoretical propositions. The details of these memories can never be checked against the facts, and we must assume that they are at the mercy of many of the same distortions of remembering that Freud was the first to warn us against. How many of our efforts (in good faith) to retrieve a clinical example in order to support this or that theoretical position have produced merely screen memories? In how many instances do we unwittingly fabricate a far-off clinical memory in our eagerness to support received theory? Precisely because of its largely memorial nature, our accumulated clinical evidence is particularly vulnerable to the influence of theory, and to an extent that can never be documented. We will come back to this issue later in the chapter.

Given the minuscule data base and the almost mythic nature of received theory, it can be seen that the research branch of the psychoanalytic family is a poor relation at best and not infrequently excluded from the more important get-togethers. It is worth noting that when members of the International Psychoanalytic Association gathered in Argentina in 1991, for their clinical meetings, the researchers had convened in London (halfway around the world from Buenos Aires) some four months before. Separated in both time and place, the sites for these two research and clinical meetings provide us with a useful metaphor for the decoupling of theory and data referred to earlier. Although clinicians were free to attend the London meeting and researchers were welcome in Argentina, the separation hardly encourages the close exchange of findings that is in the best interest of an enlightened and flourishing science. Whether these unfortunate occurrences are accidents or the result of something more ominous, their existence only encourages the separation of theory from research and provides another excuse for why theory cannot be built the old-fashioned way—from the bottom up.

But at this point we confront a paradox. Despite (or perhaps because of) its status as poor relation and marginal member of the psychoanalytic family, the research branch has been only too willing to accept standard theory as largely confirmed and in no need of challenge or extensive revision. Literature reviews are typically uncritical and permissive; major oversights are often overlooked in the service of keeping peace with standard theory. For example, in a recent review of outcome studies covering the past 100 years of psychoanalytic practice, the authors concluded that "the findings of the formal, systematic research studies to date are consistent with the accumulated body of clinically derived psychoanalytic knowledge"—despite the fact that, as they themselves noted several sentences later, "the studies all contain methodological weaknesses." The second conclusion takes much of the meaning away from the first, but the authors chose to accentuate the positive and ended up by noting that "the value of such contributions [the quantitative studies under review] should not be underestimated" (Bachrach, Galatzer-Levy, Skolnikoff, & Waldron, 1991, p. 911). Hardly a critical review, despite the promise of the abstract on the first page ("in this study we critically review . . . "). To become aware of the implications of this attitude, it is worth considering the fact that a Ptolemaic astronomer in the Middle Ages could easily have concluded that his observations of the sun, moon, and planets were consistent with his belief that the sun revolves around the earth. If a critical review refuses to be critical, few faults will be found and no damage (to existing theory) will be done.

It would seem that one of the major obstacles to translating research findings into clinical practice stems from the researchers' failure to ask the hard questions that strike at the heart of our basic assumptions. Instead, the researchers—both inside and outside the ranks of practicing clinicians—seem content to concede (1) that there is sufficient reason to believe in a dynamic unconscious; (2) that we can gain access to it through free association; (3) that mutative interpretations can bring about structural alterations in the unconscious; and (4) that the psychoanalytic process, to the extent that it is based on the preceding assumptions, is a valid form of therapy for certain types of patients—despite the fact that we have no convincing proof of any one of these beliefs. On the last point, it is worth noting that *none* of the outcome studies reviewed by Bachrach et al. (1991) used a no-treatment control group. As a result, there is no way of telling whether positive outcome stemmed from the psychoanalytic process per se or simply from the effects of time and regular meetings between analyst and analysand.

Because the basic assumptions are not generally challenged, we have no continuing investigation into such crucial aspects of the psychoanalytic process as the role of interpretation, the function of free association, or the meaning of dreams. And the research that remains tends to be divided into two main categories. "Faced with the awesome task of studying ourselves, psychologists have resorted either to impeccably scientific studies of nothing very much,[1] or to exciting but cloudy psychoanalytic speculation" (Dinnage, 1991, p. 7).

---

[1]Luborsky and Spence (1978) reached essentially the same conclusion in their review of quantitative research on psychoanalytic therapy: "Quantitative research . . . presents itself, so far, as an unreliable guide to clinical practice" (p. 358).

Research findings that we have every reason to believe (because they come from studies whose methodology is flawless) unfortunately tend to be unrelated to issues of deep clinical significance. But the more interesting, even exciting, clinical studies are flawed by their reliance on anecdote, their failure to collect a complete set of data, their untroubled reliance on metaphor and other rhetorical devices, and, last of all and perhaps most important, a medieval belief in the idea that what is sensed by one investigator must be sensed by all. Whereas children of 5 or 6 have usually become aware of the fact that their thoughts may be different from those of other persons,[2] this possibility seems to have escaped most analytic authors. As a result, there is no recognition of the play of subjectivity in the evaluation of evidence and no sign that researchers understand the need to guard against unwitting bias or the confounding effect of theory on observation.

Two conclusions stem from this state of affairs. First, the secure findings have no interest for practicing clinicians because they are impeccable "studies of nothing very much." Second, the more exciting findings are methodologically flawed. One of these flaws, as we have seen, leads clinicians to focus on what is taken for granted and adds an embellishment or some other kind of variation; as a result, these studies do not materially change either theory or practice and tend to be seen as welcome confirmation of something we knew all along. But when the author's curiosity leads him or her in a more daring direction, the study is usually so flawed by methodological problems (some of which we discuss in this chapter) as to be unreliable in its assertions and therefore a risky basis for changes in either theory or practice.

Unanswered Questions

What needs to be known? Because of the underlying investigative complacency over the past 100 years, practically everything. For example: How does a reasonably good interpretation gain its effect? How much is it constrained by the state of the transference or by the framing vocabulary of the speaker? How can a significant (mutative) effect be measured? Exactly how does it impact on the patient's psychic structure? How long does its effect last? How does the nature of the transference sometimes magnify and sometimes diminish the lexical content of an interpretation? How important is its lexical content in comparison to its nonverbal dimensions? Does this ratio vary with stage of treatment and the diagnosis of the patient? To what extent

---

[2]"Not only must I [as a growing child] be able to realize that other people ... have mental representations that I do not have; I must also be able to recognize that others often represent the same objects, situations, and events in a different way than I do" (Forguson & Gopnik, 1988, p. 230).

are analysts aware of the nonverbal dimension of their interventions? In addition, specific questions could be asked about the patient's memory: How does it change over time? How does it change in response to a reasonably good interpretation? Is there any evidence that some (screen) memories simply disappear when properly interpreted and worked through?

The experience of the patient, if not completely ignored, has certainly not been systematically investigated.[3] Aside from a handful of apocryphal clinical anecdotes (usually about patients with a so-called "negative therapeutic reaction"), we know next to nothing about the average patient's experience of the analytic situation in its various phases, that is, of his or her reaction to interventions, silence, interruptions, touch, failures of the analyst to stay awake, failures of the analyst to maintain proper boundaries, attempts by the analyst to establish rapport and to respond empathically; attempts by the analyst at being a blank screen, and so on. It is currently fashionable to conceive of the psychoanalytic relationship as an extension of the mother–infant developmental process (see Mayes & Spence, in press). To what extent does this metaphor hold true for our patients? What other metaphors would they choose in its place? To what extent do they feel deprived by the lack of visual contact and the almost total reliance on auditory cues? Or by the somewhat arbitrary nature of the analytic situation and its studied, almost ritualistic nature?

Dose-response effects are largely unstudied and, as a result, probably misunderstood. Is there any evidence that the number of sessions per week bears any relation to outcome? Is there any evidence that total hours of treatment is related to outcome?

We have seen how investigative complacency has minimized the role of the skeptical researcher in the psychoanalytic enterprise. It has also had a second unfortunate consequence: it has led to an unwarranted emphasis on the case report. In the next section, we look at some of the failings of the case report and how these sometimes conceal (paradoxically) some of its potential strengths.

How Reliable Are Anecdotal Reports?

The case report is our most popular method for communicating clinical findings, and it has a long and durable history. But because of its anecdotal base,

---

[3]This is not a new point in the caring professions. In a recent book titled *Doctors' Stories* (Hunter, 1991), the author makes the points that the narrative of the typical case is usually the doctor's story and not the patient's and that many of the ills of modern medicine stem from the difference between the two. Many aspects of the patient's story do not fit easily into a narrative frame and thus tend to be omitted from the official account.

it is open to basic questions of reliability and validity. We have already suggested that an unknown number of reports may be based on events that have either never happened or did not happen in quite the same way as described; the nature of memory (see Neisser, 1982) and the accumulating research on eyewitness testimony (see Loftus, 1979) make it only natural to raise questions of this kind. More needs to be known about the tendency to assimilate the unusual to the familiar and the tendency to remember an unexpected event as belonging to a well-established convention. The large and ever-expanding literature on memory and its fallibility needs to be introduced to the psychoanalytic community, and steps need to be taken, where possible, to immunize the case report against the more obvious sources of infection.

A classic experiment by Robbins (1963) may help to identify some of the critical issues. She compared retrospective reports by mothers of their child rearing experiences with records from the well-baby clinic to which they made regular visits. Whereas memories of well-established events were found to be more or less reliable, significant distortions were found in recall of somewhat "softer" data. This category included memories of when the infant stopped using the bottle, when bowel training was begun, when bladder training was started, and when the 2 A.M. feeding was stopped. Errors in remembering tended to follow the advice of Dr. Benjamin Spock as presented in his best-selling book on child care, *Baby and Child Care.*

Robbins's findings may be taken as a warning that applies to the way we write case reports. So-called hard data, such as the patient's fee, initial diagnosis, frequency of sessions, and the circumstances of coming into treatment, are probably better remembered and reported than other clinical happenings that are more subject to retrospective revision. The softer data may tend to be remembered in ways that make them subtly correspond to received theory. Urgently needed is a set of paradigmatic studies that would tell us how much of a given phenomenon, on average, is captured by the usual kind of anecdotal case report. A series of such studies would begin to tell us how much of the traditional literature should be believed. Even if critical details are forgotten, can the clinical gist be trusted? Or, to take the opposite point of view, are anecdotal memories largely unreliable and apt to lead to reports that are more wishful than descriptive? In that event, case studies do not deserve to be treated as data.

Part of the error in the typical case report stems from a failure to keep careful records. In a recent study on the patient's use of first names of parents (Waugaman, 1990), we are told in the first sentence that "it is rare for a patient in analysis to speak of his parents by their first name." In the next paragraph we are told that "using the parent's first name unconsciously signifies an oedipal transgression—it constitutes doing what one's other parent but not oneself is permitted to do" (pp. 167–168). Grounds for the first sentence are never given; grounds for the second statement are suggested in the course of the paper. But the argument is flawed by the fact that no special precautions were taken to keep track of *all* uses of first names, and it seems doubtful whether the ordinary kind of process notes can be relied upon to maintain an exhaustive record of all such uses. Without such a record the reported findings, largely anecdotal, and the various conclusions are largely meaningless. (The small sample size—five subjects—might be seen as another handicap, but this defect would matter much less if the record keeping had been reliable and exhaustive). Robbins's findings should make us wary of generalizations that are devoid of explicit documentation and those that seem to correspond too closely to received theory.

For an example of another kind of problem in case reporting, consider a recent discussion of the analytic "surface" by Paniagua (1991; defined [p. 672] as contents that can be "non-conjecturally apperceived"). As she entered her office one day, Paniagua accidentally bumped into a lamp and the patient (a male) laughed and said, "I do things like that all the time" (p. 679). The analyst describes how she tried to find a way to respond to this comment and could find no good opportunity until an hour, some four sessions later, when the patient, in talking about a famous sports team and its losing season, admitted that he derived "perverse enjoyment" from its failures (p. 681). The analyst felt that this remark, because it was sufficiently close in meaning to the initial incident, gave her the opportunity to explore his earlier feelings "with fruitful results in terms of associations and insight" (p. 680).

Were there other opportunities? Paniagua admits that "there are always surfaces: the patient's and the clinical ones (fifty minutes of audiovisual surfaces per session)" (p. 680) but that she could not find an "adequate workable surface" until the event described came to pass. This remark points up the issue. The study would be considerably enhanced if some way had been found to present a fuller sampling of these surfaces to allow the reader to judge whether no other opportunities for intervention had occurred, as the author concluded, or whether some opportunities had existed that the author, for one reason or another, had either not recognized or had chosen not to respond to. The report, as it stands, presents us with only a brief glimpse of a potentially fascinating problem; by not presenting either the full transcript or a fair sample of the intervening hours, the author deprives us of the chance to examine the problem of derivatives in more detail. Of particular interest would be those surfaces that seem to the reader to be related to the original incident but that were not recognized by the analyst at the time. Her oversight necessarily raises questions of the ways in which local context may disguise meanings and effectively reduce the analyst's sensitivity; the data *not* presented are undoubtedly rich in their implications for the study of different aspects of countertransference.

What does the analytic surface look like from below, that is, from the patient's perspective? If more attention could be paid to this question, we might have a way of linking the two concepts of free association and evenly hovering attention. Paniagua reminds us that "the material the analysand becomes aware of (the patient's surface) does not always become a clinical surface" (p. 670), but it is not clear under what conditions the two coincide. Nor is it entirely obvious that the average analytic surface is all that easy to define; one suspects that ten analysts would define ten different surfaces. Here is a place where the presentation of the full transcript seems an essential step to furthering the discussion; if agreement on non-conjectural apperception cannot be found, the concept is already in serious difficulty.

The ambiguity surrounding the word *surface* points up an important difference between the Paniagua and Waugaman papers. In the latter case the goal of the study was to look at how (and, in particular, how early) the parents' first names were used by patients in the course of their treatment. We have pointed to some methodological difficulties in the study, but these do not obscure the fact that the goal is straightforward and probably attainable, given the right methodological controls. But the virtues of this design are conspicuously missing in the study of surfaces because of the fact that no attempt has been made to reduce the metaphor to something more measurable. The fact that Freud himself used the word *surface* (or, more exactly, its German equivalent) 91 times (see Paniagua, 1991, p. 670) does not justify its continued use in this investigation. One suspects that its metaphoric appeal may be one reason for keeping it in play, yet its very poetic nature interferes with its scientific value. Paniagua has come under the sway of the rhetorical voice of psychoanalysis (see Spence, 1990). What makes for evocative and persuasive writing does not always make for good science, and before the problem of "surfaces" can be explored, we need to know more about its ostensive meaning, that is, what the word is pointing at.

Paniagua's study shares with Waugaman's a failure to be exhaustive in its data collection. Even though Paniagua properly observes that "any scientific study in clinical psychoanalysis should be firmly based on [the] surface evidence, making clear the distinction between observation and inference" (p. 683), she denies this opportunity to the reader because the only data supplied are those surfaces she judged to be related to the target incident. The distinction is an important one, and the only way it can be explored is to present both domains of evidence: *all* observations and *all* inferences. Waungaman could follow the same advice. Only when both domains are compared and contrasted can we begin to develop a theory of surfaces, or a theory of first names.

The failure to present the full set of data is related to another problem common to anecdotal studies. Because data collection is usually geared to a particular purpose, the findings tend to be irrelevant for any other investigator with some other goal in mind. Thus, much effort is wasted. Instead of forming the beginning of an archival data base, the average clinical paper contains nothing of interest for future generations of researchers. If we try to make data collection more systematic, even a small number of hours might answer questions posed by future investigators who will be raising issues unknown to us at this moment. Data collected with this end in mind become invaluable, and their accumulation enriches the science almost as much as the proof of a new theory would.

But a more serious difficulty, common to both the Waugaman and Paniagua papers, remains to be mentioned: a failure to fully appreciate the extent to which one's awareness of a phenomenon may not be universally shared. What is missing from the vast majority of clinical reports is what might be called a kind of Royal Society skepticism, that is, the view that all hypotheses are tentative and that psychoanalysis is, above all else, a science of subjectivity (see Lear, 1990). By presenting only a small slice of the available data, Paniagua clearly implies that her judgment can be trusted; that other analysts, listening to the same material, would react as she did; and that the hours not described are without scientific interest. The opposite is probably nearer to the truth: the interesting data in this study lie in what was *not* reported, because these happenings can teach us something about specific oversights and other countertransference manifestations.

Observational Models

It is instructive to contrast the present standing of psychoanalytic research with current developments in the field of mother–infant interaction. Over the past 10 years a number of specific observational models have been developed in our sister discipline that give us a repeatable method for studying certain kinds of processes. In the social referencing paradigm, to take one example, the child is presented with a novel task in the presence of the mother, and his or her attempts to confront and solve the task are studied with respect to the use he or she makes of the mother's facial expression and other aspects of her body language. If a 1-year-old is approaching a seemingly dangerous visual cliff, he or she will typically crawl toward it, hesitate, and then look at his or her mother's face; her expression and direction of gaze are used as guides for further progress. If she seems calm and relaxed and gazes steadily at the cliff, the infant proceeds across it without hesitation (see Sorce, Emde, Campos, & Klinnert, 1985). If she looks sad, he or she may stop and continue to monitor her face for further reassurance. If she looks fearful, he or she may go no farther. The behaviors elicited in this paradigm seem to suggest not only that the infant is seeking reassurance and affective support when confronting new tasks but also that he or she is beginning to understand that the parent will respond in a way that is organizing, protective, and facilitative. The predictability of reactions to the social referencing paradigm among normal children helps to sensitize us to their absence in autistic children. The relative simplicity of the paradigm enables the researcher to introduce meaningful complications and to study the effect under a wide range of conditions.

For another example of a useful observational paradigm, consider the so-called "still face situation": after playing with her infant for 5 minutes, the mother is asked to maintain an affectively neutral or expressionless face for 3 minutes and not to interact with the child (ages ranged from 3 to 15 months) during this period of time. Studies have examined the effects of this deprivation on both infant (see Fogel, 1982) and mother (Mayes, Carter, Egger, & Pajer, 1991); in the latter study over half the mothers experienced discomfort during the session and 21% broke off the experiment before the 3-minute period had elapsed. Here again, the demand characteristics of the paradigm are immediately apparent, enabling investigators to map out the dimensions of an average expectable reaction and to identify its absence (as with an autistic child or a depressed mother).

Third and last to be noted is the paradigm known as the "false belief situation." In the standard task the child being tested watches a toy being placed in one location and then (after the owner has left the room) moved to a second. When the owner returns, the child is asked, "Where will the owner look for the toy?" In other words, the child is asked where the owner *believes* the toy to be. Normal children between ages 4 and 6 can apparently take the perspective of the owner and conclude that he will look for the toy where he last saw it (see Moses & Flavell, 1990). Failure to take this perspective leads the child to confuse what he knows with what the owner knows and to conclude that the owner will search for the toy in the second location. Younger normal children and autistic children often take the second option.

These observational paradigms help us to understand a particular aspect of the growing child's understanding of other minds, of the difference between belief and reality, and of the way in which thoughts are sometimes invisible and sometimes displayed through expressions and actions. They allow us to rethink and investigate more carefully those situations that we tend to take for granted and to realize how complicated is the everyday task of interacting with, and making assumptions about, familiar and unfamiliar others. By repeating the measure at specific ages, researchers can learn something about developmental changes; by comparing different populations, they can learn something about the responses of different diagnostic groups.

Psychoanalytic research, in similar fashion, needs to develop its own set of observational paradigms that will identify critical aspects of the treatment process and to study them in a systematic manner. These paradigms, if carefully constructed, would provide us with an opening into what might be called the average analysand's theory of mind.[4] We might begin by asking, What are the minimal conditions for listening in the analytic situation? The successful patient must, first of all, be able to understand words and sentences in isolation stripped of their complementary body language; for some individuals, this is no easy task. Patients must be capable of extended auditory (and therefore serial) processing of frequently long and sometimes ungrammatical sentences (see Dahl, Teller, Moss & Trujillo, 1978) that may appear at unexpected moments. They must be capable of reflecting on inner thoughts and translating them into words, all the while keeping in mind the fact that the analyst cannot see or hear these thoughts, even though at times it may appear that this is so. They must become comfortable with the so-called basic rule and be able to move easily from one context to another in pursuit of a particular theme. In reflecting on their associations, analysands must be able to go back in time and remember when a certain thought began and what triggered it and (in moving to the present) to consider how it has changed and why. Analysands must learn that silence on the part of the analyst is not necessarily the equivalent of the still face, even though it may seem the same. And, finally, they must learn that visual and auditory channels are complementary, not interchangeable.

Deficits in one or more of these requirements can often be traced to specific developmental failures (see Mayes & Spence, in press), and it is not entirely clear to what degree they can be overcome in the normal course of an average expectable psychoanalysis. Deficits, in turn, can lead directly to certain types of resistance, therapeutic misunderstandings, and treatment failures. Patients who have the tendency to treat auditory and visual messages as interchangeable will probably never adapt to the long analytic silence; they will tend to treat it as the equivalent of an interminable still face situation. Failure to understand the nature of other minds may show itself in an attempt to create a mirror transference, that is, to automatically project onto the analyst all intense thoughts and feelings. A need to experience a certain minimal amount of social referencing will very likely impair a patient's ability to listen to a disembodied voice in the absence of all reinforcing visual clues, a voice that speaks intermittently, seemingly at random (and almost never conversationally), and is prone to make brief, authoritative, even dogmatic pronouncements surrounded by silence. If the purely auditory message sounds at all foreign or strange, the analyst's utterances will tend to be heard not for their lexical meaning but with an emphasis on their paralin-

---

[4]See Astington, Harris, & Olson, 1988, for a discussion of the general concept of theory of mind, some examples of how the theory changes in children from 2 to 5, and a sketch of how it becomes transformed in adolescence and adulthood.

guistic features—tone, timbre, rhythm, inflection—and these are the very features that we are almost never aware of or have under control. Thus, the stage is set for a classic kind of miscommunication: we think we are saying ABC (the intended contents of our intervention), but the patient is hearing XYZ, its paralinguistic surround.

A better understanding of the specific requirements of the analytic situation should lead to a better-grounded theory. We have many metaphors for describing the analytic process but little reliable documentation of its specific characteristics. Because patients are rarely heard from in any systematic way, we tend to project onto the analytic situation our own idealized definitions (as in E. Kris's definition of the good hour, cited earlier) and our more fanciful metaphors (for example, holding environment, transitional object). These may have nothing to do with the actual experience of a majority of patients. To further complicate the situation, a nontrivial percentage of analysands are candidates in training and are therefore in a particularly poor position to raise objections or complaints. An occasional analysand will tell us that he or she senses silence as contempt (see Renek, 1991); how many other patients have had the same thought—and for reasons that stem from the specific features of the analytic arrangement and that have little to do with the transference?

It seems clear that a certain amount of basic research must be devoted to understanding the more important features of the analytic situation, a situation we take largely for granted. What form might this research take? For starters, we might begin with the series of analyst interventions isolated by Dahl, Teller, Moss, and Trujillo (1978). In the original study these interventions were subjected to a careful linguistic analysis and found to express either no clear message or a mixture of meanings. It would be useful to gather further data by presenting these interventions (in their original format, taken directly from the audio recordings) to normal subjects and asking them to evaluate their linguistic and paralinguistic senses. In addition, comparisons could be made between the responses of subjects who have had some experience with therapy and those with no such experience. Experiments of this kind would help to identify interventions that seem good on paper but fail in practice, as compared to interventions that seem syntactically hopeless but nevertheless convey a clear message. Some of the interventions gathered by Dahl and associates may prove to be perfectly clear when spoken with suitable inflection and intonation despite their apparently opaque semantic surface. Basic studies are needed that would sensitize us to the difference between written and spoken language and enlarge our understanding of which forms of spoken language need a visual surround to be understood and which do not.

Similar attention needs to be paid to different parts of speech. Concrete nouns, for example, are traditionally considered to be less ambiguous than pronouns; does this difference continue to hold in the specific conditions surrounding the analytic situation? When the passive voice is used in interventions, does it somehow detract from their force or does it seem less intrusive to the patient? With certain types of wording, is there an occasional misunderstanding as to how much is assumed versus how much is known —that is, do patients sometimes believe that the analyst can read their thoughts and feelings? For example, consider this example from Dahl and associates (1978): "And I think it's a measure of how strong you do feel about that that you never really talked about it here" (p. 348). The analyst has managed to convey the idea that he knows, in some unspecified manner, just how strongly the patient feels; assuming the analyst is correct, the patient may wonder how he knows and whether he knows other things as well. In more abstract language, this kind of interpretation tends to convey the impression that at certain times no separation exists between the mind of the patient and the mind of the analyst.

We now have the basis for a possible paradigm that would parallel the false belief situation used in child development research. After the subject/ analysand has been settled on the couch and given a brief description of the basic rule, the experimenter/analyst lets him or her free-associate for 15 to 20 minutes and then selects a topic that has *not* been mentioned (we'll call it topic X) and says, "It may be a measure of how strong you do feel about X that you never really talked about it here." The subject is then allowed to continue for another 5 minutes. When the session is stopped, subjects are asked a number of questions about their reaction to the intervention: What was their initial response? Did they feel the intervention was in some ways correct? Did they feel that the analyst had managed in some unspecified manner to gain access to their thoughts? Did they have the fleeting thought that the analyst could and would continue to "read" their mind? Did they feel their privacy had been violated, and if so, did they feel less agreeable about continuing to comply with the basic rule?

This first set of questions might be asked while the subject is still on the couch. A second set, including many of the same items, might be asked at some later time to determine how subjects' reaction to the experience varied as a function of their state of consciousness and the demand characteristics of the situation. It might be found, for example, that whereas subjects might agree, while lying down, that they felt their mind was being read, they might change their opinion after more time elapses, either forgetting the original reaction or feeling ashamed of having had the thought in the first place. Careful comparison of the two sets of responses would give us information about what kinds of reactions can only be measured in a particular state of consciousness and the extent to which memory can and cannot be relied upon to preserve the specific quality of an experience. Memory of the original event might be measured after more extended intervals to pursue the same question.

Other paradigms might focus on the wording of specific interventions because much more needs to be known about the nature of language deprived of all visual cues. This form of communication is clearly the exception in our television age—in fact, it would be interesting to compare the success rates of psychoanalytic treatments before and after television arrived on the cultural scene and a purely auditory message became the exception rather than the rule for most people in terms of their exposure to nonprint mass media.

It is commonly assumed that casting interventions in a vocabulary used by the patient makes them more effective than a more standard phrasing, but is there any truth to this belief? Many analysts make it a point of putting their observations in a conditional mode in order to emphasize their tentative nature; in how many cases is the patient aware of this conditional phrasing? Patient awareness of niceties of this kind undoubtedly interacts with frequency of interventions: if the analyst speaks only once or twice during the session, we would suspect that the patient, starved for a response, may tend to ignore the mode of the verb and other fine points of phrasing; thus, the careful choice of tentative preamble may simply go unheard. It would not be surprising to find that much of the effort spent by the analyst in crafting a specimen interpretation goes unnoticed by patients and that, conversely, much of what they find personally meaningful is only uttered accidentally by the analyst. Once again, we badly need evidence to complement our theories.

An example of a paradigm that investigates the importance of the paralinguistic suround might be as follows: some of the interventions listed by Dahl and associates (1978) might be tried once with the original inflection and then again in a flatter and less expressive manner, with the following research questions in mind: How does the subject's reaction change? When experimenters speak in a flatter voice, do they seem to be less understanding? Less empathic? When more expression is used, do experimenters seem more intimate? More intrusive? How do these differences influence the content and form of subsequent associations on the part of the subject/analysand?

This line of reasoning brings us to the associative process and the part it plays in uncovering forgotten content. Part of Rapaport's (1942) *Emotions and Memory* was devoted to experimental investigations of remembering and forgetting; much more needs to be known. A similar kind of basic research needs to be devoted to separating one kind of association from another. Can Kris's (1990) distinction between convergent and divergent associations (p. 35) be identified in practice with suitable levels of reliability? Can we separate reluctance (defined by A. Kris as the conscious withholding of certain information) from resistance (its unconscious counterpart; see Kris, 1990, p. 27)? If it is possible to separate good and bad interventions in a reliable manner, can these differences be shown to lead to different kinds of associations?

As these examples make clear, there are any number of process questions that have only been studied in the context of the therapeutic situation. What is urgently needed is some method of formulating these issues as explicit experimental paradigms that can be taken out of the clinical arena and subjected to more systematic investigation. In this way, we could parallel work being done by infant researchers on social referencing, still face, and false belief situations and could identify features of the clinical situation that are not specific to a particular therapist or kind of therapy.

Concluding Remarks

Psychoanalytic research has been frequently criticized for its undue reliance on single-case studies, for the absence of controls, and for its dependence on anecdotal reports and various other subjective and selective methods for sampling the data. But equally pernicious has been its reluctance to ask the hard questions and to challenge basic theoretical assumptions. Once again, one of Flexner's (1910) observations seems appropriate:

> The sectarian [as opposed to the true scientist] . . . begins with his mind made up. He possesses in advance a general formula, which the particular instance is going to illustrate, verify, reaffirm, even though he may not know just how. One may be sure that facts so read will make good what is expected of them; that only that will be seen which will sustain its expected function; that every aspect noted will be dutifully loyal to the revelation in which favor the observer is predisposed; the human mind is so constituted. (p. 156)

All too frequently, one reads psychoanalytic papers with the feeling that the general conclusions are already known, that they conform to some unspecified formula, and that the purpose of the paper is only to illustrate the larger case. Conceived in this manner, such studies can never discover anything new; their authors (or readers) will never be surprised by the unexpected. Believing that everything important is largely already known (and this position has a disturbingly medieval ring to it),[5] authors present us with some new examples of the obvious. And as Flexner made clear almost 100 years ago, "the facts so read will make good what is expected of them."

[5]At the time Newton entered Trinity College, "the wisdom of the ancients still reigned supreme, while the advocates of substantive change [the Royal Society], comparatively few in number and just beginning to communicate with one another, carried on an arduous and quite lonely struggle for reform" (Christianson, 1984, p. 30).

Research in child development has at least two important things to teach us: First, we badly need an analysand's theory of mind that will allow us to understand how the average patient will tend to experience and understand certain kinds of utterances within the analytic situation. If the analyst, for example, says, "I know what you must be feeling," we might assume that for some patients, this sounds as if the analyst has access to privileged information, that he can somehow sense what is going on inside another's head (the single word *must*, spoken by the analyst, adds significantly to this conviction). This kind of statement, taken literally, defies the philosophical notion of the uncertainty of ever knowing other minds, and introduces an entirely new worldview that some patients may find invasive, even if others find it rewarding. Much more needs to be known about how these statements are heard by patients and what assumptions they make about what is private knowledge, available only to them, and what is public, accessible to others. Confusion about this distinction may be related to certain kinds of analytic misunderstandings, to failed treatments, to the development of prolonged silences, and to similar phenomena yet unexplored.

Various aspects of the analysand's theory of mind can probably be best explored through the use of specific observational paradigms, and this is the second piece of advice we can take from our colleagues in infant research. We badly need to be able to refer analytic phenomena to a set of specific and repeatable experimental frames; such a step would force us to strip off interfering metaphors and would mark the beginning of both a cumulative data base and a convergent investigative approach. Consider the problem of the analytic "surface" in conjunction with the provisional paradigm outlined earlier. After the experimenter/analyst makes his or her statement about certain topics not being discussed, the subject/patient will generate a complex analytic "surface," some parts of which are responsive to intervention; some analysts might choose one set of surfaces, others another. Not only could this issue be explored with respect to the analyst's response, but the underside of each surface, the patient's view, could also be explored and contrasted to its appearance from above. One of the fruits of this investigation would be a better understanding of the metaphor of the analytic surface and the way it can describe certain clinical happenings. From a series of such studies, we could begin to accumulate a set of specimen examples for this term that would both clarify its meaning and provide useful illustrations for its use. Future papers on the topic might begin by referencing this data base; in this way, all analysts could begin to share a common language.

We have seen how the average clinical study can be read as the tip of a data-rich iceberg that is waiting to be explored. The clinical literature contains a wealth of (largely submerged) clinical clues that need to be systematically studied and brought to light in ways that do justice to their practical and theoretical importance. Almost all of these studies need to be reshaped—and some of the core ideas are perhaps better studied by way of repeatable, experimental paradigms—but the way is open for the clinically and scientifically curious to discover any number of surprising things.

Of particular importance are rules for taking advantage of natural experiments, that is, the one-of-a-kind clinical happenings that lend themselves to exhaustive study because they spontaneously fulfill many of the conditions of laboratory research. Suppose we were tape-recording an analytic case and discovered that a dozen hours contained only a single interpretation and that it occurred about midway through each session. This accident enables the investigator to make measures of analytic process before and after the intervention; any change in the measures is very likely due to the content of the interpretation. Findings on the first half of the sample could be replicated on the second half, because all hours fulfill the same conditions. Future archives could be indexed in ways that allow the investigator to identify single-interpretation hours; gradually, over time, a series of studies of this specific clinical happening could be carried out.

As another example, imagine finding an hour in which the patient asked the analyst why he looked so haggard and without thinking, the analyst confessed that he had just lost his father. Assume further that the patient felt so burdened by this tragic and unexpected news that she broke off treatment, and then resumed several years later after she had worked through her surprise and guilt. This series of events presents us with another natural experiment, and it can be studied for the effects of unwitting expression of feelings on the therapeutic process.

There would seem to be any number of ways in which clinical reporting can be put on a more systematic footing to enable us to rebuild the science from the bottom up. But this move may never take place because of the heavy hand of theory. Whereas Holzman (1985) could ask rhetorically whether the therapy was destroying the science, we can ask (not so rhetorically) whether theory and received wisdom is standing in the way of new knowledge. The pernicious influence of bad theory can be seen in the unquestioned use of outmoded metaphor, as in Paniagua's paper on the analytic surface; it can be seen in the reluctance to challenge approved doctrine or even to gather data in its support (this move is frequently seen as wasteful and unnecessary). The dominance of theory over evidence can be seen in the widespread belief that four or more sessions per week is more efficacious than three, with the result that analysts who believe in fewer sessions are not eligible for membership in the International Psychoanalytic Association. Such a criterion for membership—which is based on a belief that has the force of law despite the absence of supporting evidence—should be a source of widespread chagrin, but no one seems particularly embarrassed by this state of affairs.

In the final reckoning, the heavy hand of theory may prove to be more of a deterrent to better research than any of the other issues discussed in this chapter. Ways can be found around most, if not all, of the methodological and conceptual difficulties surrounding the gathering of psychoanalytic data, and a number of potentially eye-opening studies are ripe for the planning. But until there is agreement that present theory is grievously flawed and stands as much on make-believe as on empirical support, there will be no incentive to challenge the 100-year-old corpus of received wisdom that we have grown to respect—and not always for the best of reasons. Until it is more widely believed that only a small part of Freud's theory has evidential backing, there will be no need to put theory to the test, no reason to accumulate a more representative and public data base of clinical specimens that can be used to validate old concepts and generate new laws.

Christianson (1984), in discussing the times of Newton, tells us that even "if an increasing number of learned men no longer looked upon the efforts of those who relied on experiment as impudent or foolish, many still looked on the new method [of experimental investigation] as a questionable expenditure of time and energy" (p. 77). A similar diagnosis could be made today. True enough, there are a few signs that the times may be changing. Research papers now appear in the *Journal of the American Psychoanalytic Association* at fairly regular intervals, and while E. Kris could discuss the good analytic hour in 1956 with no recourse to data, it would be difficult to publish a similar paper today. The evidential voice is growing louder and making itself heard. On the other hand, the word *replication* is hardly a household term to most analysts, and a literature search on the total corpus of the three leading psychoanalytic journals, using that as the keyword, yields exactly zero papers! Q.E.D.

REFERENCES

Astington, J. W., Harris, P. L., & Olson, D. R. (1988). *Developing theories of mind.* Cambridge, UK: Cambridge University Press.

Bachrach, H. M., Galatzer-Levy, R., Skolnikoff, A., & Waldron, S. (1991). On the efficacy of psychoanalysis. *Journal of the American Psychoanalytic Association, 39,* 871–916.

Christianson, G. E. (1984). *In the presence of the creator: Isaac Newton and his times.* New York: Free Press.

Dahl, H., Teller, V., Moss, D., & Trujillo, M. (1978). Countertransference examples of the syntactic expression of warded-off contents. *Psychoanalytic Quarterly, 47,* 339–363.

Dinnage, R. (1991, December 13). The wounded male. *Times Literary Supplement,* p. 7.

Flexner, A. (1910). *Medical education in the United States and Canada*. New York: Carnegie Foundation for the Advancement of Teaching.

Fogel, A. (1982). Affect dynamics in early infancy. In T. Field & A. Fogel (Eds.), *Emotion and early interactions* (pp. 25–56). Hillsdale, NJ: Erlbaum.

Forguson, L., & Gopnik, A. (1988). The ontogeny of common sense. In J. Astington, P. Harris, & D. Olson (Eds.), *Developing theories of mind*. New York: Cambridge University Press.

Holzman, P. (1985). Psychoanalysis: Is the therapy destroying the science? *Journal of the American Psychoanalytic Association, 33*, 725–770.

Hunter, K. M. (1991). *Doctors' stories*. Princeton, NJ: Princeton University Press.

Kris, A. (1990). The analyst's stance and the method of free association. *Psychoanalytic Study of the Child, 45*, 25–41.

Kris, E. (1956). On some vicissitudes of insight. *International Journal of Psychoanalysis, 37*, 445–455.

Lear, J. (1990). *Love and its place in nature*. New York: Farrar, Straus & Giroux.

Loftus, E. (1979). *Eyewitness testimony*. Cambridge, MA: Harvard University Press.

Luborsky, L., & Spence, D. P. (1978). In S. L. Garfield & A. E. Bergin (Eds.), *Handbook of Psychotherapy and Behavior Change* (2nd ed. New York:) Wiley.

Mayes, L. C., Carter, A. S., Egger, H. L., & Pajer, K. A. (1991). Reflections on stillness: Mothers' reactions to the still-face situation. *Journal of the American Academy of Child and Adolescent Psychiatry, 30*, 22–28.

Mayes, L. C., & Spence, D. P. (in press). Understanding therapeutic action in the analytic situation: A second look at the developmental metaphor. *Journal of the American Psychoanalytic Association*.

Moses, L. J., & Flavell, J. H. (1990). Inferring false beliefs from actions and reactions. *Child Development, 61*, 929–945.

Neisser, U. (Ed.). (1982). *Memory observed: Remembering in natural contexts*. New York: Freeman.

Paniagua, C. (1991). Patient's surface, clinical surface, and workable surface. *Journal of the American Psychoanalytic Association, 39*, 669–685.

Rapaport, D. (1942). *Emotions and memory*. Baltimore: Williams & Wilkins.

Renek, O. (1991). One kind of negative therapeutic reaction. *Journal of the American Psychoanalytic Association, 39*, 87–105.

Robbins, L. C. (1963). The accuracy of parental recall of aspects of child development and child-rearing practices. *Journal of Abnormal and Social Psychology, 66*, 261–270.

Sorce, J., Emde, R., Campos, J., & Klinnert, M. (1985). Maternal emotional signalling: Its effect on the visual cliff behavior of one-year-olds. *Developmental Psychology, 21*, 195–200.

Spence, D. (1990). The rhetorical voice of psychoanalysis. *Journal of the American Psychoanalytic Association, 38*, 579–603.

Waugaman, R. M. (1990). On patients' disclosure of parents' and siblings' names during treatment. *Journal of the American Psychoanalytic Association, 38*, 167–194.

CHAPTER 3

Training and the Integration of Research and Clinical Practice

Otto F. Kernberg and John F. Clarkin

We have met the enemy, and they are us.
—Pogo (Walt Kelly)

R AMPANT EMPIRICISM without a firm grounding in theoretical structures will result in multiple research projects with fragmented yield and low efficiency. Theoretical digressions without grounding in research data will result in an arid philosophizing of little practical benefit to the treatment of patients. There is, obviously, a need for the integration of research and clinical practice. The nature of this integration is seldom carefully articulated.

In the area of psychotherapy research, the literature suggests that there is tension and/or separation between clinicians and researchers: Practicing clinicians contribute very little to the research base of clinical psychology (Garfield & Kurtz, 1976; Kelly, Goldberg, Fiske, & Kilkowski, 1978). It is interesting that it is never asked in print how many researchers have experience in clinical work, and clinicians report that they do little research because the research methods are inappropriate to their task with individual patients (Haynes, Lemsky, & Sexton-Radek, 1987). It has been suggested that faculty in graduate psychology programs should serve as role models for their students in integrating clinical and research work (Goldfried, 1984) and that this can be done by teaching single-subject methodologies and by reflecting on one's own assessment and intervention practices (Alberts & Edelstein, 1990).

In some respects, these arguments miss the mark. Only a limited number of individuals will do research after formal training whereas the majority will go into clinical practice. Our field needs (1) the training and career development of researchers who will be able (for example, through funding from NIMH) to pursue research in the assessment and treatment of homogeneous patient groups and (2) the training and career development of clinicians who will treat patients with strategies infused with the latest research knowledge. In this chapter, we explore the question, How do we effectively train the clinician not only in research methods and in how to be a consumer of the journals but also in how to integrate the latest research findings into daily clinical practice? In pursuit of this question, we consider (1) the way limited and piecemeal research data must be integrated before they can be useful for the clinician and (2) a model for training clinicians that exposes them to clinical research.

Differential Therapeutics: Borderline Personality Disorder

It is imperative to consider how and in what way the clinician can integrate the research on psychotherapy and psychotropic medications for optimal use in clinical practice. While some would suggest that there is little data for matching patients with specific treatments (for example, Smith & Sechrest, 1991), many have opted for treatment specificity. The three-volume treatment planning project by the American Psychiatric Association (1989) is an example of a commitment to the concept of treatment specificity. In previous writings we (Beutler & Clarkin, 1990, 1991; Clarkin, Frances, & Perry, in press; Frances, Clarkin, & Perry, 1984) have described differential therapeutics, that is, the application of principles derived from research and clinical experience in matching the individual patient to the most efficacious treatment.

Consider, for example, the treatment of a common condition such as borderline personality disorder (BPD). How does one use the existing research results on psychotherapy, medication, and the combination of therapy and medication in the treatment of a patient with this disorder?

MODEL OF BPD AND TREATMENT-RELEVANT SUBTYPES

In the context of this chapter, it is important to note the interplay of clinical theory, the generation of diagnostic criteria that can be reliably assessed, and the subsequent phenomenological research on BPD patients. The diagnostic criteria of the American Psychiatric Association's *Diagnostic and Statistical Manual of Mental Disorders* (3rd edition, revised), or *DSM-III-R,* provide behavioral/phenomenological markers that can be reliably assessed. The eight *DSM-III-R* criteria cover five different content areas: *identity diffusion* (one criterion); *dysfunctional affects,* such as labile moods, intense and uncontrolled anger, and feelings of emptiness and boredom (three criteria); *disturbed interpersonal relations,* such as intense interpersonal relations characterized by idealization and devaluation, and fear of real or imagined abandonment (two criteria); *impulsive behavior* in two or more areas (one criterion); and *self-destructive and suicidal behavior* (one criterion). The source of these criteria are theoretical conceptualizations by Kernberg (identity, impulsivity, emptiness, and boredom) and Gunderson (unstable intense relations, impulsivity, anger, self-damaging acts, affective instability, problems being alone).

The BPD criteria in *DSM-III-R* are a mixture of behaviors and traits from various clinical orientations (Stone, 1988), doing justice to none. The initial formulation of the Axis II BPD reflected a concern to distinguish it from schizotypal personality disorder (Spitzer, Endicott, & Gibbon, 1979). Only criteria that could be reliably assessed across clinicians with different theoretical orientations and training were selected, but the resulting eight criteria are too few in number to cover the salient issues and are stated at a concrete level of abstraction that becomes simplistic at times (for example, criteria for identity diffusion). This short set of criteria from several theoretical orientations is hardly adequate for research and clinical practice.

Borderline patients often present with comorbid conditions on both Axis I and Axis II. Many BPD patients have a comorbid Axis I diagnosis of some form of depression, and often these patients apply for treatment during a depressive episode. There is an involved debate about the nature of BPD, and some suggest that it is simply a variant of an affective disorder. From a practical point of view, borderline patients with depression need initial attention for the depression, after which treatment can proceed to other disruptive BPD behaviors (Skodol, 1989).

Lists of isolated criteria selected from various theoretical orientations are adequate neither for research nor for treatment planning. A set of criteria with empirically described interrelationships is more theoretically satisfying and more useful for further research. For example, to research the origins of borderline pathology in the family environment and family genetics, clusters of symptoms with construct validity are needed. To plan medication treatment interventions, traits (not diagnostic categories) that form a coherent structure are the target of specific drugs.

FACTOR ANALYSIS OF THE BPD CRITERIA

In an attempt to obtain some conceptual coherence about the *DSM-III-R* BPD criteria, we factor analyzed the eight criteria of borderline personality disorder as they were manifested in a large group of female inpatients (Clarkin, Hull, & Hurt, 1993). The assumption behind this effort was that the interrelationships between the criteria might indicate possible underlying causal relationships and hence possible treatment foci (Hurt & Clarkin, 1990). Using this methodology, we isolated three factors of BPD symptoms:

The first factor, the identity factor, is composed of criteria concerning identity diffusion, unstable interpersonal relations, feelings of emptiness and boredom, and fear of abandonment. The second factor is composed of criteria for labile moods, uncontrolled and inappropriate anger, and suicidal behavior. The third factor is composed of impulsivity in two or more areas.

Not only are the factors empirically derived, but they also appear to have face validity. Factor 1 seems to describe the borderline patient's difficulties in relation to self and others, reflecting those issues of self/other differentiation and boundary regulation that are often hypothesized as central to borderline pathology. Factor 2 reflects difficulties with anger, mood regulation, and related suicidal behavior, an important dimension of borderline pathology that has led some authors (for example, Akiskal, 1981) to view BPD as a variant of affective illness. The close association between labile affect and suicidal and other self-destructive behaviors seems to support recent speculation that borderline patients use self-mutilation as a mechanism of affect regulation (Gardner & Cowdry, 1985; Leibenluft, Gardner, & Cowdry, 1987). Factor 3 is composed of impulsive acts. This type of impulsive behavior (defined in *DSM-III-R* as including spending sprees, sexual promiscuity, drinking and drugs, bingeing, and reckless driving) is independent of the self-destructive acts in Factor 2. The impulsivity factor is composed of actual behaviors (not personality traits), behaviors that come and go depending upon the condition of the patient and the stability of current object relations.

The most severely disturbed borderlines are those with disturbances in all three areas of functioning. The less disturbed borderline patients have the affect and/or the identity factors. Treatment response tends to involve first some change in the impulsive behavior, followed by some control of affect modulation and gradual change in identity formation. This order of change has been noted in our own psychotherapy research project (Clarkin, Koenigsberg, Yeomans, Selzer, Kernberg, & Kernberg, 1992). We also see this progression of change in the five successfully treated BPD patients documented by Waldinger and Gunderson (1984).

RELATIONSHIP BETWEEN BORDERLINE PERSONALITY ORGANIZATION (BPO) AND BPD

It is interesting to consider the empirically derived factors of BPD symptoms with the conceptualization of BPO. This consideration is in part circular, as some of the criteria for BPD were derived from the writings of Kernberg. However, while initially derived from these writings, the criteria were also tested in a survey of practicing clinicians with respect to their estimated prevalence and accuracy.

The most obvious area of compatibility is between the identity factor of the *DSM-III-R* criteria (Factor 1) and the BPO identity diffusion. The BPD criterion of identity diffusion in *DSM-III-R* is stated in superficial terms, in order (apparently) to arrive at some reliability. The BPO concept highlights a lack of coherent sense of self both cross-sectionally (that is, the patient feels like a different person in different settings and with different people) and longitudinally (that is, the patient feels a lack of personal continuity across time, or an estrangement with the past). The intense ambivalence of the borderline patient is managed by defensive splitting and a concomitant idealization and devaluation of others. Thus, the patient is prone to stormy relationships in which rapid shifts of cognitive evaluation and mood are present and in which a fear of abandonment arises. Factor 2 is composed of labile moods, lack of control of anger, and self-destructive behavior. Intense anger and its lack of integration is central to the theory of borderline personality organization.

The BPD actions of the impulse factor (impulsivity in two or more areas) are conceptualized in the BPO construct as the direct result of reduction in flexibility and ego strength. Because the self is split into contradictory aspects, the patient shows nonspecific aspects of ego weakness in the form of poor impulse control, anxiety tolerance, and sublimatory capacity. Impulsive actions, then, are the outward symptoms of the underlying structural ego weakness and primitive defensive operations.

The BPO construct of reality testing is not represented in the BPD *DSM-III-R* criteria but is proposed in the *DSM-IV* criteria. In some ways this construct was placed in the schizotypal personality disorder criteria listed in *DSM-III-R*. In fact, this is a good illustration of the kind of splitting off of criteria (that are often related in individuals) into separate disorders on Axis II, one of the reasons for the massive Axis II comorbidity in clinical samples. As is well known, there is a substantial group of BPD patients with comorbid schizotypal personality disorder. These BPD-SPD patients probably include individuals with borderline structure (variable reality testing) and those who have a psychotic structure.

BPO and Axis II Comorbidity

With the accrual of data on clinical populations using the phenomenological and behavior criteria of *DSM-III-R*, it has become apparent that the overlap of Axis II disorders is extensive—so extensive in clinical samples as to mock the very meaning of the word *overlap*, which implies some unity and distinctness in the separate disorders. This overlap, as determined empirically in clinical samples, is consistent with that hypothesized by the BPO construct. In the BPO system, neurotic personality organization is composed of the obsessive compulsive, hysterical, and depressive/masochistic personality disorders, and the borderline level of organization includes BPD, narcissistic, antisocial, histrionic, schizoid, and paranoid personality disorders.

Thus, we would expect a high comorbidity rate between Axis II BPD and the latter five disorders. With data from Widiger et al. (1991), it seems clear that the overlap is as predicted, not only in the patients but in their first-degree relatives.

Comparison and Combined Use of the Two Systems

The BPD criteria are measurable behaviors and attitudes whereas BPO is a hypothesized structural organization of behavior. The two are articulated at different levels of abstraction and thus provide alternative advantages and disadvantages. At the present time we are in a neo-Kraepelinian revolution in which the emphasis is on phenomenological criteria that can be reliably assessed (Blashfield, 1984).

Some BPD criteria are not personality traits but, rather, behaviors and symptoms that fluctuate over time. For example, the patient fluctuates in terms of impulsive behavior and self-destructive behavior. In contrast, the BPO structures are seen as relatively stable across time, with the patient's outward behavior changing depending upon the circumstances at the moment.

Finally, the eight isolated criteria of BPD are not helpful in a conceptualization of the disorder for treatment planning. An atheoretical mélange of phenomenological and behavioral criteria is not helpful in providing a conceptual approach to intervention. This is not totally surprising; in fact, this situation was anticipated by the authors of *DSM-III*, who clearly state that treatment planning involves consideration of much more than what is contained in each set of criteria. The current BPD criteria, focused at a behavioral level to ensure reliability, are most useful for considering medication and possibly for behavioral treatments, which can be focused on separate and multiple behavioral areas.

Few individuals classified as having BPD manifest all eight criteria. Because BPD, like most *DSM-III* or *DSM-III-R* diagnoses, is polythetic (that is, the number of criteria minimally required to make the diagnosis is fixed and is fewer than the total number of possible criteria), it is inevitable that individuals with the disorder will be heterogeneous with regard to the defining criteria (and probably to correlated problem areas) and to comorbid Axis I and Axis II conditions.

This heterogeneity among individuals with BPD makes it difficult to define generalized treatment strategies for the group. On the one hand, designing treatment strategies for each of the individual criteria or for the many possible combinations of criteria seems overly concrete. On the other hand, a treatment strategy designed to address the entire complex of criteria would fail to address the modal individual with the diagnosis, who has fewer difficulties than those represented in the complete set.

MEDIATING GOALS OF TREATMENT

Borderline patients are more likely than other groups to prematurely end treatment. The mediating goals of treatment include (1) control of suicidal and other self-destructive behavior; (2) induction into treatment with normalization of in-treatment behavior (for example, attendance at each session, reduction in multiple contacts between sessions); (3) normalization of labile and disruptive moods, for example, depression, anger, and irritability; (4) improvement in interpersonal relations and behavior; and (5) increase in self-esteem and identity consolidation.

Treatment Choices

Setting.   Under usual circumstances the borderline patient can be treated on an outpatient basis. Acute hospitalization may be needed periodically to control serious self-destructive behavior. The range of functioning, both psychosocial and vocational, varies widely in the borderline group, and some patients may need day hospital treatment for the development of vocational and social skills. There is no existing research on the differential effectiveness of various treatment settings for BPD patients.

Format.   While the predominant treatment format is individual, the most researched treatment formats for BPD are group treatment and a combination of individual and group treatment (Clarkin, Marziali, & Munroe-Blum, 1991). The group format has the advantage of diluting the BPD patient's involvement with one therapist and of providing multiple models for coping and interaction. This format may provide one antidote to the iatrogenic effects of individual treatment in borderline patients that have been reported anecdotally (Strupp, Hadley, & Gomes-Schwartz, 1977).

Strategies and Techniques.   There are two manual-based treatments for BPD patients: a cognitive-behavioral approach that combines individual and group formats (Linehan, 1984, 1987; Linehan & Heard, 1992) and a modified psychodynamic approach (Kernberg, Selzer, Koenigsberg, Carr, & Appelbaum, 1989). The cognitive-behavioral approach has been found to be superior to treatment as usual in a clinical trial (Linehan, Armstrong, Suarez, Allmon, & Heard, 1991) whereas the psychodynamic treatment has been tried without a comparison group (Clarkin et al., 1992).

Psychodynamic treatments show differences among themselves in the use (or lack thereof) of early transference interpretation, in emphasizing a holding environment versus exploring negative transference, and in different conceptualizations of the therapist's role (Adler, 1989). Reports of successful dynamic treatment of borderline patients suggest that early treatment goals must focus on controlling acting-out behavior, both self-destructive behavior and that which is destructive to the treatment, and that other treatment goals come later (Waldinger & Gunderson, 1984).

In summary, there is little research evidence to guide choice of treatment strategy for BPD patients. Most researched is the cognitive-behavioral approach, but this has not been compared to any other theory-grounded and standardized approach.

Medication. A range of pharmacologic treatments have been tried with borderline patients, including neuroleptics, antidepressants, minor tranquilizers, anticonvulsants, and lithium (Soloff, 1989). It is useful to relate target symptoms and the various symptom clusters in this heterogeneous group of patients to each of the classes of medications. Neuroleptics may be useful to reduce anger and hostility; the cognitive symptoms of paranoia, as well as referential thinking, derealization, and depersonalization; anxiety and phobias; impulsivity; and depression and suicidal ideation. The TCAs target depression but have the disadvantage of providing borderlines with lethal substances; moreover, they have been known to precipitate an increase in suicidal, assaultive, and psychotic behavior. The MAOIs target atypical depression (labile mood, hyperphasia, hypersomnolence, and rejection sensitivity), impulsivity, and self-destructiveness. Carbamazepine may be useful for treating impulsivity, behavioral dyscontrol, anger, suicidal ideation, and anxiety. And, finally, the benzodiazepines may be useful for anxiety, panic, volatile mood, depression, and paranoia but, unfortunately, may precipitate behavioral dyscontrol and impulsiveness. Since medication effects are only modest, medication should be a part of the overall treatment package, which includes psychotherapy.

Duration. It is generally agreed that substantial progress with BPD patients will require a treatment of long duration. Linehan's dialectical behavioral treatment is 1 year in duration, and Kernberg's dynamic treatment posits a treatment period of some 2 years. Brief treatment, however, may be effective at times of crisis for the BPD patient and may or may not be followed by long-term therapy. In particular, those BPD patients who have previously formed intense and destructive treatment relationships may need only brief treatment in crisis.

SUMMARY

In summary, when treatment is planned for the BPD patient a number of factors must be considered:

One must evaluate the action potential of the patient, including the potential for suicidal and other impulsive behaviors. There need to be parameters around these behaviors right from the start of treatment. Whether one uses dialectic/cognitive-behavioral or dynamic treatment, both of which have been manualized, it is important to structure the treatment from the start, for example, in the contract-setting phase of treatment.

One must evaluate the comorbid Axis I disorders. Depression is common, and in about 10% of the cases bipolar disorder is present.

One must evaluate for a range of comorbid Axis II disorders. The continuum of antisocial personality, malignant narcissism, narcissism with antisocial traits, and borderline personality alone is relevant for treatment planning and prognosis.

It should be clear from this review of the empirical data, however, that the research findings are too meager and tentative to extensively guide the clinician. The clinician must use what is known but cannot wait until definitive results are in. How can we best teach this combination of science and art to the clinician-in-training?

Our Approach to Clinical Research Training

We will describe a setting in which clinical training and exposure to research are combined with the goal of fostering the integration of clinical work and clinical research for psychologists and psychiatrists who are in training. We suggest that a combination of clinical theory and research is the optimal approach for the emergence of therapy research and for the training of future mental health professionals.

The aim of our research and training effort was to develop a specific (psychodynamic) treatment adapted to the particular needs of a specific patient population, those with borderline personality disorder.

Any specified treatment of a particular patient population must be based upon a congruence between the unique patient pathology and the treatment parameters (format of treatment, strategies/techniques, focus of the sessions, and so on). A model of borderline personality organization, as described earlier in this chapter, was the basis for the articulation of the treatment chosen for clinical training.

CLINICAL RESEARCH OBJECTIVES

In the process of our clinical research, we have accomplished a number of tasks: We have generated a treatment manual (Kernberg et al., 1989), and, more importantly for training, a library of videotapes depicting expert therapists using the treatment described in the manual with borderline patients. These tapes are most helpful in modeling the treatment for trainees, thus bringing the written manual alive. We have taught the manual to some 30 therapists-in-training, using the manual and videotapes in seminar fashion and in individual supervision.

We have documented some of the heterogeneity of the BPD sample, using both cluster analytic (Hurt, Clarkin, Widiger, Fyer, Sullivan, Stone, & Frances, 1990) and factor analytic techniques (Clarkin et al., 1993). We have generated a scale for measuring borderline personality organization (Oldham, Clarkin, Appelbaum, Carr, Kernberg, Lotterman, & Haas, 1985). We have assessed and treated (or are in the process of treating) 35 BPD patients. We have been able to reliably rate the contract-setting phase of the treatment and have generated a rating scale for assessing adherence to the manual and the psychodynamic treatment.

In this section of the chapter, we describe our theory of treatment, the generation and teaching of the manual, and involvement of the trainee in the investigation of this treatment.

Theory of Psychodynamic Treatment

On the basis of the formulations of BPO described earlier, we have constructed a theory of psychodynamic treatment geared to the resolution of the specific disturbances of borderline patients. The basic objective of this modified psychodynamic psychotherapy is the resolution of identity diffusion and, in the process, resolution of the primitive defensive operations characteristic of these patients and of their primitive internalized "part object" relationships into the "total object" relationships that are characteristic of more advanced neurotic and normal functioning.

Primitive internalized object relations involve part-self representations relating to part-object representations in the context of a primitive, all-good or all-bad, affect state. They are part-object relations precisely because the representation of self and the representation of object have been split into an idealized and persecutory component; this is in contrast to the normal integration of good (loving) and bad (hateful) representations of self and significant others. These primitive or part-object relations emerge in the treatment situation in the form of primitive transferences, characterized by the activation of such self and object representations, together with their corresponding affect, as a transference "unit" that is enacted defensively against a primitive transference unit that is under completely opposite affect valence or dominance.

Strategies of the Treatment. The essential strategy in the psychodynamic treatment of borderline patients consists of a three-step procedure. Step 1 is the diagnosis of an emerging primitive part-object relationship in the transference and the interpretative analysis of the dominant unconscious fantasy structure that corresponds to this particular transference activation. For example, the therapist may point out to the patient that their momentary relationship resembles that of a sadistic prison guard and a paralyzed, frightened victim.

Step 2 of this strategy is to identify the self and the object representation of this particular primitive transference and the typically oscillating or alternating attribution of self and object representation by the patient to himself and to the therapist. For example, the aforementioned therapist may point out, in expanding the previous intervention, that it is as if the patient were experiencing himself as a frightened, paralyzed victim while attributing to the therapist the behavior of a sadistic prison guard. Later on in the same session the situation may become reversed in that the patient may behave like a sadistic prison guard while placing the therapist in the role of the frightened victim, and the therapist will point this out to the patient.

Step 3 of this interpretative intervention is the delineation of the linkage between the particular object relationship activated in the transference and the entirely opposite one activated at other times, which constitutes the split-off, idealized counterpart to this particular persecutory object relationship. For example, if at other times the patient has experienced the therapist as a perfect, all-giving mother, while the patient experiences himself as the satisfied, happy, loved baby who is the exclusive object of mother's attention, the therapist might point out that the persecutory prison guard is really a bad, frustrating, teasing, rejecting mother and the victim is an enraged baby who wants to take revenge but is afraid of being destroyed by mother's anger, which is a projection of his own rage onto mother. The therapist might add that this terrible mother–infant relationship is kept completely separate from the idealized relationship out of fear of contaminating the idealized one with the persecutory one and destroying all hope that, in spite of the rageful, revengeful attacks on the bad mother, the relationship with the ideal mother might be recovered.

The successful integration in the transference of dissociated or split-off all-good and all-bad primitive object relations includes the integration not only of the corresponding self and object representations but also of the primitive affects. The integration of intense, polarized affects leads, over time, to affect modulation, to an increase in the capacity for affect control, to a heightened capacity for empathy with both self and others, and to a corresponding deepening and maturing of all object relations.

This psychotherapeutic strategy involves a modification of three basic tools derived from standard psychoanalytic technique: interpretation, transference analysis, and technical neutrality. Interpretation—that is, the establishment of hypotheses about unconscious determinants of the patient's behavior—is the major technical tool of the treatment. In contrast to standard psychoanalysis, however, interpretation here involves mostly the preliminary phases of interpretative intervention, namely, a systematic clarification of the patient's subjective experience; the tactful confrontation of the meanings of those aspects of the subjective experience, verbal communication, nonverbal behavior, and total interaction with the therapist that express further aspects of the transference; and a restriction of interpretation to the unconscious meanings in the "here and now" only. In contrast to standard psychoanalysis, where interpretation centers on the unconscious meanings of both the "here and now" and the "there and then," in the psychodynamic psychotherapy of borderline patients psychodynamic interpretations of the unconscious past are reserved for relatively advanced stages of the treatment, after the integration of primitive transferences has transformed primitive into advance transferences (which are more characteristic of neurotic functioning and more directly reflective of the actual experiences from the past).

A second modification of standard psychoanalytic technique involves the transference analysis. In each session the therapist pays attention to the longrange treatment goals of the particular patient and to the dominant current conflicts in the patient's life outside the sessions. The treatment must not gratify excessively the patient's transference needs, thus undermining the patient's initial motivation and long-range treatment goals. However, in order to prevent a splitting off of external reality from the treatment situation and the severe acting out expressed by such dissociation, transference interpretation has to be linked closely to the present realities in the patient's life. In short, in contrast to psychoanalysis (where a systematic focus on the transference is a major treatment strategy), in the psychodynamic psychotherapy of borderline patients transference analysis is modified so that attention is focused on the initial treatment goals and current external reality. This overall treatment strategy is incorporated into the manual, which spells out the therapeutic interventions characteristic of this psychodynamic psychotherapy (Kernberg et al., 1989).

The position of *technical neutrality* (the therapist's equidistance from the forces in mutual conflict in the patient's mind) is an important aspect of the psychodynamic psychotherapy of borderline patients, as well as of neurotics. However, given the severe acting out of borderline patients inside and outside treatment hours, technical neutrality may have to be limited by a structuring (limit setting) of the treatment situation. A reinstatement of technical neutrality requires an exploration of the reasons for the therapist's temporary abandonment of it.

Constructing the Manual

The manual was constructed from the theoretical formulations about borderline pathology noted earlier and from extensive clinical experience in treating borderline patients in psychodynamically oriented psychotherapy. The manual presupposes a knowledge of the central tenets and strategies of dynamic psychotherapy. Building upon the groundwork of psychodynamic therapy in general, the clinicians on this project articulated the principles of the treatment as applied to the borderline patient, the phases of the treatment, and the common complications. As the manual was being drafted, several senior therapists on the project treated borderline patients with all sessions either video- or audiotaped, and portions of these sessions were (with proper disguise) used in the articulation and exemplification of various aspects of treatment.

Early drafts of the manual were used in seminar instruction to advanced residents and psychology trainees, who then were assigned patients to treat. These treatment sessions, too, were audio- and videotaped, and supervision of the clinicians-in-training in their handling of these cases has led to a further articulation of various aspects of the treatment. For example, it was found upon supervision that often the contract-setting phase of the treatment, as described in the manual, was done incompletely or with poor affective tone. Examples from transcripts of inadequate and adequate contract-setting sessions were collected and subsequently used in the seminar series. The contract-setting phase was further articulated, and rated reliably by observers, and our instruction concerning this phase of the treatment improved. This amplification of the original treatment manual, along with our rating scale and clinical illustrations, is now in published form (Yeomans, Selzer, & Clarkin, 1992).

Clinical Research Involving the Trainee

There are widespread, profound, and perennial fears manifested by psychotherapists when their work is being observed by others. It has been the experience of the Psychotherapy Research Project of the Menninger Foundation, as well as of our own project, that senior therapists as well as junior ones have great difficulty in tolerating audiotaping and, even more so, videotaping of psychotherapy sessions. Reasons for this uneasiness include therapists' concerns about the invasion of the patient's privacy and about the distortion introduced in the transference situation by the symbolic presence of a third person. Other concerns are that patients might not be able to fully express the most intimate aspects of their difficulties, for example, intimacies of their sexual life and love life, and that a full-fledged development of the transference may be inhibited, since patients might be unable or unwilling to express their most intimate feelings about the therapist in a treatment situation that is being monitored.

On the basis of many discussions with senior as well as junior therapists, however, we have reached the conclusion that the most important reason for a therapist's uneasiness is fear of a critique, by a real or imagined third person, of the therapist's work, that is, projection onto a third person of the therapist's own self-critical attitude, which is derived from the unavoidable insecurity of a psychotherapeutic endeavor. The fear of being observed while doing psychotherapy is the most powerful illustration of what Heinrich Racker (1968) called an "indirect countertransference," that is, the therapist's fear about the reaction of third persons involved with the treatment.

Since in psychoanalytic training psychoanalytic candidates typically never observe the work of their own analyst (other than in their own analyses), it is possible that aspects of the idealization of the training analyst are never fully resolved. This may result in a silent but powerful fantasy on the part of candidates that their own analyst possessed a perfect technique that will never be matched by anything acquired in their own learning process. In that fantasy the senior analyst is never guilty of the trials and errors, the blind spots and countertransference acting out, that are practically unavoidable in psychoanalytic and psychotherapeutic treatment, particularly of patients with severe psychopathology. This typical problem in psychoanalytic training has been exported to psychodynamic psychotherapy training, where the tendency is for senior therapists to supervise junior therapists' work while junior therapists never observe the work of their seniors. In any case, the fear of being observed by senior, experienced, secure psychotherapists and failing to live up to the imaginary perfection of these masters is intensified under conditions where a manual provides a standardized approach to treatment.

Rating of Adherence to the Manual.   An additional major difficulty with a set of techniques presented in a manual is the dilemma between the desire to respect and do justice to the complexity of general psychotherapeutic concepts by reaching into their theoretical underpinnings (with the result that technical procedures may be expressed in abstract or even obtuse generalizations) and the desire to simplify the complexity of broad theories into concrete clinical interventions (with the result that these may deteriorate into a mechanical simplicity). Here, depth may be sacrificed to an illusory precision to an extent that represents a straitjacketing of the particular psychotherapeutic approach involved.

This problem arose in our efforts to write a manual commensurate with the complexity of the theory involved but with practical descriptions and illustrations. An enormous effort went into construction of the manual (Kernberg et al., 1989): we attempted to start from the most general concepts acceptable to the psychodynamically oriented clinician, representing the complexity of the corresponding theory of technique while attempting at the same time to spell out in great detail and with clinical examples the practical implications of the specific modifications of that general technique that we had developed for borderline patients. Moving frequently from general theory to practical illustrations and back to general theory permitted us to create a continuity in the text that could then be translated into a continuity between theory and practical intervention in the supervisory situation.

Still another problem is the general distrust of researchers on the part of clinicians, that is, the fear of clinicians that researchers get caught up in methodology rather than in meaning and that they may do injustice to psychotherapists' struggle to clarify meanings by focusing on methodological precision and even preciousness. The fear is that methodologists might trivialize the treatment and that the very findings of empirical research will end up in such trivializations.

In our clinical seminars for the entire group of therapists-in-training, in individual supervision of the therapists, and in periodic group reviews of videotapes to discuss technique, we attempted to diagnose and resolve the dilemma between "Bible reading" and "revolution," that is, between a slavish submission to the text of the manual that would bring about a rigid and unskilled application of its prescription and a subtle or not so subtle flaunting of the manual with the sense that it was an artificial imposition that did not do justice to the needs of the patient in the therapeutic situation. We repeatedly pointed to the temptations of these two extremes, illustrated them with clinical examples, and tried to help the trainees remain in a middle ground between them. In this connection, we also encouraged frequent ventilation of trainees' fears of the researchers, who were truly superego figures about whom a number of distortions circulated among the trainees. It was particularly helpful for the trainees to find out that the senior therapists in the research group had significant disagreements among themselves about how to handle specific clinical situations. These disagreements, watched on videotape by the entire group of therapists and researchers, did not bring about a sense of uncertainty or confusion but, on the contrary, a sense of relief and security: "If the grand old guys can't agree, then we don't need to worry so much about doing it wrong."

The standardization of our approach to particular critical situations—for example, suicide attempts, dishonesty in the transference, severe paranoid regression, and threat of interruption of the treatment—was of great help in providing the trainees with a set of guidelines that prepared them for the extreme and sudden development of complications and in reducing their sense that only the senior members of the team would be able to deal with such emergencies. Paradoxically, then, standardization, under conditions of severe complications in the treatment, provided security to even young therapists.

It was helpful that the formal leaders of the research group (the principal investigators, JFC and HK) did not coincide with the most senior theoretician of the group (OFK) and that a trainee's actual supervisory experience was tangential to the influence of that senior member of the group, thus facilitating the expression of ambivalence toward him and reducing a trainee's paranoid reaction to the monitoring of his or her sessions with the borderline patient.

To counteract hero worship, we attempted to illustrate with clinical material, as well as in our seminars, how the different personalities of senior clinicians could be expressed in a spectrum of concrete formulations, so that the same technical approach could be expressed in different ways. This facilitated the junior therapists' utilization of their own personality to adjust the theory of technique so that more comfortable ways could be found to express themselves and interact with patients. It is of interest that in spite of the differences in personal styles the invariance of our technical approach could be diagnosed by means of the instruments we used to evaluate adherence to the technique (see Clarkin, Koenigsberg, et al., 1992).

Finally, the fact that junior therapists saw their participation in the project as a significant opportunity for increasing their general psychotherapeutic skills compensated for the tensions of supervision and the fears referred to earlier; our conscious effort to maintain a nonauthoritarian attitude throughout all our encounters permitted individual dissatisfactions and protests to emerge and be explored and resolved in helpful ways.

Research Tracking of the Patient in Treatment and Feedback to Therapist. There are multiple opportunities for feedback between the clinical treatment and the empirical information that is gathered on a continuous basis, from patient evaluation, through treatment, to follow-up status. Since this is a pilot study and not a double-blind design, there are opportunities to provide the clinician-in-training with feedback, in terms of his or her performance in the treatment, the patient's response in the sessions, and therapeutic outcome:

- At initial evaluation the clinician/therapist is provided with research data on the patient. This includes Structured Clinical Interview for *DSM-III-R* (SCID) Axis I and Axis II ratings, dimensional ratings of BPD severity, and so on.
- After the contract-setting period of the treatment (fifth to seventh sessions), the ratings of this process, which is captured on audiotape, are provided to the supervisor and the therapist.
- At intervals in the treatment the research team rates (from audiotapes) the therapist's skill and adherence to the manual. In effect, this is a check that the therapist is targeting the most important themes and that the inter-

ventions are psychodynamic (that is, consist of clarifications, confrontations, and transference interpretations) rather than supportive.

- Patient progress is evaluated on a regular basis. Every 4 months the patient completes self-report data on his or her general symptoms, borderline behavior, and social and vocational adjustment. On a yearly basis the patient is interviewed by an independent assessor who rates progress in each of the salient areas.

Summary and Future Directions

There are no all-good guys or all-bad guys, researchers or clinicians, in this realm of clinical research. Rather, the question at hand is, How does one integrate research and its relevant results into clinical practice for the optimal care of the patient? One answer is in the training of future clinicians and researchers. In this chapter we focused on the training of clinicians who are exposed to and involved in clinical research. That is, clinical research and clinical practice are integrated at the personal level, within individuals who work in the mental health field. This integration is a goal and is not a completed task at the time of graduation from a mental health training program, such as a residency in psychiatry, an internship or fellowship in psychology, or a course of training in a postdoctoral setting like a psychoanalytic training institute. On the other hand, if some stimulation toward integration of research and clinical practice is not fostered in the training period, such integration may not develop in future years.

In our clinical research project we did not set out to integrate clinical practice and research. Rather, our intent was to create an environment in which faculty and students could examine the results of therapeutic intervention in patients with a particular diagnosis and psychostructural condition. We have found this process to be a productive one in terms of both training and clinical research outcomes. A productive feedback loop develops between the clinical researchers and their data, and the clinicians-in-training and their supervisors.

As noted earlier, there was a tendency for both the patients and the therapists to see the researchers as formal, rigid, intrusive, critical, and fault finding. The researchers, on the other hand, complained at times of the lack of organization of the therapists and of some inconsistency in their adherence to the manual. There were a number of forces that countered these tendencies toward splitting and alienation of researchers and clinicians. The leading theoretician and clinician consistently supported the objectification of the treatment (that is, the manual) and the procedures used to collect data (for example, semistructured interviews to diagnose BPD, rating scales to rate adherence to the treatment). The trainees were encouraged to take both research and clinical roles in the project. All were trained in using the manual to guide treatment, and some conducted research projects using data generated by the study. Joint meetings of both clinicians and researchers, in which videotaped sessions were viewed and discussed, brought out research/clinical dilemmas and disagreements, as well as agreements. Polarization was reduced by discussion.

The goal of the integration of research and clinical practice is multifaceted: clinicians who have an inquiring, empirically oriented mind-set; researchers who are clinically astute and attuned to the complexities of patients and their treatment; research in which hypotheses are infused with data acquired in clinical practice; clinical practice that is always in the process of modification by the latest research findings.

All is not perfect, however. There are, indeed, signs that our current educational processes do not always have the desired yield:

- The journals are filled with much research that is trivial, clinically useless, or devoid of theoretical rationale. Clinical research should be theoretically based with a clear goal in mind. Single-shot research should be replaced by research in which issues are investigated in multiple studies that build upon one another.
- Assessments of isolated behaviors are limited in value and should be replaced by meaningful constructs that have been operationalized. While the leap from behaviors to constructs is difficult to achieve, it is necessary for progress. The diagnostic criteria for BPD are a case in point. While the semistructured assessment of the eight criteria of BPD in *DSM-III-R* is an advance, the understanding of how these criteria co-vary and relate to theoretical constructs is imperative.
- The body of clinical research is useful to clinicians only if it is integrated. This integration must involve clinical judgment; that is, clinicians and researchers alike must contribute to this integration.

Central to these goals is the training of clinicians and researchers who are not wedded to traditional concepts and formulations but are open to increasing information and data. Flexible clinicians and researchers must forge the future. It is our impression that patient care is maximized in a setting of clinical research that is combined with clinical training.

By now the not so subtle analogy between defensive splitting in the BPD patient and the polarization of researchers and clinicians in our field will be familiar to the reader. Black-and-white, judgmental thinking is not limited to patient populations. Our field can only progress if patient care is advanced by active research, which in turn will only be as good as the clinical experience upon which it is based. Polarization is fostered when the two groups read separate journals, join separate professional organizations, operate out of separate settings, and have no training in common. The educational model in which the resident or psychology graduate student does an independent project or dissertation may be appropriate for future researchers, but it has probably failed by not involving the future clinician in the research enterprise. We argue here that the process of integration, which can only be carried out within the individual, is fostered by a training experience that is organized to break down projection of inevitable difficulties and limitations onto the other group.

REFERENCES

Adler, G. (1989). Psychodynamic therapies in borderline personality disorder. In A. Tasman, R. E. Hales, & A. J. Frances (Eds.), *Review of Psychiatry* (Vol. 8, pp. 49–64). Washington DC: American Psychiatric Press.

Akiskal, H. S. (1981). Subaffective disorders: Dysthymic, cyclothymic and bipolar II disorders in the "borderline" realm. *Psychiatric Clinics of North America, 4,* 25–46.

Alberts, G., & Edelstein, B. (1990). Therapist training: A critical review of skill training studies. *Clinical Psychology Review, 10,* 497–512.

American Psychiatric Association. (1987). *Diagnostic and statistical manual of mental disorders* (3rd ed., rev.). Washington, DC: Author.

American Psychiatric Association. (1989). *Treatments of psychiatric disorders: A task force report of the American Psychiatric Association.* Washington, DC: American Psychiatric Association.

Beutler, L. E., & Clarkin, J. F. (1990). *Systematic treatment selection: Toward targeted therapeutic interventions.* New York: Brunner/Mazel.

Beutler, L. E., & Clarkin, J. F. (1991). Future research directions. In L. E. Beutler & M. Crago (Eds.), *Psychotherapy research: An international review of programmatic studies* (pp. 329–334). Washington, DC: American Psychological Association.

Blashfield, R. K. (1984). *The classification of psychopathology: Neo-Kraepelinian and quantitative approaches.* New York: Plenum.

Clarkin, J. F., Frances, A. F., & Perry, S. (in press). Differential therapeutics: Macro and micro levels of treatment planning. In J. Norcross & M. Goldfried (Eds.), *Handbook of psychotherapy integration.* New York: Basic Books.

Clarkin, J. F., Hull, J. W., & Hurt, S. W. (1993). Factor structure of borderline personality disorder criteria. *Journal of Personality Disorders, 7(2),* 137–143.

Clarkin, J. F., Koenigsberg, H., Yeomans, F., Selzer, M., Kernberg, P., & Kernberg, O. F. (1992). Psychodynamic psychotherapy of the borderline patient. In J. F. Clarkin, E. Marziali, & H. Munroe-Blum (Eds.), *Borderline personality disorder: Clinical and empirical perspectives,* pp. 268–287. New York: Guilford Press.

Clarkin, J. F., Marziali, E., & Munroe-Blum, H. (1991). Group and family treatments for borderline personality disorder. *Hospital and Community Psychiatry, 42(10),* 1038–1043.

Frances, A., Clarkin, J. F., & Perry, S. (1984). *Differential therapeutics in psychiatry*. New York: Brunner/Mazel.

Gardner, D., & Cowdry, R. (1985). Suicidal and parasuicidal behavior in borderline personality disorder. *Psychiatric Clinics of North America, 8*.

Garfield, S. L., & Kurtz, R. (1976). Clinical psychologists in the 1970's. *American Psychologist, 31*, 1–9.

Goldfried, M. R. (1984). Training the clinician as scientist-professional. *Professional Psychology: Research and Practice, 15*, 477–481.

Haynes, S. N., Lemsky, C., & Sexton-Radek, K. (1987). Why clinicians infrequently do research. *Professional Psychology: Research and Practice, 18*, 515–519.

Hurt, S. W., & Clarkin, J. F. (1990). Borderline personality disorder: Prototypic typology and the development of treatment manuals. *Psychiatric Annals, 20*, 1–6.

Hurt, S. W., Clarkin, J. F., Widiger, T., Fyer, M., Sullivan, T., Stone, M., & Frances, A. (1990). Evaluation of DSM-III decision rules for case detection using joint conditional probability structures. *Journal of Personality Disorder, 4*, 121–130.

Kelly, E. L., Goldberg, L. R., Fiske, D. W., & Kilkowski, J. M. (1978). Twenty-five years later. *American Psychologist, 33*, 746–755.

Kernberg, O., Selzer, M., Koenigsberg, H., Carr, A., & Appelbaum, A. (1989). *Psychodynamic psychotherapy of borderline patients*. New York: Basic Books.

Leibenluft, E., Gardner, D., & Cowdry, R. (1987). The inner experience of the borderline self-mutilator. *Journal of Personality Disorders*, 317–324.

Linehan, M. M. (1984). *Dialectical behavior therapy for treatment of parasuicidal women: Treatment manual*. Unpublished manuscript, University of Washington, Seattle.

Linehan, M. M. (1987). Dialectical behavior therapy: A cognitive behavioral approach to parasuicide. *Journal of Personality Disorders, 1*, 328–333.

Linehan, M. M., Armstrong, H. E., Suarez, A., Allmon, D., & Heard, H. L. (1991). Behavioral treatment of chronically parasuicidal borderline patients. *Archives of General Psychiatry, 48*, 1060–1064.

Linehan, M. M., & Heard, H. L. (1992). Dialectical behavior therapy for borderline personality disorder. In J. F. Clarkin, E. Marziali, & H. Munroe-Blum (Eds.), *Borderline personality disorder: Clinical and empirical perspectives* (pp. 248–267). New York: Guilford Press.

Oldham, J., Clarkin, J. F., Appelbaum, A., Carr, A., Kernberg, P., Lotterman, A., & Haas, G. (1985). A self-report instrument for borderline personality organization. In T. H. McGlashan (Ed.), *The borderline: Current empirical research* (pp. 3–18). Washington, DC: American Psychiatric Press.

Racker, H. (1968). *Transference and countertransference*. New York: International Universities Press.

Skodol, A. E. (1989). *Problems in differential diagnosis: From DSM-III to DSM-III-R in clinical practice*. Washington, DC: American Psychiatric Press.

Smith, B., & Sechrest, L. (1991). Treatment of aptitude X treatment interactions. *Journal of Consulting and Clinical Psychology, 59*(2), 233–244.

Soloff, P. H. (1989). Psychopharmacologic therapies in borderline personality disorder. In A. Tasman, P. E. Hales, & A. J. Frances (Eds.), *American Psychiatric*

Press review of psychiatry (Vol. 8, pp. 65–83). Washington, DC: American Psychiatric Press.

Spitzer, R., Endicott, J., & Gibbon, M. (1979). Crossing the border into borderline personality and borderline schizophrenia. *Archives of General Psychiatry, 36,* 17–24.

Stone, M. H. (1988). Borderline personality disorder. In R. Michels & J. O. Cavenar, Jr. (Eds.), *Psychiatry* (Vol. 1, pp. 1–18). Philadelphia: Lippincott.

Strupp, H. H., Hadley, S. W., & Gomes-Schwartz, R. (1977). *Psychotherapy for better or worse: An analysis of the problem of negative effects.* New York: Aronson.

Waldinger, R. J., & Gunderson, J. G. (1984). Completed psychotherapies with borderline patients. *American Journal of Psychotherapy, 38,* 190–202.

Widiger, T. A., Frances, A. J., Harris, M., Jacobsberg, L. B., Fyer, M., & Manning, D. (1991). Comorbidity among Axis II disorders. In J. Oldham (Ed.), *Personality disorders: New perspectives on diagnostic validity* (pp. 165–194). Washington DC: American Psychiatric Press.

Yeomans, F. E., Selzer, A. M., & Clarkin, J. F. (1992). *Treating the borderline patient. A contract-based approach.* New York: Basic Books.

CHAPTER 4

Can Psychotherapy Research Answer This Psychotherapist's Questions?

Marshall Edelson

THE PRACTICE OF PSYCHOTHERAPY is cut off from the findings of psychotherapy research. As a psychotherapist, I do not look to those findings for help in doing psychotherapy or for answers to questions that come to my mind as I do psychotherapy. I do not look to those findings to settle disagreements I have with psychotherapists who apparently do psychotherapy differently from the way I do it or to decide which of two ideas I have about what is going on in my patient's mind here and now is the better or more accurate idea.

Why should research play such a small part in this very demanding, complicated, and puzzling enterprise? I think that one reason for the difficulty of translating research findings into clinical practice follows from differences in the interests clinical researchers and clinical practitioners pursue. The questions that psychotherapy research is eager to address are not the questions in which a psychotherapist qua practitioner is most interested. The questions psychotherapists ask as they are doing their work are questions psychotherapy research has shown little inclination to tackle.

Psychotherapy research is interested, on the one hand, in big theoretical questions, that is, in general theories of personality, pathogenesis, and psychotherapeutic process, and, on the other hand, in urgent practical questions: the outcome or efficacy of one form of psychotherapy compared to another or

Parts of this work were presented at a departmental forum entitled "Clinical Practice and Clinical Research: The Story of a Troubled Marriage," in the Department of Psychiatry, Yale University School of Medicine, April 19, 1991. This chapter has previously appeared, in somewhat different form, in *Contemporary Psychoanalysis*, 1992, 28(1): 118–151.

of psychotherapy compared to other kinds of treatment. The psychotherapist is interested in a particular patient and in the particular stories that patient stories that patient tells or enacts: "Therapy is a work of particulars, not generalities. It follows the patient's interests and concerns in the particulars of his life. . . . [The therapist responds] session by session to the patient as he seems at the time" (Shapiro, 1989, p. 204).

The indifference of psychotherapy research to the psychotherapist's questions is not then simply due to a deficiency in the state of the art. It is not that psychotherapy research evades the psychotherapist's questions because answering them requires a sophisticated methodology, techniques, or instruments of measurement that are not now, but may perhaps some day be, available. Rather, the very observations psychotherapy research selects, what it regards as an observation, and how it describes its observations are determined by its interest in the general. And so the observations it considers relevant are different from the observations the psychotherapist, who is inquiring into here-and-now particulars, finds relevant.

The second reason for the difficulty of translating research findings into clinical practice has to do with selecting and describing observations, that is, with the data themselves. Quarrels among psychotherapists about what inferences are justified by some specific clinical material are notorious. They never seem to get settled. Clinical research certainly does not seem to be able to settle them. What's the problem?

As things stand now, clinicians who present or discuss a clinical report, much less clinical researchers, can't even agree upon what the relevant observations are and how to describe them. Since you can't report everything, you have to select what to report. And since any observation can be described in multiple ways, and at different levels of abstraction, you have to select the kind of description you're going to use.

Our problem is that we lack generally agreed upon criteria for selecting what is to count as an observation and for selecting a way of describing these observations. Such criteria must satisfy the following conditions: (1) These criteria have to capture those observations that are responsive to psychotherapists' interests; these are just the observations they will find useful in accomplishing their objectives. (2) These criteria have to ensure that we do not continue to leave out those observations that contradict an idea we hold dear. (3) These criteria have to ensure that we do not give our attention only to those observations that prove our point. (4) These criteria must prevent us from describing our observations in a way that infects them with the very ideas we want to test.

I think it is fair to say that psychotherapy research has not provided the community of psychotherapists with criteria that make sense and are compelling because they satisfy these four requirements. I have some suggestions to make toward that end, which are based on conclusions I have come to as a result of an attempt to make explicit how my mind works as I do psychotherapy.[1]

A Dialogue

Here and now I imagine myself, a clinician, talking with you, an interlocutor, a colleague, a friend, not a vague general figure but someone I can see in my mind, alert, leaning forward, with an inquiring facial expression. I imagine myself responding to your expression with these words: "You have a question?"

As I ask you in just those words for the question you seem to have, I am reminded of the voice and look of Claude Rains in the movie *Kings Row*, which in my mind are now my voice and look. In the role of Dr. Tower, Rains teaches medicine to Parris Mitchell (Robert Cummings), who one day, puzzled and upset for reasons we the audience are aware of, stands up, leans toward his teacher, and in an urgent, challenging tone begins, "Dr. Tower. . . " Dr. Tower responds (very evenly): "You have a question?" We, the audience, are in suspense: Will Parris go on to ask his question? If he does, how will Dr. Tower respond? But why am I reminded at this moment of that scene and story? This experience of being reminded, along with the inquiries and suspense evoked by a remembered scene from a remembered story, exemplifies what happens in psychotherapy and is part of the process of psychotherapy.

I do have questions. What do you mean "the psychotherapist is interested in different questions"? Don't you as a psychotherapist draw upon those general theories you just mentioned in interpreting your observations and making your interventions? Don't you care whether what you do works or not and whether some other treatment might work better?

I care. The general theories and the practical problems in which psychotherapy research takes special interest are important for knowledge and for the credibility and future of the enterprise itself. But that does not mean that questions about general theory or relative efficacy are the questions that are central for practicing psychotherapists. The answers to these questions are not the knowledge to which they turn as they practice psychotherapy; they are not what helps them decide which interventions to make, for example.

---

[1]This method of inquiry is not too different from that used by some cognitive psychologists interested in artificial intelligence. They simply asked people how they actually thought when trying to solve a problem. Of course, I do not claim that all such workings of the mind (some preconscious, some unconscious) are accessible to introspection.

What *is* the best, or most effective, kind of psychotherapy for which patient having which kind of problem? That is a policy question; it concerns the choice of treatment that offers the best *chance* of success if it is repeatedly made in dealing with cases drawn from a particular population of patients, but that does not in each particular case necessarily result in success. Psychotherapists who are already engaged in trying to carry out a particular kind of psychotherapy with a particular patient will not be centrally concerned with that kind of question, unless the difficulties they encounter in that endeavor make them wonder whether deciding to make the attempt was itself a mistake.

Suppose I am trying to decide whether to recommend psychotherapy to a patient. In the specific instance, diagnosis is not always a good indicator of what will happen in psychotherapy. I match a patient who brings me some problems against memories of patients I have previously encountered. (Let us ignore for the moment the question of how I made this decision before accumulating a file of such memories.) I have a hunch about whether psychotherapy will go or not. Since I know that first impressions can lead me astray, I usually offer a patient a trial of psychotherapy of a few weeks or a few months even if all signals are go: "let's try it out and both of us see how it goes." This way of proceeding—deplorably sloppy as it may sound—works well enough in most cases so that I am not likely to turn to research, which classifies patients rather more grossly than my memory bank does, for answers to the question, Should I do psychotherapy with *this* particular patient?

With respect to general theory, I have a confession to make: as time goes on, I am less and less reminded of some general theoretical truth or general rule of technique by what patients tell me. Neither generalizations supported by research findings nor timeless characterizations of the patient (for example, diagnostic classifications) pop into my head as my patients talk, at least when I am working well.

In connection with making a recommendation to your patient, you used the expression "works well enough." How do you know your hunches that a patient will or will not do well in psychotherapy work better than probabilistic predictions made on the basis of knowledge gained from clinical research? It sounds to me as if the questions you are raising about the relevance of research to your work as a psychotherapist have to do with ignorance of statistical reasoning.

How do I respond to you without defensiveness? It is true that many psychotherapists are ignorant of statistical reasoning, which is a major form of argument used by clinical investigators in deciding whether evidence justifies believing one conjecture rather than another about what caused an observed effect (a difference in outcome, for example). But it is possible, and you should be able to recognize this possibility, that psychotherapists may eschew attempts to quantify clinical phenomena (including those attempts that are necessary if statistical reasoning is to be applied to such phenomena) not because they are ignorant of statistics or phobic about numbers but because of their belief that the stuff in which they are interested is not structured like mathematics.

I know that clinical investigators depend upon quantification when they try to show, for example, that their observations are reliable. Reliable means that different observers will count the same phenomenon as being the same sort of thing and that the same observer will consistently count similar phenomena as the same sort of thing whenever he or she encounters them. I have to tell you that psychotherapists are likely to find it difficult to be interested in this problem, because they take it for granted that what is selected or what counts as an observation will differ from observer to observer; that different observers will see some particular phenomenon differently; and that the same observer will, from one time to another, classify similar phenomena differently depending on the context in which a phenomenon occurs. Rather than get rid of this variability, the psychotherapist wants to know why it should be the rule and what difference it makes if it is.

Furthermore, and this is old ground we have covered before, a psychotherapist is interested in a particular patient. That, technically put, is his or her domain of inquiry. If he or she is interested in generalizations at all, he or she is interested in those that are true over many observations of that patient. But were he or she to turn to a typical piece of clinical research, he or she is likely to find that the clinical investigator is instead interested in generalizations that hold over a relatively crudely defined population of patients.

Along the same line, I wonder if the conclusions derived from clinical research are applicable in the "contaminated" situation in which I do psychotherapy, where these conclusions are, at best, approximately true because many things are going on at once and some causes may cancel the influence of others. Clinical investigators, on the other hand, are more likely to be interested in whether they are justified in holding their conclusions to be true or false in a model experimental situation. This model experimental situation has been purified of factors that might otherwise have interfered with the expression of causal powers in which the investigators are interested or that might have influenced the outcome of their investigations, irrespective of the truth or falsity of their conjectures.

The psychotherapist, like most clinicians, tends to give greater weight to what is called external or ecological validity (that is, Does a conclusion hold up in different natural settings?) whereas the clinical investigator is likely to give greater weight to what is called internal validity (Do the observations in an experimental situation support one conclusion over others about what is going on in that experimental situation?). In any piece of research, if one kind of validity, whether external or internal, is maximized, it is, unhappily, always maximized at the expense of the other.

You say generalizations don't pop into your head when you are working well. What do you mean "working well"? "Well" in what sense? How do you know when you are working well and when you are not?

The question about which I am puzzled is, Do I mean "doing well" as a physician knows he is doing well when he tries to cure a patient with pneumonia or as a sculptor knows he is doing well when a figure emerges from stone?

Is it possible that after all these years of stubborn opposition to the hermeneutic stance, you are giving up on science? You have always seemed to prefer ideas, tough rigorous thinking, and abstraction over feeling, metaphor, and pleasure in particulars? But if you now think doing psychotherapy is an artful performance like sculpting or swimming, why are you so concerned with science? Why do you care whether the findings of psychotherapy research are translated into clinical practice?

Well, the problem, if it is a problem, is that I am drawn to science. For me, science is nothing more than a way of asking questions and getting answers to them, the main idea, and a pretty good one, being that this way of getting the answers is fair. Science keeps me from stacking the deck to guarantee my getting just those answers I want. Science means the world won't submit to my wishes, won't simply be the way I want it to be. Science means that I am still capable of being surprised by things as they are.

So I wish I could reply to your questions by pointing to all the times I have turned to psychotherapy research for answers to the questions I ask myself as I do psychotherapy. To my chagrin, I can point to no instance, not one, where I have done so. I do not believe that, among psychotherapists, I am an exception.

The important question in thinking about the relation between the work psychotherapists do and the knowledge that research can provide them is, Upon what knowledge do they actually draw as they do psychotherapy? Doing psychotherapy, I draw on all sorts of things that do not have much to do with science, scientific findings, or technical knowledge. I learned to do psychotherapy through an apprenticeship and through my own participation as a patient in psychotherapy. I learn from the patients with whom I work as a psychotherapist, who share with me things about themselves no one else knows. I learn from psychotherapists-in-training, whom I teach and who teach me, as do other colleagues, by sharing with me their own particular experiences doing psychotherapy. Doing psychotherapy, I draw also on happenings from my childhood; on my attempts to make and keep friends; on my experiences as a husband and father; on my work as an intern with patients in pain and their anxious, grieving families; and on movies, plays, and novels.

My patients' stories in all their particularity remind me of other particulars, other stories they have told me or events, characters, and scenes in my own life. It is these particulars, and the different kinds of relationships I seem to detect among them, that determine my responses to what my patients tell me. The important point here is that which particulars present themselves on any occasion depends on a thousand contingencies that enter into that occasion, and perhaps no other occasion. The occurrence of such ad hoc contingent particulars cannot be predicted from general laws.

You may want to compare what I have said here about my commitment to science, coupled as it is to my interest in particulars, with what Levenson (1988) wonderfully has to say on "the pursuit of the particular," though problematically for me, in a hermeneutic frame of reference.

I find it hard to believe that you do not make use of psychodynamic theory in doing psychotherapy. As you do psychotherapy, don't you think about the ego, superego, and id or at least about conflict, defense mechanisms, and the relation between the past and the present?

Perhaps psychodynamic theory should be seen not as a set of causal laws but as a theory of stories, that is, as a way of organizing stories, of understanding communications as stories, of helping us to see that there is a story where we might otherwise have missed it.

You do want me to tell you what I am actually doing when I am doing psychotherapy, don't you, and not some fiction, however respectable? Let me first separate and set aside the perhaps important role of theory in preparing and enabling me to notice, to receive, what the patient is saying and doing. For me, the more problematic role of theory is in determining what comes to my mind and what I say in response to what I have taken in. It is this role I call into question when I tell you that I have become more and more aware that it is the relationship between particulars, such as those from my life experience (including my experience with a particular patient), and not theory that leads me to my interventions. I am reminded by one scene or event of another that called up the same emotion. Or one scene or story has the same theme as another (for example, revenge, rivalry). Or a similar constellation of characters; for example, a story has one, two, or three characters or is about two couples or features characters of the same generation or of different generations or of the same gender or different genders. I am struck that different scenes or stories contain the same props (for example, elongated objects, food) or settings (for example, dark, enclosed spaces). Or it suddenly occurs to me that one of two apparently disconnected events leads to the other, that they are actually episodes in the same story.

More and more, I find that as I listen to patients in psychotherapy, the central facts of which I am aware (the "data," if you prefer that term) are their stories; there are two kinds of stories: the stories they tell me and the stories they enact in which I am one of the characters. A model of the kind of psychotherapy I have in mind is the story of Scheherazade. Scheherazade tells stories to her husband, the king, who has gotten into the cynical habit of beheading his queen after one night of love. Scheherazade's stories are great stories in their own right, but she also tells these stories in a certain way, to achieve a certain purpose of her own, which is part of the story she enacts with the king. She keeps him asking, "What will happen next? How does the story come out?" Each night she stops the story just at the moment of greatest suspense, and each night she avoids being beheaded at least one more time. Scheherazade tells the King wonderful stories for a thousand and one nights—and then their own story has a happy ending.

Patients, too, tell their psychotherapist stories about their current life, about their childhood and figures important in their early life, or about themselves and the psychotherapist. Unlike Scheherazade, they are the hero of most of the stories they tell. Quite unlike Scheherazade, patients are at the same time the hero and the real adversary of the hero in most of the stories they tell, although as adversary they often enter the story disguised as someone else. Like Scheherazade, they also tell their stories at a particular time for particular reasons or to achieve particular ends, which often have to do with avoiding certain subjective states that, for one reason or another, they dislike, reject, or disown. Often they use the story they tell to influence the psychotherapist. Just as we can differentiate the story of Scheherazade and her husband from the stories she tells, so what a patient hopes to accomplish by telling his or her story is part of another story, a story involving the patient and psychotherapist, which the patient is enacting rather than telling.

The reasons or purposes patients have for telling a story can be inferred from the way they tell it, from its position in a series of stories, and from the nature of the event in the internal or external world that evoked it. It is especially interesting when the event that evokes a story is another story the patient has just told or enacted. Patients often reject what their story seems to tell about them, what it arouses in them, where it seems to be leading them, or what they imagine it may cause the psychotherapist to feel about or do to them. So they tell another story to undo the first or to mitigate its effects.

I follow where a story leads me. My interventions are responses to how a story unfolds or ways of encouraging it to unfold. I ask myself, "How did this story begin? What got the sequence of events going? What was the triggering event? How does this scene fit in? What will happen next? Will the hero make the deadline? What obstacle prevents the hero from getting what he or she wants? How will the hero overcome it? How will it all end?"

Don't you think you ought to tell me what you mean by "story"?

I am in no hurry to define it. Sometimes it is better to leave a concept you're working with a little vague, a little fuzzy at the borders. I mean by story what mothers tell children before they go to sleep, when they say, "Mama, tell me a story." I mean by story what a friend tells another who asks, "What's been happening with you?" A story is an ordered sequence of events. One event leads to another. The sequence has an initial or triggering event, which gets things going, and a final event, which is how the story turns out. There is a character who wants something, who wants to bring about (or sometimes just to maintain) a state of affairs. There is one or more than one obstacle to that goal. An obstacle may be something inside or about the character, or it may be another person, a group, society, or nature. By various means, the character tries to overcome the obstacle and either succeeds in bringing about the wished-for state of affairs or fails to do so. A story, then, is an account of an attempt to solve a problem. A good story holds our interest, gives pleasure, and often has some point to make.

Do all stories fit this description in all ways? I doubt it. But any story will resemble in some way those stories that do fit the description. That is enough of a notion to get us started.

Are you saying that a critical skill upon which psychotherapists depend is, of all things, their skill as a storyteller? Do you really want to say that the essential knowledge upon which they depend is knowledge of narrative?

Yes. Do you feel I denigrate psychotherapy as an enterprise by saying so? If I do, that would seem to be an unhappy and unintended consequence of my coming to believe that psychotherapists must be able to detect what scenario absorbs a patient and into what scenario the patient has drawn them. They must be able to fill in missing pieces of the story the patient tells or enacts. They must be able to take apparently disconnected scenes, events, props, settings, and constellations of characters, which both they and the patient first hear or experience as fragments, and to see suddenly and often with surprise the story these fragments come together to make. Then they must be able to tell that story to the patient so that the patient recognizes it as his or her own.

When psychotherapists tell that story, would you say they are doing what we call "making an interpretation"? Are you saying that we really should advise a patient who is looking for a psychotherapist to find someone who is a story maven, an expert when it comes to following all the twists and turns of a complicated story, and no slouch when it comes to telling a story?

Maybe. What seems to me to be going on more and more as I do psychotherapy, when I am working well, is giving myself over to feelings and the images or scenes feelings evoke, to processes of "being reminded," and to making inferences based on metaphoric reasoning rather than "logic."

How do you understand "being reminded"? How does "being reminded" work? What determines that you will be reminded of this particular rather than that particular by what your patient says? Why are you reminded of one scene or event whereas another psychotherapist who hears an account of what the patient said will be reminded of some other scene or event? Does it make any difference just what a particular psychotherapist is reminded of? Do differences in the brains of psychotherapists make a difference to how psychotherapy goes? Might not psychotherapy research help you with questions like these?

Where, oh where, is *that* psychotherapy research?! You know, maybe I do use theory when I am doing psychotherapy after all. Maybe this "theory" is a rather loosely or oddly organized set of concepts rather than a hierarchically arranged set of laws; maybe it does not deserve the name "theory." But theory or no, it determines how I classify particulars, under what rubrics I file them in memory, and thus whether I will have access to some particular when I "need" it, that is, whether I will be reminded by some particular of another. What if the concepts I use in classifying particulars the patient tells and enacts do indeed belong to a "theory of narrative" rather than to some psychological theory or other? What if this story reminds me of that story, which is the same kind of story? What if an episode reminds me of a story in which just such an episode occurred? What if these two scenes cry out for a third scene that connects them and I inquire of my patient, who is my collaborator, "Did the third scene actually take place?" Would that be disgraceful? After all, the concepts and theory I use in interpreting perceptions and making sense of my experiences in everyday life are dramatistic.

If you do not have explanatory laws, how do you understand what patients tell you? How do you explain to patients why they have the symptoms they do, why they suffer so, what causes their illness? How do you predict what will happen when you make an interpretation?

I find it very difficult to respond to those questions without getting into a lot of dry technicalities. Psychotherapy research is interested in explanatory laws. Here is an example of an explanatory law: An event having a property X will bring about an event having a property Y. So if an event having a property X occurs, we can predict with certainty or with some degree of certainty the likelihood that an event with property Y will follow. More often than not, psychotherapy research offers the psychotherapist correlations, which come down to saying, "If you have X, then predict that you also have Y or that Y will follow."

But psychotherapists do not want primarily to improve their ability to predict. They are all too aware of the extent to which contingencies—not to mention the incalculable interactions of more variables than investigators could ever make part of their research—can disrupt the most dependable of correlations. Psychotherapists do not pin their hopes on prediction. When they are interested in causal explanation at all, they are interested not only in what causes what but in how any number of causes combine to bring about an effect by specific means or mechanisms. But psychotherapy research rarely explicates causal mechanisms or even traces the steps leading from one state of affairs to another.

But most of all psychotherapists are interested in explanation, which even after the fact can help them make sense out of what has happened. They make sense out of what has happened by using a narrative frame of reference to see how the fragments they observe go together, rather than a set of laws that explain what can be deduced from them. But that does not mean they can tell or piece together any old story they want. They must have evidence for their inference that it is this story rather than another that makes the pieces fit together, that it is this story rather than that one that a patient is enacting, that it is this episode rather than that episode that connects two apparently unconnected episodes. Evidence for the inference is the data that support one of these paired rival inferences over the other.

The data that may provide such evidence might be the details of an apparently unconnected story of another kind, for example, daydreams, fantasies, dreams, stories told by relatives or others about the patient and repeated by him or her, stories about things that "really" happened. Evidence may be a story told about some other domain, for example, the past, the extratherapeutic present, the future, the psychotherapy situation. Evidence may also be a story previously untold or an episode the patient now remembers, a missing piece until just this moment misplaced, a detail to which the patient never paid attention before.

Perhaps I do have a theory of a kind. But it is not a theory made up of covering laws linking observable variables. Rather, it is a theory that asserts, first, that a theoretical entity (an unconscious master story) *exists* and, second, that this theoretical entity brings about or causes—by means of theoretical mechanisms or transformations—the observations in which I am interested and in that sense explains them.

The theory that seems plausible to me on the basis of my own and others' clinical experience is that the stories told or enacted in psychotherapy are caused by (technically put, "are derivatives of") an unconscious master story ("an unconscious fantasy," "repressed daydream," "an unconscious traumatic memory," or "repressed memory").[2] I am interested in inferring the specific master story that generates these told or enacted stories by means of various mental operations (for example, "condensation," "displacement," "iconic symbolization," "pictorialization," "mechanisms of defense").

The master story generates the told or enacted stories essentially because it is a story in which wish fulfillment occurs and the patient is determined to find a way to get more of that good stuff; because it is a story of a problem (a dilemma or conflict) that remains unsolved (a story that remains unfinished) and the patient wants to solve it (or bring about an ending); or because it is a story of pain and failure and the patient wants to repeat it to make it come out differently.

[2]For my previous discussions of unconscious fantasy as a core concept and of the research methodology that seems relevant to investigations informed by such a concept, see Edelson (1988, 1989). Arlow (1969a, 1969b) has also emphasized the causal role of unconscious fantasy in psychoanalytic psychology.

Patients do not imagine the story as if it were someone else's story. They imagine themselves in it; they are immersed in it, preoccupied with it, dominated by it. They keep looking for ways to realize it. It determines what they choose to perceive, including what perceptions they act to bring about, how they interpret what they perceive, and how they respond to these perceptions.

That they are in the grip of this story helps to account for the stereotypy and repetitiveness of their moods, imaginings, and experiences, when there is no other plausible explanation for these qualities. That they are unconscious of the story or of the relation between it and their emotions, beliefs, and actions, helps to account for the fact that these emotions, beliefs, and actions may not make sense to them. Patients may disclaim or disown them, regard them as alien intrusions, or present them as puzzling symptoms.

I am getting some ideas about the kind of question clinical research might help you answer that would make a difference to what you do when you talk to a patient in psychotherapy. Is the hypothetical master story in the patient's head like a daydream, its specific content already fixed? Or is it merely an abstract schema that will generate many stories depending on how the conceptual "slots" are filled in? Is it not a story at all but simply a (mysterious) disposition to respond to certain kinds of events in a certain way?

Now you are with me! You can see why I find it difficult to connect my practice and clinical research. For psychotherapy research offers very little in the way of answers to questions like these. It tends to deal with how the world *is*, independently of any observer of it (this comes down to intersubjective agreement), rather than how things or events seem to some one person (however differently the same things or events might, and most probably will, seem to another person). It tends to deal with correlations between observable phenomena, not with theoretical, nonobservable entities whose properties explain a variety of observable phenomena.

A patient has a story in his or her head—a "comparator," if you want a technical word from cognitive psychology—and he or she matches particulars of his or her experiences to that story to see how similar they are. Patients want a good match because of their strong interest in the story and their desire to actualize it. The patient's mind is a "black box" into which we cannot look directly. This story in that black box to some extent determines what patients make out of what they perceive and how they then respond to it. There is no direct causal connection between incoming information and outgoing response. What is in the black box mediates the relation of perception and response.

In a way, what patients carry in their head takes the bare particulars of their experience and turns them into characters, settings, props, events in stories. Patients are more or less unaware of the stories in the black box, which produce manifestations when triggered by information from their internal or external world. These manifestations are their responses to that information, including the inferences they make from it about their internal and external world and therefore their interpretation of its meaning or significance. Their response in one form or another constructs out of their experience, or realizes in some experience, more or less disguised transformations of the stories in the black box.

The complexity of a patient's story, the many subplots, the tortuous way the entire scenario unfolds over a number of sessions, the way the patient as director changes his or her mind about who will play what part, the many disguises the patient as adversary wears, and above all the unlimited inventiveness with which different components (events, characters, props, settings) can be stitched together to make a novel story, suggest that even psychotherapy research that focuses on stories told and enacted during psychotherapy is going to face difficulties. How will investigators locate in a transcript the basic unit of observation, the story, especially when the story is enacted rather than told or when the enactment occurs over several sessions and has a lot of missing pieces ("behind the scenes")? How will observers come to agree what particular story is being enacted? Will investigators find a system for classifying these stories that is particular and complex enough to capture what is essential and that, at the same time, can be applied reliably? How will they convince themselves that their classifications are exhaustive and mutually exclusive? (It always seems possible, for example, given human inventiveness, to mix the distinguishing characteristics of one movie genre with the distinguishing characteristics of any other movie genre in making a particular movie, and surely patients can be expected to be equally inventive.) Also, if I know clinical investigators they will start by reducing 36 dramatic situations (Polti, 1921) to 8 or 9 so that their unsophisticated observers will have no trouble remembering the list and agreeing about assignment of an observational unit to a class. Unfortunately, the level of generality reached with the 8 or 9 classifications sacrifices just that particularity that is the psychotherapist's stock in trade.

Would you agree that what you have been saying about the relation between the practice of psychotherapy and psychotherapy research might be true for one kind, and not other kinds, of psychotherapy?

I regret having to confirm what your question implies you have noticed, namely, that there certainly are as many kinds of psychotherapy as there are kinds of art. One form of psychotherapy has as its primary (although not necessarily only) objective the alteration of a situation that is the cause of, or that exacerbates and aggravates, a patient's difficulties. That objective is achieved mainly through the psychotherapist's directions, suggestions, or direct actions. Another kind of psychotherapy seeks primarily (although not necessarily exclusively) to correct patients' false beliefs about the world or to provide them with beliefs about the world of which they are merely ignorant. Still another psychotherapy aims chiefly at undoing maladaptive habits or correcting deficiencies in the patient's social or cognitive skills; these objectives are accomplished mostly through training, didactic intervention, or modeling by the psychotherapist. And yet another psychotherapy tries for the most part to provide the patient with some environmental nutriment necessary for development or psychological functioning, delivered in the form of the psychotherapist's responses, when the patient lacks or has lacked such nutriment.

Although some of what I have said about the practice of psychotherapy and psychotherapy research may transcend the differences among psychotherapies, we probably do need, for these other kinds of psychotherapy, a discussion very different from the one I am offering here. Different kinds of psychotherapy generate different kinds of questions. I suspect, with some uneasiness, that the practitioners of other kinds of psychotherapy are more likely to get answers to their questions from psychotherapy research than I am. I am most interested in a psychotherapy that focuses on stories told or enacted and that aims to loosen the grip scenarios have on patients, inexorably determining what they experience and how they respond to it. Is this relative insulation from research, as it is currently carried out, a reason to think that doing my kind of psychotherapy cannot be justified? It is easy to be assailed by doubts as soon as the question of the relation between psychotherapy and research is brought to the fore, which is why I am not altogether pleased by your question.

Don't you think that perhaps some psychotherapists don't pay any attention to psychotherapy research because they want to stay with what they know how to do? After all, if psychotherapists are compelled by the evidence to change not only what they are thinking but what they are doing, they might find themselves out of a job, or at least forced to look around for a new one. I don't want to be cruel, but it is not so easy after a certain age to acquire new knowledge or skills.

There is, regrettably, always the inertia factor. Yes, we tend to stay with what we know how to do. We do not change our most central beliefs easily. I wonder what kind of psychotherapy research might be most effective in counteracting this conservatism, which paradoxically enters as a criterion of selection in the very evaluation of alternative theories in science itself.

Certainly, if in doing psychotherapy we turn to knowledge of the particulars of our concrete experiences, rather than to general theory or research findings, we may not move easily from one way of doing psychotherapy to another. How do the brains of psychotherapists work? Can psychotherapy research tell us that? In making sense of particulars we see and hear, do we primarily refer to other particulars we know, as I have suggested, or to general rules? Do our particulars fall under general or abstract concepts, or do they become constituents of narratives? Is the difference an idiosyncratic one, depending on who the psychotherapist is, or is this something basic about how psychotherapists (or one kind of psychotherapist—or any kind of psychotherapist?) work?

I don't mind sticking with one kind of psychotherapy for now. But I do have trouble with the notion that people can suffer from stories the way they suffer from lesions or genes. Can you tell me more about how your kind of psychotherapist thinks about what is wrong with the patient and how the psychotherapy will make the patient better? Shouldn't psychotherapy research be able to help you decide, at the very least, between rival answers to that question?

When I was a child I was impressed by the radio program "The Shadow." ("Who knows what evil lurks in the hearts of men? The Shadow knows!") In one episode an enemy of the Shadow invents a time machine in order to wreak vengeance on him. This enemy captures the Shadow and spends one 24-hour period visiting unspeakable tortures upon him. Then the time machine is set, dooming the Shadow to repeat this 24-hour ordeal throughout eternity.

I reject the view that patients really suffer only if they have a physical disease, that they are otherwise simply well persons with "problems of living" like the rest of us "normal" people. I see patients who are trapped in master stories of unslaked desire, relentless punishment, and horrifying dangers, and their suffering seems quite terrible enough to me. Being trapped in such a story (*trapped* is the operative word here) is an important cause of their psychopathology, which is often not only a manifestation of what it is like to be caught and to participate in such a scenario but also a result of the patient's efforts to cope with, counter, or escape the effects of being caught and participating in such a scenario.

Perhaps I had better be specific about the kind of psychotherapy I am talking about, acknowledging at the same time that it is certainly only one kind and not necessarily in all cases the best kind of psychotherapy.[3] Some terms used to describe it are the following: psychodynamic psychotherapy, psychoanalytic psychotherapy, psychoanalysis (a more rigorous or specialized form of psychoanalytic or psychodynamic psychotherapy). (There is no need to struggle here, given the purposes of this discussion, with the question of what the differences between psychoanalysis and these less specialized forms are.)

Patients tell or enact stories because they are in the grip of one—or, usually, more than one—unconscious story. All the stories they tell or enact are, to some extent at least, more or less disguised spinoffs of such unconscious stories, variants resulting from the use of such devices for presenting or representing objects or states of affairs as condensation, displacement, iconic symbolization, and pictorialization.

---

[3]I have been moving toward this formulation in other works; see Edelson (1988), especially the material on a cinematic model in chapter 9, and a reworking of the same material in Edelson (1990); and Edelson (1992, 1993).

Some patients are in the grip of a more or less unconscious story because they have gotten and continue to get so much of a certain kind of sensuous pleasure when they effectively imagine themselves into this story. They wish more of the same.

Other patients are in the grip of a story because it once had and continues to have the power to mitigate, counteract, or reverse some intolerably painful experience. The painful experience is, of course, a constituent of the story they tell or enact. It is the triggering event or situation that gets things going. So, for example, telling or enacting a story in which a patient is proud or triumphant follows an experience of shame. Telling or enacting a story in which a patient is shown to be completely justified follows an experience of guilt. Telling or enacting a story in which a patient is bold and brave follows an experience of fear. Telling or enacting a story in which a patient exacts compensation or revenge follows an experience of injury. Patients tell or enact a story in which they control, possess, or are reunited with something or someone following an experience of loss of control (or the anticipation of loss of control) or the loss of someone or something. They tell or enact a story in which they repair someone or something following an experience of remorse over ragefully wishing or seeking to destroy someone or something.

Some patients are in the grip of a story because it remains (necessarily, for a variety of reasons) an unfinished story for which they are trying over and over again to find a happy ending (in vain if, for example, a vicious cycle, dilemma, or unresolvable conflict is a component of the story). Other patients are in the grip of a story because telling or enacting some version of it (however disguised) serves many different current purposes at once. (It is important to distinguish the content of a story from the function or purpose it serves on a particular occasion or for a particular patient. The same story may serve more than one function or purpose.)

In the psychotherapy I have in mind, the primary objective is to extend the range of what patients permit themselves to experience fully and directly. This kind of psychotherapy is designed to enable patients to come to know and to articulate fully what it feels like to have certain wishes, beliefs, or emotions, which they had previously, for a variety of reasons, rejected and have continued to reject. Using a variety of mental operations, they have prevented these from coming into awareness at all or have paid them little (or, at the most, peripheral) attention. But these wishes, beliefs, and emotions continue to play a part, however disguised or transformed, in the stories patients tell and enact.

The objectives of this psychotherapeutic process are achieved as patients increasingly come to know the particulars of a favorite story, which over and over they write and direct and in which they assign themselves first one and then another part. As such stories take center stage in consciousness, as they are sharpened and made explicit, as the details are filled in, as the twists and turns in the plot and the many revisions are traced out, patients become focally and fully aware of the wishes, beliefs, or emotions they have when immersed in these stories. As they come to have direct knowledge of what it feels like to have a certain wish, belief, or emotion, they are able to appreciate how having that wish, belief, or emotion might have disabled them, led them to see themselves or others, or caused them to act, in ways that hitherto they found puzzling. As they come to recognize what evokes their playing out the story on still another occasion, they increasingly understand its value to them—the uses to which they are able to put it, the purposes it serves.

Such a psychotherapy is appropriate to the extent that the patient's difficulties or problems—whether these be formulated in terms of psychological dysfunction, developmental deficiencies in capacity, or interpersonal vicissitudes—have their main source in some sort of internal psychological structure that mediates the patient's response to his or her own perceptions of the internal and external world. The master story is just such a psychological structure. Such an internal psychological structure determines what patients notice (that is, what perceptions they select to have), including certain kinds of experiences that are rejected by them because of what they imply about them. It determines how patients interpret information reaching them from their inner or external world (that is, what they infer from such information about their inner or external world) and therefore how they feel or act in response to that information.

That internal psychological structure may be defined differently and given different content by different psychotherapists. It may involve traumatic memories, unconscious conflicts, unconscious fantasies, self-ideals, or paradigms of interpersonal interaction. (For the present discussion, it does not matter which of these is favored by the psychotherapist; all of them can be an aspect of, or used as material in creating, a narrative.)

Please give an example of how you work with observations of stories told and enacted in a psychotherapy.

All right, here is an example.[4] My story begins with a patient who has arrived late to the psychotherapy session, as she often does, and who tells a story about her current difficulties in completing a work assignment on time. The story about the work assignment seems to serve the purpose of countering the disapproval she imagines the psychotherapist feels in response to her coming late. The psychotherapist is reminded of stories the patient has told in other sessions illustrating how her father dominated and criticized her and how she devised secret strategies for defeating him. The psychotherapist notices the similarity or thematic affinity between these stories about the past, what is going on currently in her work life, and the story that the patient seems to be enacting in the psychotherapy situation.

---

[4]Other versions of the following clinical material appear in Edelson (1992, 1993).

The psychotherapist offers an interpretation, connecting the story of coming late, the story of the work assignment, and the stories of the defeated father. The patient discusses the interpretation calmly and with great interest, expressing admiration and appreciation of the psychotherapist's ability to bring all these stories together. She adds some details and remembers some other incidents that fit the narrative pattern the psychotherapist has detected.

The psychotherapist's interpretation turns out to be what someone writing a screenplay would call a triggering event (example: a stranger riding into town). A triggering event stirs things up, upsets a balance, gets a story going. In the next session the patient tells a story about a fight she has just had with a younger brother. It is clear that even before the fight she had been irritable, belligerent, and provocative. She is still fuming in the session, beside herself with rage toward her brother, who is, as far as she is concerned, a troublesome adversary, blocking her from achieving what she wants. (In a screenplay the brother would be the villain.)

"But why," the psychotherapist wonders, "does the fight story follow my giving an interpretation? Was my giving the interpretation a triggering event in a story that has more to it than the episode of the fight?" It is certainly not immediately clear that this giving-the-interpretation episode and the fight-with-the-brother episode belong to the same scenario.

The psychotherapist reminds the patient of similar episodes in which she was truculent and provoked a fight. The patient complains bitterly that the psychotherapy has done nothing to change her, that she still acts as she always has. The psychotherapist notices that he feels bad when the patient says this. The patient soon settles down and becomes reflective: "Why do I get so angry? Why do I make life so difficult for myself by behaving this way with others? I know that there was no reason for acting so provocatively. I just defeat myself. I am my own adversary!" Now she is remorseful and wishes there were some way to make up to her brother for her treatment of him. She thinks of ways to undo the bad effects of the quarrel.

The psychotherapist remembers the patient's reasonableness in the last session and contrasts it with the fulminations and irrationality with which this session began. Reminded of a number of stories in which the patient became furious in situations in which, it turned out later, she had felt denigrated, the psychotherapist wonders if in the previous session the patient felt humiliated by his superior performance (making an interpretation). The patient then remembers she was peripherally aware of such a feeling: "But, of course, I couldn't tell you I envied you or that I felt resentful that you are always the superior, and I the inferior, one. After all, you were helping me. You would become offended. Then you would really send me away."

If the psychotherapist had been less involved in an attempt to follow and piece together a complicated story, he might have relied instead on a theoretical formula. He might have thought, "The patient's rage was displaced from me to her brother." This rather lazy shortcut would miss some essential details of what turned out to be a more complex scenario.

The patient now tells an additional story, what a screenwriter would call a flashback. The psychotherapist hears it as an episode that has to be interpolated between the story of the interpretation and the story of the fight; it connects them. Here is the additional story: Later in the day of the previous session the patient had a conscious sexual fantasy in which she had oscillated between scenes in which she was powerful and was forcing someone to do what she commanded and scenes in which she was submitting to someone.

A fantasy like this was a favorite of the patient's. It seemed always to be readily available in the patient's mind, easily recruited for a variety of purposes in response to many different kinds of triggering events. But it seemed especially likely to be evoked in circumstances the patient interpreted as humiliating. At this point in the psychotherapy various versions of this favorite fantasy were relatively accessible to consciousness, although the patient, embarrassed, was always reluctant to tell these stories.

These sexual fantasies are cut off from any contact with the patient's everyday life and, as far as she is concerned, have nothing to do with it. Why she has such fantasies is a mystery to her. They make no sense. The patient is not aware of any connection between her conscious sexual fantasy and her feelings in the previous session and therefore is certainly not aware that the fantasy is the fulfillment of a wish stirred up in that session. The psychotherapist wonders whether the patient had wished, following the previous session, to be superior and powerful, as she had experienced the psychotherapist, and capable of humiliating someone inferior, as she felt she had been humiliated. Her fantasy seemed to gratify this wish, at least in imagination. The connection between her sexual fantasy and the actual event that had triggered it now becomes apparent to her.

Further details emerge. Why couldn't she stay with the scene in which she tortured her victim? Uncomfortable with an image of herself as a cruel person, she softens the torture and disguises it, so it seems less like torture and more like teasing. Then she reverses roles; as the director of this scene, she assigns herself the role of the character who is kind, gentle, and submissive, the "teasee." In talking with the psychotherapist she begins to recapture some details of the original scene, where she was the torturer, and she is horrified by the details.

The psychotherapist begins to realize that the patient has omitted a piece of the story because she is unaware of it as an episode in a continuous scenario. She habitually fails to connect any act or feeling that occurs in her everyday life or in a psychotherapy session to what she more or less obscurely feels and thinks as she observes herself playing a particular part in a sexual fantasy. (It is just this piece of the story the psychotherapist would have lost, had the story of the fight reminded him of a theoretical formula about "displacement.")

The psychotherapist finally wonders aloud if after having the fantasy the patient had worried that the submissiveness she experienced in her imagined drama might emerge in a real relationship. Seeing that she is submissive, someone might despise or take advantage of her. In response, the patient remembers that just before the fight she interpreted something that had happened as indicating that she had unwittingly invited her brother to treat her as an inferior. This was especially galling to her, because her brother is younger than she. It was her desire to cancel this invitation, which she rejected with all her heart, that, she now believes, compelled her, as it had on so many other occasions, to be obnoxious and domineering.

Further details of this story about herself and her brother suggest its links to the sexual fantasy. I think it inaccurate, therefore, to regard this fight-with-the-brother story as *only*, or even primarily, a disguised expression of "the transference."

Finally, the patient's telling the psychotherapist the story about her brother is part of an enactment in the psychotherapy session of a story of vindictive attack and reparation. For telling this story makes it possible for her to take the psychotherapist down a peg or two by showing him that the psychotherapy is not working: she still behaves in the same way she has always behaved. At the same time, by cooperating with the psychotherapist in doing the work of psychotherapy, she repairs the damage she fears she has done him, both by the acts of cruelty in her fantasy and by what she feels are ungrateful, cruel reproaches about the inefficacy of the psychotherapy, reproaches she hurls at him because of her envy and resentment.

Even if we stick to psychotherapists who think along the same lines you do, isn't there an awful lot of disagreement among them about just what kind of psychological structure is mediating patients' interpretation of and response to what they perceive, disagreement about the nature of that structure, its content, and how it brings about the effects in which the psychotherapist is interested?

As I have already said, a major problem for both the clinician and the clinical investigator is what criteria to use to select and describe the clinical observations themselves. It should be clear that we cannot make use of every bit of information available in a domain, every utterance in a months-long or years-long psychotherapy, for example. Nor can we allow the selection of information to depend on just those theoretical predilections of the observer that are in question.

All the schools of psychotherapy in which we are here interested agree in postulating some hypothetical internal psychological structure as the cause of what is observed. But members of each school tend to favor different conjectures about the properties, including contents, of the hypothetical internal structure and about what is responsible for the effects of that structure.

Usually, whether or not an observation belongs to a category that is a constituent of a hypothesis about these hypothetical internal psychological structures favored by a particular school of psychotherapy determines whether or not members of that school select or ignore it, that is, count it as an observation at all, and further determines how it is described if it is counted as an observation. But evidence is evidence, after all, just because it is capable of deciding in favor of one hypothesis over another as to the properties, content, and effects of a hypothetical internal psychological structure. These usual observations, then, cannot be used as evidence capable of deciding among rival hypotheses about a postulated structure, because confirmation of conjectures is made inevitable by biased selection of observations and the very way of describing what is to count as an observation. Clearly, observations selected or described according to one or another theoretical preference cannot serve as evidence when that theoretical preference is the progenitor of one of the rival hypotheses competing for evidential support.

My own belief is that we can go far toward finding a way to decide among these conjectures by choosing as the observational units of interest the stories—all the stories—told and enacted by a patient during psychotherapy.[5] Such a choice makes it less likely that the theoretical preferences of one school of psychotherapy will determine how observations are selected and formulated. Furthermore, in my experience, psychotherapists of different schools can agree at least about what the observations *are*, when they are at just this level of abstraction.

The choice of a narrative or part of a narrative as the unit of observation is determined by the conjecture that the internal psychological structure, whatever its nature or content might be, has a narrative form. Traumatic memories or unconscious fantasies are symbolic representations of organized sequences of particular events (episodes, scenes), or they are schemes or prototypes (for example, sequences of *classes* of events rather than particular events) that are capable of generating many such representations. Different psychotherapists, of course, may disagree about what is important in these representations—the ideals exemplified by the characteristics of the hero or heroine of the narrative, the interpersonal paradigms exemplified by the interactions of the various characters of the narrative, or the conflicts exemplified by the obstacles and dilemmas that must be overcome by the hero or heroine as he or she tries to execute a plan to reach an objective. But all these are coexisting aspects of a narrative that are abstracted from it; as perspectives on the phenomena, they do not exclude each other.

---

[5]See, for example, Luborsky and Crits-Christoph (1990), especially chapter 17, for a description of a large number of measures reflecting the interest current psychotherapy research takes in the narratives of patients.

*I begin to see how psychotherapy research might be of help if not in doing psy-
chotherapy then in teaching psychotherapy. After all, it has taken you much experience to arrive at your present views. Wouldn't it be useful in teaching psychotherapy to beginners just to give them a set of stories often told or enacted by patients so
that they would recognize what story they are hearing or are caught up with the patient in enacting? Psychotherapy research might come up then with a set of stories
from its empirical studies that a psychotherapist should have ready at hand when listening to patients. Maybe psychotherapy research can even show that patients with
different personality or character disorders, for example, are partial to particular
kinds of stories.*

"A set of stories ready at hand?" I don't think so, for a variety of reasons. I
am, as you can tell from what I have said so far, leery of anything that promotes reliance on formulas, even if these are archetypal narratives rather than
abstract or general concepts. I would recoil from the prospect of stretching
the patient's material on still another procrustean bed instead of focusing on
the particulars in the narrative the patient tells. But I don't think there is a finite list of stories any more than I think there is a finite list of sentences in a
natural language. Narrative competence can generate an infinite set of stories,
including completely novel stories, just as linguistic competence can generate
an infinite set of sentences, including completely novel sentences, from a finite set of components. A first approximation to such a set of components for
narrative competence might include the following: theme (some general idea,
the point or "moral" of the story); kind of event, episode, situation, scene, or
state of affairs, multiples of which can be linked together in many ways; constellation of characters (varying in number, generation, gender, species, type);
prop (various kinds of objects, natural and cultural); setting; and mood or
feeling (sometimes called style, although that is not an adequate term).[6]

One of the reasons that I like stories as a taking-off point in considering
psychotherapeutic process is that I don't have to start with a blank slate in
teaching someone how to do psychotherapy. I can rely on the person's narrative competence; he or she not only comes to me knowing how to create
stories but how to recognize and respond to them as well.

A psychotherapist who cannot get into a patient's story imaginatively because of a lack of narrative competence may be experienced by the patient as
lacking in empathy. The ability of psychotherapists to respond sympatheti-
cally and empathically to their patients is related to their narrative competence—to their propensity to listen for stories, to how good (involved, responsive) an audience they are, to how many stories they know. Knowing as an

---

[6]For example, see the computer software program designed "for the writer of novels,
short stories, plays, screenplays and television episodes" called "Plots Unlimited"
(Sawyer & Weingarten, 1990) and described as "a creative source for generating a virtually limitless number and variety of story plots and outlines."

audience how to identify with characters in stories is part of narrative competence. Given a dramatic situation and some appreciation of what a character is like, an audience knows directly how that character is feeling in that situation, as well as how other characters are feeling about that character. An audience grasps those feelings because identification with a character in a story includes feeling as that character feels.

So my first task becomes to convince psychotherapists-in-training that something they already know and know how to do is relevant to this new enterprise. My second task is (by example usually) to help them hear the stories in what their patient says and does and to get into these imaginatively. Their answers to the following questions indicate whether they are into the story imaginatively: Are they seeing a particular scene in their mind, or are they simply processing words and concepts? Are they curious, in suspense, anticipating what happens next? Are their feelings engaged?

To hear the stories, psychotherapists-in-training must learn the importance of adopting a mind-set in which in response to what a patient says and does they ask themselves such questions as: "Where is the story?" and "What is the story?" They learn to give priority to helping the patient tell his or her stories, as many of them as possible, and as fully as possible, holding nothing back. Because of their own narrative competence, they will notice that there are pieces missing and will inquire after them or settle back to wait for them to show up. They appreciate that a story about the past is a flashback and is relevant to—is a comment upon—the present.

The psychotherapist learns to consider a patient's story in terms of such questions as these: What purpose, what function, does this story serve here and now? What problem does it help the patient to solve? To answer such questions, psychotherapists learn to pay attention to what event or situation, internal or external, evoked the story, for the content of that event or situation is often a clue to the problem the patient now faces and, therefore, to the purpose the story serves. For the same reason, they learn to pay attention to how the patient tells or enacts the story, to what gets emphasized or put in the foreground and what is slipped into the background. (A complication: the event or situation evoking the story may not pose a problem for the patient, but one of the features of the event or situation may have reminded the patient of another event or situation that does pose a problem for him or her; thus, the importance of the inquiry "What does that remind you of?")

Since the patient usually tells and enacts multiple stories, the psychotherapist is called upon to understand their relation to each other. Are the stories about the past, the present, and the patient–therapist relationship similar? Are the stories that are told and those that are enacted in the psychotherapeutic situation similar, suggesting the power of some master story of which these stories are variants or versions, or are the stories different? Are they pieces in a more comprehensive plot or scenario as yet only dimly apprehended? Are they related to each other as theme and countertheme, that is, with one a response to the other, with one set against, rejecting, evading, canceling, or undoing the other? When theme and countertheme are from different (earlier and later) periods of life, the technical phrase describing their relation to each other might be "the defensive use of regression or progression."

A more complicated problem faces psychotherapists as they begin to suspect that a story told or enacted is a condensation of more than one master story, borrowing a piece from this one and another piece from that one. Each piece needs to be followed up until the condensation is undone, until all the stories stand forth fully told, before the task of determining their relation to each other, and determining what effects each is responsible for, can begin.

You look a bit taken aback or overwhelmed. I did not mean to suggest by talking about stories that psychotherapy is easy, only that the knowledge involved is narrative competence rather than general psychological theory as it is usually formulated.

I notice that you put a great deal of weight on what psychotherapists are reminded of as they listen to the patient and on what events or situations remind the patient of the master story. How do you know that what the psychotherapist is reminded of has something to do with what is going on in the patient, with what the patient is reminded of? And how do psychotherapists convince themselves and others of the credibility (with respect to accuracy) of their inference concerning the existence, content, and causal efficacy of a master story? Given your pessimism about the contribution of psychotherapy research to practice, I am beginning to worry that you have landed yourself in one of those "touchy feely," "it depends on who does the psychotherapy, but the different stories psychotherapists tell are all acceptable," "no one is right or wrong," "anything goes" approaches to doing psychotherapy.

Be clear that I am not pessimistic about the contribution that any kind of research might make to the practice of psychotherapy; my skepticism is directed to the kind of research that is currently done under the rubric of psychotherapy research. I am quite taken with the possible relevance to psychotherapeutic practice of some theoretical work in cognitive psychology and the research that it has generated and to which it refers—for example, work on memory (see, for example, Schank, 1982, 1990); work on how we form classifications and how different kinds of classifications determine how we file memories and therefore our access to them (see, for example, Johnson, 1987; Lakoff, 1987; Lakoff & Johnson, 1980); work on emotions defined in terms of paradigm scenarios (see, for example, de Sousa, 1987; and "A Case Study: Anger," Appendix 1 in Lakoff, 1987); work on knowledge structures in terms of scripts, plans, and goals (see, for example, Miller, Galanter, & Pribram, 1960; Schank & Abelson, 1977; Schank, 1982, 1990); and work on mental representations, computations, and desire/belief explanation (see, for example, Fodor, 1975, 1981, 1983, 1987, 1990; Holland, Holyoak, Nisbett, & Thagard, 1986; Pylyshyn, 1984).

Case studies take pleasure in particulars and focus on their patterns. The case study has a fond affinity for narrative patterns. My emphasis (Edelson, 1988, 1989) on the potential value of the case study as a method of research and my formulation of canons that, if followed, would result in more rigorous case studies than those now found in our literature are appropriate to my focus on stories in psychotherapeutic work and on the particular rather than the general. Case studies following those canons, and therefore capable of testing and not merely generating hypotheses, would be at least a first step toward psychotherapy research that might have an impact on psychotherapeutic practice.[7]

I won't elaborate upon that proposal here but merely wish to mention the importance in case studies, as well as in the practice of the psychotherapist, of three major ways to argue that one inference or conjecture, given the evidence, is more credible than another (for details, see Edelson, 1988, especially chapter 15). The first way, analogy, involves fitting detailed data to a familiar model; you already know how the model works, and you argue that similar entities and causal mechanisms are operating to produce the phenomena you observe. The second, consilience, involves arguing that different kinds of data converge on the same conclusion. The third, abduction, involves arguing that a postulated entity and/or causal mechanism is the best explanation, that is, that there are no other plausible rival explanations. Case studies, by focusing on particulars, can also provide decisive counterexamples to some universal generalization or dogmatically held generality and can therefore lead to its deserved extinction or at least revision.

With respect to checks on the accuracy of the psychotherapist's inferences (interpretations), I would make three comments: First, it does not matter with respect to an assessment of accuracy *how* the psychotherapist arrived at the inference. If one psychotherapist makes one inference about the patient (based, for example, on what the patient's talk reminded him of) and another psychotherapist can be imagined making another, a rival, inference about the same patient, based on what the patient's talk reminded him of, then the choice between the two inferences as to which is the more accurate does not depend on assessing the quality of either psychotherapist's "reminding apparatus." It depends, rather, on whether there is evidence, other than what either psychotherapist was reminded of, that would favor one of these inferences over the other.

Second, in view of the inevitable degree of indeterminateness and ambiguity in clinical material, I encourage myself and those I teach to generate more than one inference from the same material. It is a good idea to get out of the habit of thinking "Obviously this patient is . . ." or "This patient's story is certainly . . ." and into the habit of thinking "What is going on

---

[7]Freud's case studies, whatever their shortcomings with respect to what is required for testing hypotheses, may be included here as steps in the right direction.

with this patient today, given what I have observed, could be this *or* this," or "The story the patient is most concerned today to tell or enact could be this *or* this."

Do you remember the report of four psychoanalytic sessions by M. Silverman (in Pulver, 1987, pp. 147–165)? A structural theorist, two developmentalists, a self psychologist, a Kleinian, an interpersonalist, an eclectic, and an object relations theorist responded to the report, their commentaries designed to clarify the way in which theory shapes technique. In the psychoanalytic sessions the patient alluded to three stories: the film *Now Voyager*, the novel *Don Quixote*, and the story of Helen Keller and her teacher Anne Sullivan. What do these stories have in common? They are stories in which someone rescues someone else. Does the patient wish to be rescued by the psychotherapist? Is she enacting a story of rescue? But the three stories are also stories of wondrous transformation. Does the patient wish to be transformed by the psychotherapist? Is she enacting a story of transformation? These two kinds of stories are not incompatible. Both may be of interest to her. But surely one is closer to consciousness and therefore more appropriate as a basis for interpretation on this particular day, in this particular session, here and now. Which one? The patient reports a fantasy in which a mad scientist does something to give her bigger breasts. That fantasy provides some evidential support, however weak, for the inference from the other three stories (which are not reported as fantasies) that a story of transformation, rather than of rescue, is on the patient's mind. (Multiple instances of evidence providing weak inductive support may add up to relatively strong inductive support.)

It is important to me that one cannot read off someone's theoretical preference from their descriptions of their observations in terms of stories of rescue and transformation. In the eight commentaries on these four sessions only two mention *Now Voyager*, although the psychoanalyst writes in an aside, "She repeatedly brings up *Now Voyager*. Is that the script for the analysis?" None consider the story of *Now Voyager* in any detail. One commentary mentions the allusion to Helen Keller. No commentary mentions the allusion to *Don Quixote*. Infatuation with theory, and with explicating theory, leads to ignoring details in the clinical material solely on the grounds, as far as I can see, that they don't lend themselves to promoting a general theory (see Pulver, 1987; there are, of course, many other details to consider in constructing the story or stories most on the patient's mind in these particular sessions). The mischievous witch, Theory, banishes what otherwise might be fascinating particulars right out of the picture.

Third, in assessing the credibility of an inference or conjecture I have communicated to a patient, I give priority to the patient's actual subjective experience. My conjectures are not about any story that might be somewhere in the patient's mind but about a story I believe is engaging the patient here and now. If I am in touch with a story the patient is telling or enacting in the here and now, I will be dealing with accessible versions or transforms ("derivatives") of stories that in other versions may be at this particular time inaccessible to the patient. I am looking for the following kinds of responses to my communications: "Now I remember an episode just like that which I forgot to tell you"; "On the way here today, I thought [or wondered or imagined] . . ."; "Just yesterday [this morning, right after the last session] I . . ."; "That reminds me of something that happened with my mother . . ." These new events are of a time or place. They complicate, enrich, or complete the story; that is, they add a missing piece to it, provide a clarifying flashback to an earlier event, or give some necessary background. The patient's response to my communication may provide me with other stories that are similar to—or constitute an attempt to counteract—the story the patient has told or enacted that I have commented on. The patient may deepen a mood evident in the story we are discussing or may give more details about its setting. The patient may burst through to an emotional state that is clearly appropriate to the unfolding story and that therefore—no matter how awkward, embarrassing, or painful—makes sense.

I am inclined to think I am on the right track if the patient's response to my communication tells me more than I knew before, surprises me, adds a new twist to a story, carries the story further, or involves an intense expression of feeling (such as when we begin to laugh or cry, sometimes quite unexpectedly, when something about a movie—we are not always sure what it is—touches us). I am inclined to think I am on the wrong track if the patient convincingly challenges what I say by pointing out particulars that are inconsistent with it or not encompassed by it or if the patient ignores what I say (what I say has no impact on the patient or the story he or she is telling or enacting). Mere assent or dissent are evidentially irrelevant. Timeless generalizations or generalities, no matter how eagerly or enthusiastically the patient offers them, are evidentially irrelevant.

But I see you are getting weary. We have posed enough questions for the present. Let us see how others will answer them.

REFERENCES

Arlow, J. (1969a). Unconscious fantasy and disturbances of conscious experience. *Psychoanalytic Quarterly, 38,* 1–27.

Arlow, J. (1969b). Fantasy, memory, and reality testing. *Psychoanalytic Quarterly, 38,* 28–51.

de Sousa, R. (1987). *The rationality of emotion.* Cambridge, MA: MIT Press.

Edelson, M. (1988). *Psychoanalysis: A theory in crisis.* Chicago: University of Chicago Press.

Edelson, M. (1989). The nature of psychoanalytic theory: Implications for psychoanalytic research. *Psychoanalytic Inquiry, 9,* 169–192.

Edelson, M. (1990). Defense in psychoanalytic theory: Computation or fantasy? In J. L. Singer (Ed.), *Repression or dissociation: Implications for personality theory, psychopathology, and health* (pp. 33–60). Chicago: University of Chicago Press.

Edelson, M. (1992). Telling and enacting stories in psychoanalysis. In J. Barron, M. Eagle, & D. Wolitzky (Eds.), *Interface of Psychoanalysis and Psychology,* pp. 99–124. Washington, D.C.: American Psychological Association Press.

Edelson, M. (1993). Telling and enacting stories in psychoanalysis and psychotherapy: Implications for teaching psychotherapy. In A. Solnit, P. Neubauer, S. Abrams, & A. S. Dowling (Eds.), *The Psychoanalytic Study of the Child,* vol. 48, pp. 293–325. New Haven, CT: Yale University Press.

Fodor, J. (1975). *The language of thought.* New York: Crowell.

Fodor, J. (1981). *Representations.* Cambridge, MA: MIT Press.

Fodor, J. (1983). *The modularity of mind.* Cambridge, MA: MIT Press.

Fodor, J. (1987). *Psychosemantics.* Cambridge, MA: MIT Press.

Fodor, J. (1990). *A theory of content.* Cambridge, MA: MIT Press.

Holland, J. H., Holyoak, K. J., Nisbett, R. E., & Thagard, P. R. (1986). *Induction: Processes of inference, learning, and discovery.* Cambridge, MA: MIT Press.

Johnson, M. (1987). *The body in the mind: The bodily basis of meaning, imagination, and reason.* Chicago: University of Chicago Press.

Lakoff, G. (1987). *Women, fire, and dangerous things: What categories reveal about the mind.* Chicago: University of Chicago Press.

Lakoff, G., & Johnson, M. (1980). *Metaphors we live by.* Chicago: University of Chicago Press.

Levenson, E. (1988). The pursuit of the particular. *Contemporary Psychoanalysis,* 24, 1–16.

Luborsky, L., & Crits-Christoph, P. (1990). *Understanding transference.* New York: Basic Books.

Miller, G., Galanter, E., & Pribram, K. (1960). *Plans and the structure of behavior.* New York: Holt, Rinehart & Winston.

Polti, G. (1921). *Thirty-six dramatic situations.* Boston: The Writer, Inc.

Pulver, S. (1987). How theory shapes technique: Perspectives on a clinical study. *Psychoanalytic Inquiry, 7*(2), 141–299.

Pylyshyn, Z. (1984). *Computation and cognition.* Cambridge, MA: MIT Press.

Sawyer, T., & Weingarten, A. (1990). *Plots unlimited.* Malibu, CA: Ashleywilde.

Schank, R. (1982). *Dynamic memory: A theory of reminding and learning in computers and people.* New York: Cambridge University Press.

Schank, R. (1990). *Tell me a story: A new look at real and artificial memory.* New York: Scribner.

Schank, R., & Abelson, R. (1977). *Scripts, plans, goals, and understanding: An inquiry into human knowledge structures.* Hillsdale, NJ: Erlbaum.

Shapiro, D. (1989). *Psychotherapy of neurotic character.* New York: Basic Books.

CHAPTER 5

Some Suggestions for Making Research More Applicable to Clinical Practice

Leston Havens

ONE IMPEDIMENT to applying psychotherapeutic research in the clinic is the contrast between the global nature of research recommendations and the usually specific character of clinical dilemmas.

Much clinical work involves recognizing and resolving impasses. By impasses I mean the development or discovery of features of the patient–therapist relationship that complicate it or complicate other relationships outside it. For example, recommendations for a warm, interactive style or the use of empathic statements may have to be fit into paranoid developments in which warmth is misunderstood as an attack. Intractable self-deprecatory attitudes or failure to maintain an integrated selfhood or will are also responsible for impasses in clinical work.

In this chapter I attempt to operationalize the recognition of three such impasses, the means of their resolution, and evidence of that resolution. I close with a discussion of four more general psychotherapeutic goals, with suggestions for their achievement.

Starting with specific clinical impasses and testing different interventions should make the application of research results to the clinic easier. What follows is an attempt to outline such a strategy. The mode of analysis undertaken here closely parallels that of Greenberg and Pinsof (1986), who present the following set of questions, which are designed to bring investigators "closer to studying what people actually do in therapy":

1) What client in-therapy performances suggest themselves as problem states requiring and ready for intervention?

The author is indebted to Dan Giacomo and Peter Weiden for help with the manuscript, as well as to the editors of this volume.

2) What therapist operations are appropriate at these markers? What therapist performances will best facilitate a process of change?

3) What client performances following the markers lead to change? What are the aspects of the client performance that seem to carry the change process and what does the final in-therapy performance, that is, problem resolution, look like? (p. 717).

Paranoid Developments

RECOGNITION OF THE IMPASSE

One would be well advised to use the criteria of paranoid states put forth in the American Psychiatric Association's *Diagnostic and Statistical Manual of Mental Disorders* (3rd edition, revised), or DSM-III-R. Because paranoid patients are unlikely to be willing contributors to research studies, however, it may be necessary to define paranoid development more narrowly, that is, as a paranoid attitude during the treatment process, whether toward others or the therapist. I suggest the following criteria: sustained attacks on the therapist or others, evidence of externalization of blame or responsibility, and signs of pain or rage at feared or experienced attacks. I believe a compelling operationalization of such features will only be achieved by comparative studies, that is, by studies that also use subjects in whom the opposite attitudes are apparent, namely, attacks on self, internalization of responsibilities, and depressive signs.

MEANS OF RESOLUTION

Sullivan (Havens, 1977) made the original observations on which interventions against the paranoid development are based. Part of the clinical reputation he made in his own lifetime rested on his ability to reverse such developments, particularly as they arose between patients and members of the hospital staff. In the 1970s I began collecting anecdotes and supervisory advice that Sullivan gave, much of which pertained to management of these occurrences. This was necessary because Sullivan himself had not explicated the specific clinical steps necessary to the intervention. My conclusions were published in a series of books and articles (Havens, 1972, 1977, 1979, 1986a).

The recommended intervention involves three aspects of the therapist's, or intervenor's, behavior: physical position, content of speech, and emotional force. First, the intervenor is to place himself or herself beside the patient, neither in front nor behind (as in medical interviewing and psychoanalytic treatment, respectively), so that the two look out at the world together.

The value of this position springs from its avoidance of the projections that inevitably settle on whoever is in the center of the patient's gaze; in the side-by-side position projections tend to be deflected outward.

Second, the intervenor speaks of the conspirator. He or she avoids speaking to the patient. The personal pronouns *I* and *you*, as in orders or questions, are not to be used, but *it, he, she* , and *they* figure largely in the intervenor's speech. Again, the purpose is to deflect projections away from the patient–intervenor interactions and toward the external world. Above all, no attempt is made to correct or contradict the patient or to test reality (these can be used as alternate interventions to test the effectiveness of the recommended ones). The patient's account is accepted as reality.

Finally, the intervenor's attitudes and emotional expressions toward the "conspirator" must mirror the patient's, in empathy with the patient's rage. Again, the patient's feelings are not commented upon or corrected but simply restated. The intervenor's emotional expressions should be taken up to the point, and slightly beyond, where the patient corrects the intervenor (for example, "Don't be so paranoid, Doc"). This is confirmation of the paranoid content having been transferred from the patient to the intervenor. In chronic paranoid states the comparable point is the appearance of depressive signs; the emergence of depression, and the disappearance of rage, signals the end of the intervention. It is necessary to bring the patient to the point of sharing, that is, apportioning or dividing, the attitude of rage, which constitutes the paranoid position. It is only in such an alliance that the paranoid position can be modified.

The assumption underlying these techniques is that in a paranoid state the patient cannot "hold on to" rage. He or she is overburdened and must project the unpleasant content outward. Until the patient's coping mechanisms are strengthened, as by the described interventions, no attempt should be made to hand the projected content back. Instead, the intervenor takes it on himself or herself.

EVIDENCE OF RESOLUTION

The principal evidence of resolution of the impasse in paranoid development is a decline in the sustained attacks, in the externalization of blame, and in the signs of pain and rage at feared or experienced attacks. As indicated, the opposite of these may also occur (globally, as depression). Long-term outcome studies could be done by sampling subsequent interviews or behavior.

Marked Self-Deprecatory Trends

RECOGNITION OF THE IMPASSE

Patients with marked self-deprecatory trends are, as a rule, at least moderately depressed; however, the clarity of the depressive picture varies greatly. By self-deprecatory trends I mean a tendency to comment negatively on one's own performance. A rough quantification can be achieved by counting the number of such remarks in a given period. There is an accompanying tendency not to blame others, which could be similarly counted. A central difficulty of this assessment is the patient's frequent reluctance to voice self-deprecatory thoughts.

MEANS OF RESOLUTION

The intervention again involves three aspects of the therapist's, or intervenor's, behavior: physical position, content of speech, and emotional content. The position is face-to-face (because the intervenor addresses those aspects of the patient under self-attack), the content is admiration for those aspects, and the emotional tone is approval.

In selecting what to admire, special note should be made of whatever tendencies are addressed by the self-deprecatory remarks. These tendencies are often the personal characteristics most spontaneous in the individual's reactions, characteristics that have been targeted by someone in the family as unacceptable. A common example is tenderness in a male patient, a trait that has been targeted as unmanly, or spontaneity itself, which has been proscribed by a rigid or inhibited elder.

The intervenor's admiring statements are easily counted. It is more difficult to quantify levels of approval. The latter is important, however, for several reasons: Allegedly admiring statements can be said in a begrudging or sarcastic tone (especially by professionals accustomed to making references only to pathology). Approval is also best given cautiously at first, in case the patient is closely identified with the self-deprecatory trend; this is often the case with schizophrenic patients. Finally, approval needs to be sincere, just as a convincing expressiveness is necessary in empathizing with rage against paranoid developments. I suspect sincerity is even more difficult to quantify than emotional approval.

The method's rationale is as follows: Self-deprecatory trends are sometimes a function of identification with the aggressor, for example, a critical parent. The presence of a critical parent and the young child's identification with parental standards threaten the development of the criticized aspects of the child's emerging identity. For example, intellectual parents may depreciate a child's athletic interests. Depression in such cases can be seen as one result of a crushed or depreciated identity or true self. Intervention attempts to redress this state.

The intervention involves the use of a "performative," a speech form named by Austin (1962; see also Havens, 1984) that refers to statements deriving their power simply from being made, provided the right circumstances and people are involved—for example: "I pronounce you man and wife" in a proper marriage ceremony or "I knight you Sir Lancelot." Umpires also speak performatively in declaring balls or strikes. Statements of admiration, in turn, create the state of being admired, which has special power when performed, for example, by experts on mental health (who define personal characteristics as evidence of a sick or well mental condition). When mental health experts use performative interventions, the action of similarly powerful parents can be redressed. The point is to provide the patient with a colleague in support against the internal critics that have hitherto been unopposed.

The two established psychotherapeutic strategies for dealing with an impasse characterized by a marked self-deprecatory trend have been mourning the lost, ambivalently held objects and using the devices of cognitive therapy. These strategies could be used in conjunction with performative intervention or as competitive procedures.

EVIDENCE OF RESOLUTION

The process of resolution of marked self-deprecatory trends is generally slow. Therefore, counts of self-deprecatory comments need to be made at widely spaced intervals.

Psychotic Breakdown (Collecting Lost Mental Parts)

RECOGNITION OF THE IMPASSE

It is not frivolous to suggest that the mind can be lost in just the way one's wallet can be lost. One knows a wallet is lost because it is not where it's supposed to be. Similarly, in a state of losing one's mind, the search for a center of consciousness and will fails; thoughts and actions become autonomous. One also discovers that one's wallet has been lost if it appears in an unexpected place; the mental equivalent is hearing voices, for example, coming from a corner of the room or from one's foot.

The observer's recognition of a mind's being lost depends upon a number of familiar signs. Central to the process is a failure of will, in the sense of a coherent center of action capable of integrating thoughts, feelings, and behavior (which is what we mean by mind). Hence, thoughts are scattered or dissociated; feelings are volatile, inappropriate, or absent; and behavior is unpredictable or sharply contradictory (as in psychotic ambivalence).

MEANS OF RESOLUTION

The impasse of lost mental parts requires an intervention that is not so easily described as in the first two. The physical position of the therapist, or intervenor, is readily described: one is slightly to one side of the patient and not staring; one aims for an easy accompanying, a physical expression of the air of quiet confidence that is needed. Content of speech is easily described, too: little is said except for allusions to the patient's presumed state of mind, to wandering and feeling aimless, frightened, bewildered, vulnerable. These are best rendered by short empathic statements: "How awful"; "It must be frightening" (Havens, 1978). What is difficult to detail is the emotional state of the intervenor.

One wants to be able to sit with such patients and, at the same time, to leave them alone, giving them their own space. The opposite is intrusiveness or possessiveness. Those intervenors who are unfamiliar with the state of being alone with another have to be carefully instructed. It is important to contrast this state with indifference toward the patient or distancing; many therapists feel that unless they are actively reaching toward the patient and inquiring, they are indifferent or hostile.

The importance of this careful respecting of boundaries has to do with the mental state of individuals losing their minds. Patients in this state are extraordinarily vulnerable. As a rule, their own boundaries are lost or very permeable, and they are sensitive to minute emotional changes in the world around them and quick to feel distorted or overwhelmed. The boundaries of such patients must be maintained for them.

The described intervention is also useful for those patients who need to be left alone in order for the therapist to establish what they can do on their own. Such patients may evoke from therapists unnecessary and dependence-continuing help. I have argued elsewhere that this is the specific treatment discovery of psychoanalysis (Havens, 1989; see Freud's Invention).

EVIDENCE OF RESOLUTION

Resolution of the impasse is evident in signs of the recovery of will, that is, in signs of self-possession: the ability to initiate ordered movements and thoughts and a decrease in emotional scattering, inappropriateness, and in expressions of turbulence and bewilderment.

I do not include among these relatively well-defined interventions the steps a therapist can take with a patient who is mourning a loss, because Freud (1917/1957) gave a clear account of the mourning process, from which the intervention is easily described. I also do not discuss a direct empathic understanding of the patient's plight, as this occurrence and intervention have been well described, too (see, for example, Squier, 1990, p. 332). The final four impasses are less well defined, and the interventions themselves are still imprecise. Evidence of resolution is also either slow to appear or hard to pin down. These impasses are included, however, because all, I believe, are important to the psychotherapeutic process and are perhaps broader and more fundamental in their personal impact than the first three. Future students should be able to improve on these descriptions.

Expansion of Psychological Perspective

By expansion of psychological perspective, I mean seeing things from a different point of view. This includes the realization that there are different points of view.

The impasse is any situation for which the patient's present point of view proves unhelpful, confusing, or self-defeating. Commonly, the situation is a repetitive one in which the patient has again and again foundered, for example, in dating or when working under someone's authority. The fixed point of view might be, for example, that a date will always dislike the patient or that a boss must invariably be obeyed or disobeyed. The intervention is supplying another point of view.

In my experience, enlarging the patient's perspective depends upon four steps:

Recognizing the patient's point of view: Of course, a point of view varies greatly, in fixity, obviousness, and consistency. One is looking for a constant attitude, especially with respect to the difficult situation. The most reliable place to look is the patient's attitude toward the therapy, since that can be directly observed.

Establishing that it is only one point of view: As a rule, whatever is discovered about the patient's point of view should not be directly pointed out. In the absence of massive evidence to the contrary, one assumes that the patient's point of view is believed in, even cherished, and highly learned or overdetermined. Assertions that it is just a point of view must therefore be avoided. People dislike being pigeonholed. How does one indicate respect for a perspective while signaling its limitations? Here are three rules: (a) The first is a respectful, even loving, recognition of the development of the point of view in question. The intervenor should understand why this particular point of view is necessary. (The principle is that of Alcoholics Anonymous: Advice must come from the like-minded). Only when this is fully established is criticism possible. (b) The therapist should not assume that any difficulties encountered are the patient's doing. (To return to our earlier examples, it is possible that the patient's date and the boss are themselves difficult; such possibilities must be explored first.) (c) Self-defeating attitudes should be described positively. For example, overgenerous or consistently obedient character traits can be referred to as good-natured or modest (as opposed to masochistic or self-defeating). This method has been called the "right hand–left hand" technique: one feeds with one hand while pointing out with the other. What may seem a ponderous or timid approach is required not only because of the sensitivity people have with regard to personal traits but because of the extent of the demand on the patient, namely, to examine his or her whole way of seeing.

Supplying an alternative: Properly handled, patient's supply their own alternatives. These are worth waiting for if only to avoid slavish obedience or dependence on the therapist and their frequent backlash. A research protocol may include measures of the relative success of homemade (patient-generated) versus imported (therapist-generated) alternatives.

Experimenting with alternatives: Alternatives need to be described to the patient as experiments, to prepare for failure or even for those successes that are obscured by the patient's anxiety. The latter is a frequent finding. So great is the usual fear and confusion surrounding any new action that the most striking success can be lost to view. As a result, therapists should not be content with their patients having achieved a fresh perspective until it has been taken up to acknowledged success. Even then one looks for clear evidence of the new attitude being reinforced by favorable results. The goal is an affective competence in the face of deeply feared actions (Russell, 1990).

Beyond this point one hopes for a growth in the patient of philosophical or psychological mindedness, that is, an awareness of the divergent points of view people have and the capacity to empathize with many of them.

Seeing Ourselves As Others See Us

Three aspects of this self-seeing, which are discussed in detail in the following paragraphs, are (1) the experience of meeting steady reflections of oneself, (2) the discovery of self-elusiveness and commonality, and (3) the discovery of what one might become (future-self).

MEETING STEADY REFLECTIONS OF ONESELF

A research protocol could be designed to match strategies of self-reflection used by therapists against evidence of patients' increased self-awareness.

Strategies of self-reflection widely used by therapists are mirroring (repeating patient's statements and/or reproducing patient's feelings), clarification (of patient's behavior, thoughts, or feelings), and self-descriptions (that is, the intervenor says to the patient, self-descriptions "You make me feel . . . "). Evidence of increased self-awareness includes direct statements, with examples to that effect; acknowledgment of previous behaviors; and changed self-presentations. It is important to note, however, that self-descriptions are frequently erroneous: frugal people, for example, often think of themselves as generous, just as narcissistic types often see themselves as other-centered, simply because any departure from their regular behavior is so striking to them and overvalued. In contrast, people who call themselves narcissistic are, in my experience, usually the reverse.

DISCOVERY OF SELF-ELUSIVENESS AND COMMONALITY

Difficulties of self-seeing arise from the elusiveness and volatility of the sense of self and from the fact that people have as much, or more, in common with each other as they possess individually. Looking inward at the stream of consciousness one meets scant evidence of the distinct self. (This is part of William James's and the Buddhist critique of selfhood.) In addition, the lack of quantitative measures of self attributes makes for widely varying personal descriptions. Even overt behaviors can suggest conflicting and changing centers of selfhood. Moreover, psychotherapists often claim discovery of an overwhelming number of common elements—whether fantasies, wishes, conflicts, or prohibitions—in patients of widely different background and experience. Knowing oneself can therefore mean accepting one's humanity rather than a distinct individuality.

Research protocols aimed at evaluating the growth of self-seeing need to measure both distinct and universal elements in order to identify persons going from thinking themselves distinct to appreciating their commonality, as well as those who are making the opposite discovery. The protocols must therefore establish baselines of distinctness and universality for the individuals evaluated.

DISCOVERY OF WHAT ONE MIGHT BECOME

An element of self-knowledge of particular interest to therapists is the patient's view of the self in the future. Does the patient have a vision of a self-in-future (as opposed to a static self-conception)? Can the patient conceive of a means for achieving that self-in-future? (An investigation of patients' views of the self-in-future would be a positive analogue to studies of suicidality, which pose questions such as "Does the patient have suicidal ideation?" and "Are there suicide plans?") For example, unentitled patients, perhaps those deeply imprisoned in institutions or substantially alone, sometimes achieve a vision of independence and freedom of response and initiative; they may also learn the tactics necessary for successful action to these ends.

The impasses in clinical work would be scenes of unentitlement or imprisonment, that is, the belief that one does not have the right or ability to alter one's circumstances. The interventions would be (1) admiration and support for independent selfhood (what is sometimes called belief in the patient or alliance with the patient), (2) instruction both in the recognition of predatory, imprisoning others and in the means of successful independent action, and (3) support and encouragement throughout action trials. Therapeutic success could be measured by the extent of change from unentitlement to entitlement and by evidence of tactical knowledge and success.

Getting to the Real Person and Modeling Understanding

Discovering the true self and modeling understanding are both fundamental actions in psychotherapy. They are not elaborated here because a beginning has been made in operationalizing them in the sections Collecting Lost Mental Parts and Marked Self-Deprecatory Trends, respectively. Getting to the real person is begun when lost mental parts are collected. In treating better-organized personalities it is also important not to be distracted by less authentic aspects of personality; one is seeking to reach and celebrate what is real. Elsewhere I have discussed defining and recognizing the authentic self (Havens, 1986b).

Modeling understanding is partly operationalized in my earlier discussion of marked self-deprecatory trends. The patient's negative understanding is replaced by one more reflective of his or her real interests. The same process has often been termed modifying superego or hostile introjects. A more complete discussion of modeling of understanding would take up identification with the therapist, a fundamental process in psychological change.

Concluding Remarks

The present chapter can be seen as contributing to what Greenberg and Pinsof (1986) have called "a typology of problem states or conditions that would help to organize the domain of client process" (p. 717). Evaluating interventions against problem states or impasses that arise during therapy should best proceed, in my opinion, from the descriptions of impasses in individual patients. My experience is largely restricted to the study of individual occurrences, with some comparative studies (Havens, 1972, 1977, 1979, 1986a), and does not include coding behaviors in ways necessary for group verification research.

REFERENCES

American Psychiatric Association. (1987). *Diagnostic and statistical manual of mental disorders* (3rd ed., rev.). Washington, DC: Author.

Austin, J. L. (1962). *How to do things with words*. Cambridge, MA: Harvard University Press.

Freud, S. (1957). Mourning and melancholia. In J. Strachey (Ed. & Trans.), *The standard edition of the complete psychological works of Sigmund Freud* (Vol. 14, pp. 243–258). London: Hogarth Press. (Original work published 1917)

Greenberg, L. S., and Pinsof, W., (Eds.). (1986). *The psychotherapeutic process: A research handbook*. New York: Guilford.

Havens, L. (1972). Clinical methods in psychiatry. *International Journal of Psychiatry, 10,* 7–28.

Havens, L. (1977). *Participant observation*. New York: Aronson.

Havens, L. (1978). Explorations in the uses of language in psychotherapy: Simple empathic statements. *Psychiatry, 41,* 336–375.

Havens, L. (1979). Harry Stack Sullivan's contribution to clinical method. *McLean Hospital Journal, 2,* 20–32.

Havens, L. (1984). Explorations in the uses of language in psychotherapy: Counterintrojective statements (performatives). *Contemporary Psychoanalysis, 20,* 385–399.

Havens, L. (1986a). *Making contact*. Cambridge, MA: Harvard University Press.

Havens, L. (1986b). A theoretical basis for the concepts of self and authentic self. *Journal of the American Psychoanalytic Association, 34* (2), 363–378.

Havens, L. (1989). *A safe place*. Cambridge, MA: Harvard University Press.

Russell, P. (1990). *Trauma, repetition and affect*. Unpublished manuscript.

Squier, R. W. (1990). A model of empathic understanding and adherence to treatment regimens in practitioner–patient relationships. *Social Science and Medicine, 30,* 325–339.

CHAPTER 6

Research-Based Knowledge as the Emergent Foundation for Clinical Practice in Psychotherapy

David E. Orlinsky

THE CHAPTERS that compose this volume both express and reflect the fact that they have been written during a peculiarly complex time of crisis in the development of modern psychotherapies. At the heart of the crisis is a widespread questioning among psychotherapists about the scientific basis of their practice.

This questioning is compounded by the radical reevaluation of the total health care system that is currently under way, especially in the United States, including the psychotherapies as a source of mental health care. Evidence is being sought inside the therapeutic professions and out concerning the value and efficacy of therapeutic practice.

A third facet of the crisis is the sheer ignorance shown by all parties of precisely the field of study—psychotherapy research—that has data relevant to the questions being asked. A mitigating factor in this ignorance is the fact that the field of scientific research on psychotherapy is small (Beutler & Crago, 1991) and thus, perhaps, easily overlooked, although the results of at least one project have been featured as front page news by the *New York Times*— the NIMH Treatment of Depression Collaborative Research Program; Elkin, in press.

Work on this chapter was partially supported by research grant R 01 MH42901 from the National Institute of Mental Health. Portions of it were previously presented at the Second Scandinavian Conference on the Supervision of Psychoanalysis and Psychotherapy, Linköping, Sweden, May 12, 1993.

The ignorance of those who need to know is matched only by the shyness of those who do know—but who are more acutely conscious of how much they don't know (as good scientists should be). In fact, they don't yet realize how much is known already because so much of that has been learned only in the past decade and only now has begun to be comprehensively reviewed (Orlinsky, Grawe, & Parks, in press). At the time this chapter is being written, the volume to which investigators will turn for summaries of this accumulated research knowledge is still in galleys (Bergin & Garfield, in press). Even when that volume is published and read, a vital strut will still be missing from the bridge that needs to be built across the chasm dividing research findings from clinical practice. Textbooks have to be written to distill research findings into a coherent body of knowledge[1] and, in applied fields such as medicine or engineering, to expound their implications for practice. There is no equivalent in psychotherapeutic education yet to the practice-oriented research compendiums that other professions use as scientific texts.

The aim of this chapter is to contribute toward bridging the chasm by describing the task to be accomplished and trying to do one small part of it in order to show that it can in fact be done. The first section comments further on the core of the crisis confronting the modern psychotherapies and reflects briefly on the chapters contributed to this volume by the clinical authors. The second section introduces a research-based model of psychotherapy to serve as a framework for building a bridge across the chasm so sadly represented by the clinicians' chapters. The third section uses that framework to put in place a first span of the bridge from the research side of the canyon.

The Current Crisis of Legitimacy Within the Psychotherapies: The Chasm Between Research Findings and Clinical Practice

The modern psychotherapies draw an aura of legitimacy and operating authority from their standing as forms of science applied to the human condition. Yet the science of which most of them were born is not that of today but of the *belle époque*, a century past. From the point of view of the present, especially in the social and psychological sciences now grown to maturity, the mantle of authority in which the older forms of therapy were wrapped seems particularly threadbare—not least to sophisticated internal critics

---

[1]"Finished scientific achievements" as Kuhn (1970) observed, "are recorded . . . in the textbooks from which each new scientific generation learns to practice its trade" (p.1).

such as Spence (this volume).[2] As Yeats said: "Things fall apart; the centre cannot hold."

This is not an age that honors prophecy or venerates tradition. Healing practices associated with older forms of cultural authority, such as Asclepian incubation (Meier, 1967) and the "king's touch" (Geertz, 1983), have been forgotten, discarded, or relegated to the possession of a lunatic fringe. Rational authority, derived from sustained critical reflection on verified observations, is the standard of modern culture, and science is the supreme embodiment of rational authority in the cognitive domain (as law is in the political domain), the ultimate warrant for all secular knowledge and technique.[3] Psychoanalysts and other therapists have shown an amazing ability to endure the cavils and calumnies of external critics, but when they lose faith in their own claims to legitimacy, they stand like Oz without wizardry behind his emerald curtain. "The best lack all conviction, while the worst are full of passionate intensity" (Yeats, *The Second Coming*).

When Breuer and Freud (1895/1955) introduced their cathartic method for the treatment of hysteria one hundred years ago, they did so in the belief that they were presenting a scientifically grounded approach, developed empirically in the course of clinical work. They expected or at least hoped that their colleagues would respect the clinical evidence they adduced to indicate the method's effectiveness. Subsequently, Freud transformed the cathartic method into psychoanalysis, but even after 30 years of gradual modification he viewed what he did as a scientific method for the investigation and treatment of psychological problems (Freud, 1922/1955).

Now there are two senses in which psychotherapies may be called scientific. The first refers to the character of the theories used to explain the nature and origins of patients' problems and the processes and outcomes of treatment. These theories are scientific in a cultural sense insofar as they are *naturalistic* (rather than supernaturalistic), invoking only known or potentially knowable biophysical, social, or psychological agents and conditions. They do *not* need to be reductionistic, positivistic, or materialistic. However, factors such as spirit possession and violation of a cosmic moral order are not possible explanations for the origin of disorders, any more than exorcism and redemptive punishment are explanations for the action of therapeutic interventions. Theories that are scientific in a cultural sense therefore also tend to be pragma-

---

[2] These comments include all modern psychotherapies, but they apply most poignantly to the original and therefore older therapies—that is, the rival versions and variants of psychoanalysis and their psychodynamic descendants—as well as to the various experiential-humanistic therapies that first opposed and now seem to share so much with them. Nor are the more recently developed behavioral and cognitive therapies exempt, although their self-questioning tends to focus on whether they have been overly narrow in their concerns rather than on whether they are appropriately or sufficiently scientific (for example, Goldfried, 1982; Safran & Segal, 1990).

[3] The threefold typology of rational-legal, traditional, and charismatic authority is based on the work of Max Weber (1978).

tic and nonjudgmental rather than moralistic in tone. With marginal exceptions and to varying degrees, it may be said that all modern psychotherapies qualify as scientific in this sense. However, their plausibility increases to the extent that they draw appropriately on concepts currently accepted in other scientific disciplines, and thus they tend to need periodic updating and reformulation (in the case of psychoanalysis, see, for example, Laplanche, 1989; Pribram & Gill, 1976; Schafer, 1976).

The second sense in which psychotherapies can be scientific depends on the degree to which clinical understanding and interventions are based on systematically validated research findings. Their showing in this respect is much poorer than in the first. Clinical psychoanalysis, in any of its forms, has virtually no basis in systematically validated research (as the term *research* is currently understood in either sociopsychological or biomedical science). Some of the contemporary psychodynamic-interpersonal therapies do have a basis in systematic research,[4] but it is a historical irony—indeed, part of the chasm being discussed in this book—that this research base is not well known by psychodynamic clinicians.

Among the humanistic-experiential therapies, only the client-centered school of Rogers took research seriously; In fact, it contributed strongly to the creation of the field of psychotherapy research (for example, Rogers & Dymond, 1954). But the movement founded by Rogers has turned in other directions, and only a few continue in the research tradition (Lietaer, Rombauts, & Van Balen, 1990; Rice & Greenberg, 1984). The systemic-strategic therapies also have little foundation in scientific research (for example, Gurman, Kniskern, & Pinsof, 1986). Only the behavioral and cognitive-behavioral therapies have sought to ground themselves extensively in systematic research and confidently claim to be scientifically legitimate in this second sense, but that research base is somewhat narrowly focused (in comparison to the range of variables included in the investigation of other therapies) and depends partly on the extension by analogy of findings from the study of animal behavior.

The core of the crisis confronting the modern psychotherapies concerns their scientific standing in the second sense defined earlier, and therefore the crisis is more strongly felt by nonbehavioral therapists. The contributors of the clinical chapters to this volume, all well-known figures in American psychoanalysis, show symptoms of this crisis, either through an agonizing search for a new research foundation (as Spence hopes to find in developmental research) or by rejecting science—or, rather, an outmoded view of science—as relevant at all (as Edelson does). Although current research on psychotherapy

[4]Reported in a rich journal literature (recently augmented by a special section, Curative Factors in Dynamic Psychotherapy, in the *Journal of Consulting and Clinical Psychologist* for August 1993) as well as in the following books: Dahl, Kächele, & Thomä (1988); Frank, Hoehn-Saric, Imber, Liberman, & Stone (1978); Luborsky, Crits-Christoph, Mintz, & Auerbach (1988); Miller, Luborsky, Barber, & Docherty, (1993); Orlinsky & Howard (1975); Strupp, Fox, & Lessler (1969).

has much to offer them, they show varying degrees of ignorance about it in their essays for this volume. Clarkin, of course, is a leading investigator and fully conversant with current research in this field (for example, Beutler & Clarkin, 1990); Kernberg and he have simply chosen to focus on their own project to illustrate one particular linkage between research findings and clinical practice. Havens shows some awareness of psychotherapy research in his reference to the task-analytic paradigm of Rice and Greenberg (1984), along with a genial, if naive, willingness to conceive a study that he would view as relevant. Edelson, on the other hand, creates a lengthy dialogue in which he battles quixotically against psychotherapy research as a kind of fantasy-dragon of his own devising. However, Spence's essay was a greater disappointment, since at one time he did know something about psychother-apy research (Luborsky & Spence, 1978). Unfortunately, he gives no evidence of having read any further in this field during the past 15 years.

The systematic empirical study of the psychotherapies began as long ago as the late 1940s and early 1950s, but it is probably fair to say that for the first 25 or 30 years (till 1975 or 1980) the results of studies revealed as much about how to improve research techniques as they did about how to improve clini-cal practice (Orlinsky & Russell, in press). Clinicians and clinical theorists who turned expectantly to these early studies for validation or guidance were inevitably disappointed, and many turned away (like Spence, per-haps). For a long time, practitioners could, in fact, afford to disregard the re-sults of psychotherapy research as largely irrelevant to questions of clinical practice, but this is no longer the case. From rather uncertain beginnings, the field of psychotherapy research has grown with increasing rapidity and dur-ing the last 10 years has truly come of age. Although research, by its nature, is an open-ended enterprise, not given to declaring certainties or making broad generalizations, the accumulated research has finally begun to consti-tute a sufficient base of knowledge to guide clinical practice. Some findings have been so well replicated that they can be accorded the status of *estab-lished facts*, facts practitioners need and ought to know.

Process–Outcome Research and the "Generic Model of Psychotherapy"

An area of psychotherapy research of particular relevance for clinical prac-tice is that of process–outcome studies. Originally, in the '50s and '60s, when the field was very young, researchers typically distinguished between out-come studies and process studies. Outcome studies attempted to evaluate the effectiveness of treatments. Some patients were assigned to "regular treatment," while others were assigned to comparison or control groups on a random or matching basis, without any attempt to specify or assess what occurred in treatment. On the other hand, many studies focused on the process rather than the outcome of treatment. These sought one of two basic goals. Proponents of specific clinical theories attempted to document the presence and operation of their favorite therapeutic technique—interpretation, for example, in the case of psychoanalytically oriented researchers or empathic reflection of feeling in the case of client-centered researchers. Other investigators, less committed to a particular clinical model, simply sought to describe objectively what "actually" occurs in therapy sessions. Inevitably, subsequent studies have become more finely differentiated. Among these, process–outcome research examines the relation between treatment effectiveness and *specific aspects* of therapeutic process.

Process–outcome research is one of the fastest growing areas in studies of psychotherapy. In an extensive review just completed, Orlinsky, Grawe, and Parks (in press) tabulated a total of 2,343 separate process–outcome findings published in English and German from 1950 through 1992. When compared to the approximately 1,100 findings that were published in this field between 1950 and 1985 (Orlinsky & Howard, 1986), the number of research findings can be seen to have more than doubled in the last 7 years! Little wonder that even researchers in the field are not yet fully aware of the extent and implications of their results.

To transform this mass of findings into a coherent body of knowledge required a theoretical model of therapy adapted to and based upon the needs of research rather than practice, one that could organize the many different variables that have been studied into a small but comprehensive set of conceptual categories. To meet this need, we developed a framework, called the "generic model of psychotherapy" (Orlinsky & Howard, 1986, 1987a, 1987b, in press), that distinguishes three broad types of research variables: *input* variables, which determine the form and content of psychotherapy; *process* variables, which describe the events of therapy itself; and *output* variables, which specify the consequences of therapy (including, most importantly, consequences for the patient that are usually referred to as "outcome").

Research to date has led to the differentiation of six categories of process variables, summarized in table 6.1. These six categories are conceived as functionally interdependent aspects of therapeutic process.

First is the formal aspect of process, usually referred to as the *therapeutic contract*. This defines the respective goals and roles of patient and therapist and specifies formal characteristics of the treatment, such as the frequency and duration of sessions, the length of the treatment, whether it will be conducted as individual or group therapy, and so forth. The therapist's treatment model is a key element in the therapeutic contract, especially as it shapes therapist and patient roles, but of course the treatment model only becomes effective if the participants understand it, agree to it, and implement it in a competent fashion.

Table 6.1   Aspects of Therapeutic Process in the "Generic Model of
Psychotherapy"

---

1. THE FORMAL ASPECT: THERAPEUTIC CONTRACT
Definition of therapeutic situation and reciprocal roles of patient and therapist
(and other contracting parties); stipulation of treatment arrangements, including
therapeutic collectivity (individual therapy, group therapy, and so forth),
schedule, fees, term, and so on *(contractual provisions)*; negotiation of working
consensus in goals and expectations and implementation of reciprocal roles
through various phases of treatment *(contractual implementation)*.

2. THE TECHNICAL ASPECT: THERAPEUTIC OPERATIONS
Application of professional expertise to (1) eliciting the patient's subjective
complaints and characteristic patterns of thought, feeling, and action *(patient
presentation)*; (2) understanding these in terms of a relevant treatment model, for
example, by making a diagnostic evaluation or ongoing case formulation
(therapist construal); (3) selecting an appropriate intervention strategy and
techniques, guided by the treatment model *(therapist intervention)*; (4) eliciting the
patient's participation in these efforts *(patient cooperations)*.

3. THE INTERPERSONAL ASPECT: THERAPEUTIC BOND
Interpersonal involvement or alliance between patient(s) and therapist(s)
reflecting their joint contributions to the global quality and atmosphere of the
emergent dyadic/group process and characterized in particular by varying levels
of therapeutic teamwork *(personal role-investment)*

4. THE INTRAPERSONAL ASPECT: SELF-RELATEDNESS
Interactive self-experience of persons participating in therapy roles *(patient self-
relatedness, therapist self-relatedness)*, with each participant's self-awareness, self-
control, self-esteem, and so forth, being manifested clinically in varying degrees
of openness versus defensiveness.

5. THE CLINICAL ASPECT: IN-SESSION IMPACTS
Positive and negative effects of therapeutic interactions on participants within
sessions, especially impacts on patients, such as insight and self-understanding,
emotional catharsis, encouragement, skill enhancement, and so forth *(patient
therapeutic realizations)*, and concurrent impacts on therapists, such as self-efficacy
and emotional intimacy *(therapist accruals)*.

6. THE TEMPORAL ASPECT: SEQUENTIAL PROCESSES
Interaction sequences unfolding over time within sessions *(session development)*
and events characterizing the overall treatment episode *(therapeutic course)*.

The instrumental or technical aspect of process consists of the *therapeutic
operations* that are performed by the patient and therapist. These include the
patient's presentation of information to the therapist, verbally and nonver-
bally, and the therapist's construal or interpretation of that information in
terms of the diagnostic and explanatory constructs provided by the thera-

pist's treatment model. On the basis of an assessment of the patient's underlying problem, the treatment model indicates which technical interventions should be most helpful. Finally, to be successfully carried out, any type of therapeutic intervention requires a complementary mode of cooperation from the patient. Thus, if the problem the patient presents is judged to be caused by dynamically unconscious conflicts of motivation, then interpretation of the latent content of the patient's preconscious associations is a relevant technique for making the unconscious conscious and spontaneous free association is the optimal way for the patient to cooperate with this procedure.

The third category of process variable, the interpersonal aspect, is called the *therapeutic bond*, since it focuses on the person-to-person relationship between patient and therapist. In group therapy, where the bond is multilateral rather than bilateral, this is described in terms of cohesiveness and group atmosphere. In contrast to the technical aspect, the quality of the therapeutic bond is largely shaped by the ways in which patients' and therapists' personalities interact and combine. The quality of the bond is manifested in two ways: One is through the caliber of teamwork, that is, the participants' personal investment and ability to coordinate action in their respective roles. The other is the quality of their personal rapport, that is, the resonance of their communication and the feelings they elicit in each other.

A fourth aspect of therapeutic process is the intrapersonal, rather than interpersonal, aspect; this reflects the participants' immediate states of personality functioning. Participant *self-relatedness* refers to the way persons respond to themselves in the course of responding to the people and things and forces around them. It refers to the way persons experience their internal activation; formulate their self-awareness; control and direct their ideas, feelings, and urges; and evaluate themselves. In therapy this is often referred to globally as openness versus defensiveness. Individuals in an "open" state can absorb what is offered or available to them in their surroundings, adapting to take advantage of what is useful. Individuals in a defensive state need to screen and filter their responses more stringently (in order to maintain their self-control, self-esteem, or inner sense of safety), and they are only able to avail themselves of whatever matches the limitations they impose on themselves.

The fifth aspect of therapeutic process that researchers have focused on concerns the immediate clinical productivity of therapeutic work, that is, *in-session impacts* such as insight, emotional relief, and remoralization. These "therapeutic realizations" presumably have an intimate connection with treatment outcome, yet they should not be counted as outcome until they are effectively applied by the patient in life situations outside of therapy. In-session impacts also include the personal rewards and frustrations that accrue to therapists as a result of their efforts to help their patients.

The final aspect of therapeutic process is temporal in nature. It may be thought of in terms of strands of *sequential processes* that unfold through the events occurring in sessions and combine over successive sessions to define the distinctive phases of treatment. These temporal strands represent successive intersections of the other aspects of process, intersections that constitute a series of momentary configurations of the contract, operations, bond, self-relatedness, and in-session impacts that cumulatively determine the overall course of treatment. The salience of this temporal aspect is demonstrated, for example, through interaction effects indicating that the character of events is partly determined by whether they occur early, middle, or late within a session and early, middle, or late in the course of treatment.

The "generic model of psychotherapy" is not a clinical theory designed to guide therapists in their daily work with patients. It is a research theory whose main theoretical value lies in its ability to explain recurrent empirical findings in terms of testable hypotheses concerning the direction and nature of relations among process categories (see, for example, Ambühl, 1991, 1993; Kolden, 1991) and whose main practical value lies in its ability to function as a framework for comparing and integrating specific clinical treatment models (Orlinsky, in press). In the present context, these hypotheses are used as simplifying constructs to aid in reviewing the accumulated mass of process–outcome research findings.

Process–Outcome Research Findings and Their Relevance to Clinical Practice

One of the most interesting facts that researchers have had to recognize is a partial divergence between different observational perspectives in reports on both process and outcome. Ratings of therapy sessions by patients, therapists, and external observers using recordings typically do not correlate highly even when focused on what is nominally one concept, such as empathy. The same has been found true with regard to evaluations of outcome, where—as Strupp, Hadley, and Gomes-Schwartz (1977) have shown—divergent ratings are typically made by therapists, patients, family members, and independent experts.

This differs strikingly from epistemological expectations based on the natural sciences, where high levels of agreement between observers can be achieved and residual disagreements can be discounted statistically as error. That we are not just dealing with error is shown by the fact that lawful relations between process and outcome are found within and between observational perspectives. The epistemological situation in the human sciences is simply more complex than it is in the natural sciences, because human perceptions partly determine the situations in which they occur. This greater embeddedness of observation in the phenomena being observed requires rigorous adherence to a basic principle of relativity, namely, that findings validated within a given observational framework cannot be viewed as valid across perspectives until that has been empirically demonstrated.[5]

To observe this basic principle, process–outcome findings were sorted by observational perspective on process and on outcome within each process category. The results are summarized at length in table 6.2 (adapted from Orlinsky, Grawe, & Parks, in press) where they are aggregated across outcome perspectives but are presented separately for each observational perspective on process.[6] From among these, the *therapist's perspective on process* must be the principal point of reference if therapists are to be able to translate research findings into terms they can utilize in clinical practice. (By the same token, the patient's process perspective would be the principal point of reference if one were writing a consumer's guide for patients in psychotherapy.)

The column on the left side of table 6.2 presents the specific variables that have been investigated within the six process aspects defined by the "generic model of psychotherapy." Second from the left are two columns, the first giving the percentage of process-outcome findings recorded for the corresponding variable that are both statistically significant and "positive" in direction, and the second giving the total number of findings (in brackets). In the next columns, from left to right, the subtotals from each observational perspective are recorded, with the percentage of "positive" findings indicated if greater than 50%. (Groups of three dots in the body of the table indicate that there are no findings for a given perspective.)

The term "positive," as used in table 6.2 can mean that a higher level of that variable was associated with better outcome *or* that a lower level was associated with poorer outcome. Most of the nonpositive findings were statistically nonsignificant (that is, null findings), but a few were statistically significant and "negative," meaning that a lower level of the process variable was associated with better outcome *or* that a higher level was associated with poorer outcome. While relatively rare, these "negative" findings can be clinically important and will be mentioned where relevant.

---

[5]This is particularly important for practitioners (example, therapists and supervisors) to keep clearly in mind as they try to understand the events of psychotherapy. None may assume that their perceptions and evaluations of events constitute privileged data or that those who see things differently are likely to be wrong. Each must assume that he or she has access only to part of the data, that there are other legitimate viewpoints to be considered, and that the responses made by each party on the basis of partial perceptions and partisan values will contribute further to the ongoing construction of the situation.

[6]Thus, the count of significant process–outcome associations reflects each variable's association with outcome judged from any observer's perspective. The summary of data in table 6.2 allows a comparison of the separate process perspectives of patients, therapists, external raters (for example, supervisors), and objective indices–but not their separate perspectives on outcome.

Clearly, not all of the process variables that have been studied are found in psychoanalytically oriented therapy. By the same token, not every aspect of psychoanalytic therapy has been well studied. In what follows, I limit my comments to findings that are broadly relevant to the psychoanalytic threatment model and recognize their provisional character. However, I take a conservative approach and focus for the most part only on process–outcome connections that have been replicated in a substantial number of cases. These are highlighted by being underlined in table 6.2.

THERAPEUTIC CONTRACT

The research variables associated with *therapeutic contract* were divided into those reflecting *contractual provisions,* that is, the organization of the therapeutic frame, and those reflecting aspects of *contractual implementation.* Inspection of table 6.2 indicates that particular *contractual provisions,* considered separately in and of themselves, have not been consistently associated with outcome. There is little evidence to suggest, for example, that individual therapy is more (or less) effective than group or family therapy; that a once-weekly schedule of sessions differs in effectiveness from more (or less) intensively scheduled sessions; that time-limited therapy is consistently more (or less) effective than treatment of unlimited term (not to be confused with short versus long therapy, where there are differences); or that variations in fee levels and payment arrangements make much difference with respect to outcome.

These statements, of course, are subject to the condition of "other things being equal." It is quite possible, as clinical experience suggests, that individual therapy may be better for certain types of patients whereas group or family therapy may be the treatment of choice for other's. It is also possible that certain combinations of contractual provisions (for example, combinations of treatment modality and session frequency or limited versus unlimited term) may be more effective for all or for some patients. These interactions need to be studied more fully. Nevertheless, it is reasonable to note that while psychoanalysis has typically emphasized individual treatment with frequently scheduled sessions and an unlimited term, the process–outcome evidence thus far accumulated does not suggest that these are important therapeutic conditions.

Inspection of the variables listed under *contractual implementation* in table 6.2 indicates several robust findings. Both the appropriateness of the patient for the particular form of treatment and the therapist's skillfulness in carrying out the treatment were consistently associated with outcome in a large number of observations and from each of the process perspectives that have been studied. Objective measures (in the *index* column of table 6.2) of pa-

Table 6.2 Salience of Process–Outcome Findings by Process Perspective

Process Variable	Total % [n]	Process perspective			
		Patient % [n]	Therapist % [n]	Rater % [n]	Index % [n]
THERAPEUTIC CONTRACT					
Contractual provisions					
Collectivity (individual vs. group/family)	20% [30]	...	...	...	[30]
Schedule (weekly vs. other frequency)	16% [25]	...	...	...	[25]
Term (time-limited vs. unlimited)	33% [12]	...	...	...	[12]
Fee (normal vs. reduced)	25% [12]	...	...	...	[12]
Use of cotherapist	0% [2]	...	...	...	[2]
Use of patient self-monitoring	67% [3]	...	...	...	67% [3]
Contractual implementation					
Goal consensus/clarity	51% [35]	63% [8]	[7]	[8]	67% [12]
Timeliness vs. delay	43% [14]	...	...	...	[14]
Patient role preparation	57% [42]	...	...	...	57% [42]
Patient verbal activity	64% [14]	...	...	[2]	67% [12]
Therapist verbal activity	37% [38]	[5]	[3]	[12]	[15]
Therapist skill	67% [36]	59% [17]	[2]	71% [17]	...
Patient suitability	68% [40]	75% [4]	67% [27]	67% [9]	...
Use of supervision	40% [5]	...	[1]	...	75% [4]
Stability of arrangements	83% [6]	[1]	...	100% [3]	[2]
Adherence to treatment model	100% [3]	[1]	...	100% [2]	...
Procedure for termination	32% [19]	...	[8]	[6]	[5]
THERAPEUTIC OPERATIONS					
Patient presentation					
Focus on problems	64% [11]	67% [3]	[2]	67% [6]	...
Focus on "here and now"	26% [19]	[2]	[8]	[9]	...
Focus on core relationships	75% [8]	[2]	[2]	100% [4]	...
Cognitive & behavioral presentation	93% [15]	100% [4]	...	100% [6]	80% [5]

tients' verbal activity suggest that the patient's verbal engagement in the therapeutic process is a prerequisite for successful treatment. Accumulating evidence also suggests the importance of contractual consensus and stability in treatment arrangements as conditions contributing to favorable outcome. These are important but commonsense considerations, applying to psychoanalysis as well as other treatment models. However, a finding that might be usefully remembered by psychoanalytic practitioners is that instruction of therapeutically naive candidates for treatment about what to expect in the

Table 6.2   Salience of Process–Outcome Findings by Process Perspective   (*Continued*)

Process Variable	Total % [n]		Process perspective						
			Patient % [n]		Therapist % [n]		Rater % [n]		Index % [n]
Therapist construal									
Focus on patient problems	53%	[19]		[2]		[8]	67%	[9]	...
Focus on patient affect	50%	[18]		...		[1]		[17]	...
Focus on "here and now"	9%	[11]		...		...		[11]	...
Focus on patient self-understanding	27%	[11]		...		[5]		[6]	...
Focus on family of origin, transference, & core relationships	37%	[27]		...		[5]		[22]	...
Technical intervention									
Change strategies (heuristics)	50%	[22]		...		[10]		[11]	[1]
Interpretation	63%	[38]	83%	[6]		[10]	65%	[20]	[2]
Exploration	39%	[41]		[4]		[6]		[31]	...
Support	34%	[38]		[8]		[12]		[18]	...
Experiential confrontation	71%	[22]	60%	[5]	100%	[2]	78%	[9]	[6]
Paradoxical Intervention	100%	[13]		...		...		...	100% [13]
Advice	20%	[5]		...		[1]		[4]	...
Reflection/clarification	7%	[14]		...		[2]		[9]	[3]
Self-disclosure	14%	[14]		[3]		[1]		[9]	[1]
Patient cooperations									
Cooperation vs. resistance	69%	[49]	58%	[12]	73%	[22]	71%	[14]	[1]
Self-exploration	30%	[79]		[7]		[7]		[65]	...
Patient total affective arousal	50%	[10]		[5]	100%	[3]		[2]	...
Positive affective arousal	100%	[9]	100%	[3]	100%	[6]		...	...
Negative affective arousal	27%	[40]		[8]		[2]		[24]	[6]
Internalization of therapist function	100%	[3]	100%	[2]		[1]		...	...

patient role does seem to facilitate contractual implementation. Such patients may be helped to make better use of psychoanalytic treatment if they are given some preparation, either in the form of a trial analysis or by more active means, such as role-induction procedures (see, for example, Strupp & Bloxom, 1973).

The overall impression left by process–outcome findings to date with regard to the contractual aspect of process is that skillfulness, appropriateness, and stability are more important than specific formalities in the structure of treatment.

Table 6.2 Salience of Process–Outcome Findings by Process Perspective (*Continued*)

Process Variable	Total % [n]	Patient % [n]	Therapist % [n]	Rater % [n]	Index % [n]
THERAPEUTIC BOND					
Global Relational Quality					
Bond/group cohesion	67% [134]	76% [51]	66% [32]	65% [37]	[14]
Therapist contribution	53% [110]	67% [42]	58% [12]	[56]	...
Patient contribution	67% [55]	100% [6]	69% [16]	61% [33]	...
Personal-role investment					
Patient engagement	65% [54]	68% [19]	92% [13]	[22]	...
Patient motivation	50% [28]	80% [5]	56% [16]	[7]	...
Therapist engagement vs. detachment	57% [37]	78% [18]	[9]	[10]	...
Therapist credibility vs. unsureness	59% [37]	53% [15]	60% [5]	67% [6]	[1]
Reciprocal investment	75% [4]	[2]	...	100% [2]	...
Interactive coordination					
Therapist collaboration vs. directiveness/permissiveness	43% [46]	64% [11]	[22]	[13]	...
Patient collaboration vs. dependence/controlling	64% [42]	75% [12]	63% [16]	57% [14]	...
Communicative contact					
Patient expressiveness	63% [51]	55% [11]	67% [9]	61% [28]	100% [3]
Therapist empathy	54% [112]	72% [47]	[19]	[40]	83% [6]
Therapist expressiveness	44% [16]	[3]	...	[10]	67% [3]
Patient empathy	42% [12]	100% [3]	...	...	[9]
Reciprocal attunement	62% [42]	83% [6]	[6]	56% [9]	67% [21]
Mutual affect					
Therapist affirmation vs. negation	56% [154]	65% [63]	[39]	52% [52]	...
Patient affirmation vs. negation	69% [59]	64% [25]	68% [22]	78% [9]	100% [3]
Mutual affirmation vs. negation	78% [32]	73% [15]	[3]	91% [11]	100% [3]

THERAPEUTIC OPERATIONS

The next block in table 6.2 shows research variables divided into four groups, each reflecting an aspect of *therapeutic operations*. The aspect of *patient presentation* includes the patient's conversational content (problems in living, in-session here-and-now matters, and core personal relationships) as well as the patient's cognitive and behavioral manner. With the exception of in-session here-and-now content, these variables often were differentially related to outcome. This may not be apparent to therapists or to supervisors whose access to process is limited to therapist reports, but patients who focus on their problems in living and on their core personal relationships tend to have better outcomes. Further, patients who show more adaptive modes of cognitive and behavioral functioning during sessions also seem to have consistently better outcomes. The finding relative to content may re-

Table 6.2 Salience of Process–Outcome Findings by Process Perspective (*Continued*)

Process Variable	Total % [n]	Process perspective			
		Patient % [n]	Therapist % [n]	Rater % [n]	Index % [n]
SELF-RELATEDNESS					
Patient self-relatedness					
Patient openness vs. defensiveness	80% [45]	70% [10]	90% [10]	82% [22]	67% [3]
Patient "experiencing"	51% [39]	100% [2]	75% [4]	[33]	...
Therapist self-relatedness					
Therapist self-congruence	38% [60]	[25]	[11]	[23]	[1]
Therapist self-acceptance	42% [12]	...	[9]	...	[3]
IN-SESSION IMPACT					
Patient impacts					
Patient "realizations"	67% [79]	64% [33]	[14]	79% [24]	88% [8]
Therapist impacts					
Therapist "accruals"	100% [4]	100% [2]	100% [2]	...	...
TEMPORAL SEQUENCE					
Session development					
Sequential interaction	56% [18]	...	...	[2]	56% [16]
Therapeutic course					
Treatment duration	64% [155]	...	...	...	64% [155]
Stage of treatment	72% [58]	...	...	...	72% [58]

Note. Derived from Orlinsky, Grawe, and Parks (in press). Number in brackets indicates number of findings within category; percentage cited for individual process perspectives if findings greater than 50% positive. "Positive" finding indicates "high" process level associated with "better" outcome, or "low" process level associated with "poorer" outcome.

flect the fact that such patients are well prepared for treatment, and the finding relative to cognitive and behavioral functioning during sessions probably reflects an initially higher level of adaptive ego functioning.

The variables grouped under the heading of *therapist construal* all reflect the focus of therapist interventions, as studied mainly from the perspective of nonparticipant raters. No strongly consistent trends stand out, although a substantial number of findings indicate that good outcomes are often associated with attention to the feelings and problems presented by patients during sessions.

Technical interventions from a wide range of treatment models have been studied by process–outcome researchers, and the strongest associations with outcome so far have been demonstrated for "paradoxical interventions" (although only in experimentally controlled therapy situations) and for "experiential confrontation" (as in the Gestalt two-chair technique). A number of other intervention modes—for example, exploration, support, self-disclosure, or giving advice—were much less consistently related to outcome. On the other hand, the use of interpretation, the mode of intervention favored in psychoanalytic treatment, has shown a fairly consistent association with good outcome. However, positive findings on interpretation came primarily from the process perspectives of external raters and patients, rather than from that of therapists, which again indicates a potential problem in supervisors relying exclusively on therapists' process reports.

The patient's participation in and response to technical interventions completes the cycle of therapeutic operations. The strongest predictors of outcome in this quarter are the patient's cooperativeness versus resistance and the patient's experience of positive affect. Patients who actively cooperate with technical interventions and feel better during sessions are most likely to have favorable outcomes. On the other hand, arousal of negative affect in itself is one of the most consistent predictors of poor outcome. Thus, it appears that patients who manifest resistance and who experience negative affect without also feeling better tend to have less favorable outcomes. This, at least, is salient from the therapist's process perspective. Supervisors dealing with cases in which this configuration of patient response persists should seriously consider whether it might not be in the patient's best interest to transfer the case to a different therapist or shift to a different treatment model.

THERAPEUTIC BOND

A glance at the process–outcome findings concerning the *therapeutic bond* shows that this area has been richly studied and includes many highly consistent indicators of patient outcome. To take one example: there were 134 separate findings linking the *global relational quality* of the therapeutic bond to outcome; two-thirds of those were significant and positive overall, and three-quarters were significant and positive when the bond was observed from the patient's process perspective. In all, 8 of the 18 variables reflecting general and specific aspects of the therapeutic bond had more than 50 findings, and 4 of these variables had more than 100 findings each. The mean percentage of significant positive associations for the total of 1,025 research findings on these 18 variables was 60%. Given the range of methodological sophistication and quality in studies done over the past 45 years, this mass of data must be taken as strong evidence for the importance of the therapeutic bond. A comparison of observations drawn from patients, therapists, raters, and objective indices further indicates that the patient's experience of the therapeutic bond is particularly salient, although the findings are generally consistent across all process perspectives.

Four specific aspects of therapeutic bond were examined: the personal investment and interactive coordination of participants in their roles as patient and therapist, which determined the quality of their therapeutic teamwork, and the qualities of communicative contact and mutual affect, which reflected their interpersonal rapport.

Personal role-investment includes variables such as patient engagement, patient motivation, therapist engagement versus detachment, and therapist credibility versus unsureness. Patient engagement was a very consistent predictor of outcome from the therapist's process perspective. Also, therapist engagement as viewed from the patient's process perspective was consistently predictive of good outcome whereas therapist detachment tended to predict poor outcome—a fact with some relevance for the psychoanalytic treatment model.

Questions of *interactive coordination* between patient and therapist focused on whether the relationship was one of collaboration between equals or, alternatively, it involved the therapist being either directive or permissive and the patient being either dependent or controlling. From all process perspectives, the patient's collaborative participation strongly predicted a favorable outcome, while the development of a dependent or an oppositional attachment to the therapist was associated with poorer outcomes. Similarly, from the patient's process perspective, the therapist acting in a collaborative rather than a directive or a permissive manner was a good predictor of outcome. This also has relevance for the psychoanalytic treatment model.

Communicative contact includes variables such as patient expressiveness, therapist empathy, and the reciprocal processes of therapist expressiveness and patient empathy. The importance of patient expressiveness for outcome was evident from all process perspectives. The importance of therapist empathy and of the reciprocal attunement of the participants for outcome was demonstrated mainly through objective measures of process and from the patient's perspective. These findings could be interpreted as strongly implying that the patient and therapist who are not well attuned to each other—who are not "on the same wavelength" but, instead, "talk at" or "talk past" each other—are likely to produce rather unfavorable outcomes.

Finally, the feeling attitudes that patient and therapist evoke in each other determine the relational quality of *mutual affect*. The evidence shows that when therapy is moving toward a successful outcome, these feelings are positive and reciprocal. A strong sense of mutual affirmation tends to develop in both participants but more differentially in the patient than in the therapist, since therapists are inclined by the nature of their clinical commitment toward a proactively friendly stance; in other words, patients' feelings tend to be more discriminating with respect to outcome. In every process perspective, the patient's affirmative attitude toward the therapist was consistently predictive of favorable outcome; by the same token, patients' negative attitudes also consistently predicted poorer outcomes.

What do these findings about mutual affect imply about the practice and supervision of psychoanalytic therapy? First, I think it would be a serious error to interpret them merely as positive and negative transferences or to conclude that these are only "transference cures"—if that is taken to mean that these phenomena reflect only the patient's early emotional attachments rather than the current therapeutic situation vis-à-vis the therapist. Transference implies a solipsistic and conflictual mode of experience that is more likely to lead to therapeutic impasse or failure than to success if not resolved. I think that Winnicott's (1965) concept of the "holding environment" provides a more adequate model of how the therapeutic bond may contribute to outcome. If patients experience the therapeutic bond as a holding environment providing safety and support for independent exploratory behavior, their ability to suspend defensive reactions is strengthened and they are thus enabled to learn more adaptive ways of coping with previously threatening situations. The impression that current reality, not just regressive fantasy, is involved in this is reinforced by findings concerning the importance of empathic rapport and communicative attunement.

Findings concerning the importance of a collaborative relationship for good outcome also imply that the adult egos of the patient and the therapist need to be jointly involved as partners in a therapeutic alliance. This alliance evidently can be threatened by an excessive detachment, under the guise of analytic neutrality, on the part of the therapist. The alliance can also be subverted if the patient's dependency is actively encouraged in the belief that this is necessary for the production of an "analytic process." The patient's neurotic condition is sufficient to ensure that regressive fantasies and transference conflicts will emerge spontaneously in the course of treatment, and when they do so, successful conflict resolution will depend to a great extent on supporting the functioning of the patient's adult ego and preserving the integrity of the working alliance.

SELF-RELATEDNESS

The greatest vindication of the psychoanalytic treatment model by process–outcome research may be seen in findings concerning *patient self-relatedness*, especially in the very consistent association of outcome with the patient's openness versus defensiveness. This underscores the urgency of Freud's (1913/1958) recommendation that therapists deal with their patients' defenses before attempting to work with their conflictual wishes. If patients are open to insight and support, they should be able to benefit from working with any "good enough" therapist, including the trainees we supervise. On the other hand, even expert clinicians can be defeated in their therapeutic efforts by highly defended patients unless they can find ways to reduce the patient's level of defensive.

A convergent aspect of self-relatedness is the patient's "experiencing" level, which reflects an ability to articulate implicit but deeply felt meanings. Typically, patients bring whatever skills they have in this regard to therapy, but when the patient is nondefensive these skills can be enhanced by practice.

As could be expected, therapist self-relatedness was less clearly related to outcome. Although there is evidence to suggest that markedly self-rejecting therapists may have a harmful influence (Henry, Schacht, & Strupp, 1990), even highly self-congruent and self-accepting therapists will often fail with very defensive patients or with patients who have serious difficulties forming and sustaining a therapeutic alliance. This touches closely on the rationale for requiring therapists to have adequate personal therapy and on the supervisor's responsibility to monitor and support the therapist's self-relatedness.

IN-SESSION IMPACT

A substantial body of findings indicates that favorable *in-session impacts* on the patient are consistently predictive of favorable outcome, except from the therapist's process perspective. Supervisors who have direct access to the process can tape record the patient's ongoing therapeutic realizations (such as insight, catharsis, and encouragement) as a sign that treatment is progressing well. These same findings, of course, indicate that a prolonged lack of therapeutic realizations by patients should be taken as a signal for supervisory intervention. Much more limited data on therapist in-session impacts, such as feelings of efficacy or frustration, suggest that these also may be useful in monitoring the course of treatment.

SEQUENTIAL PROCESSES

Finally, with respect to *temporal sequence*, the variable that has most often been studied is treatment duration. More than 150 findings have been accumulated on this point, and they show rather consistently, within studies, that longer treatments tend to be more successful than shorter treatments. This fact is certainly compatible with the psychoanalytic treatment model. However, to evaluate it properly, two other facts need to be kept in mind.

First, the average treatment case tends to be very short, especially by psychoanalytic standards, with patients often leaving outpatient therapy after only five or six sessions (Garfield, 1986; Phillips, 1985). In fact, only a small proportion of patients who come for treatment become long-term cases— though this tends not to be noticed by therapists, whose practices fill up after a while with long-term cases. Treatment duration should also be carefully distinguished from the contractual variable of treatment term, especially since time-limited treatment contracts (which are often for 16 to 20 or more sessions) may involve longer treatments than cases without a preset term. Thus, the tendency in the psychoanalytic treatment model to leave the term open-ended may not in fact facilitate longer treatment durations, or better outcomes.

Second, available dose–response data suggest that therapeutic benefit is a negatively accelerated function of treatment duration (Howard, Kopta, Krause, & Orlinsky, 1986). That is, patients tend to experience more benefit per session early in treatment and to require progressively longer periods for progress later in treatment. This is understandable if we reflect that "remoralization" and symptom relief tend to happen quickly, leaving enduring maladaptive dispositions, such as the patient's unconscious conflicts, as the material that must be dealt with in later phases.

The Psychoanalytic Treatment Model

Having presented the most salient findings of process–outcome research and commented in passing on their relevance for psychoanalytic psychotherapy, I want at last to focus directly on the psychoanalytic treatment model.

Every treatment situation begins with the formation of a therapeutic contract. In the psychoanalytic approach, as in others, it is the therapist's responsibility to ensure that patients fully understand and willingly accept the goals, methods, and practical arrangements for treatment, as well as the rationale of the treatment model. When patients are unsophisticated, they need to be educated about what to expect. It is also the therapist's responsibility to ensure that the patient is a suitable candidate for use of the treatment model, showing appropriate levels of necessary cognitive and behavioral skills. The traditional though no longer common practice of starting with a time-limited "trial analysis" could be one way to meet these responsibilities. Once a contract has been formed, it is the therapist's further responsibility to protect its integrity, either from disruption by external circumstances or, particularly in the psychoanalytic model, by unconscious attempts from the patient (or, indeed, from the therapist) to distort or subvert the contract.

In practice, the psychoanalytic treatment model guides therapists toward a specific therapeutic operation and a particular style of relating to the patient. Process–outcome findings indicate that the psychoanalytic model correctly emphasizes the importance of the patient's participation. It is important for patients to talk, to be genuinely engaged, to communicate expressively, and generally to be cooperative rather than resistant. Process–outcome findings also agree with psychodynamic thought by suggesting the importance of the patient's focusing on core personal relationships, past and present, and their influence on his or her current problems in living. This may be supported by the therapist's focusing interventions on the patient's problems and on the patient's feelings, to the extent that the patient's ego can tolerate it. Affective arousal, especially positive affective arousal, promotes or predicts favorable outcome, but negative affective arousal, if unrelieved or overwhelming, can lead to the opposite result.

The research evidence supports the effectiveness of interpretation, and in particular supports the primacy given by the psychoanalytic model to patient defensiveness as a target for interpretive intervention—with the important proviso that these interpretations be supportive and not blaming in character. Additionally, interventions typically discouraged by the psychoanalytic model, such as therapist self-disclosure and the giving of advice, have not been shown to be effective. The evidence also suggests that psychodynamically oriented therapists might want to consider related modes of intervention, such as "paradoxical intervention" and "experiential confrontation," as particularly effective when used appropriately with patients who can tolerate their intensity. (Paradoxical interventions may be the technique of choice for obsessive—compulsive patients, and experiential interventions (such as the Gestalt two-chair technique) for intellectualized patients.)

The style of therapeutic relationship proposed by the psychoanalytic treatment model poses a somewhat more complex question. There are at least two levels to be considered: one represented by the concept of therapeutic alliance, the second by the concept of transference. This follows from the psychodynamic understanding of personality as functioning concurrently at an age-appropriate level of maturity (usually consciously) and at an infantile level of unresolved emotional conflict (usually unconsciously). The shifting balance and momentary interplay of these forces determine the individual's experience and behavior in a given situation.

Process–outcome findings agree with the psychoanalytic treatment model in stressing the crucial importance of the alliance formed between the adaptive, age-appropriate ego of the patient and the mature, role-appropriate ego of the therapist. At the level of therapeutic alliance, collaborative engagement and affirmation define the most appropriate and effective stance for the therapist vis-à-vis the patient, not detachment and emotional neutrality. However, within the context of a positive alliance, detachment and neutrality, together with close empathic attunement, are probably the most appropriate stance for the therapist vis-à-vis the patient's active transference projections. Managing these different levels of relationship appropriately is particularly difficult, and should be a constant focus of supervision. Therapists who confuse the two levels by affecting detachment and emotional neutrality or by encouraging regressive dependency in the patient at the level of conscious therapeutic alliance are likely to exert a destructive influence. Likewise, therapists who become actively engaged at the level of unconscious transferences risk subtly exploiting the patient's vulnerable states of regression.

A final point may be made with respect to the importance of different observational perspectives on process in the supervisory process. Using tape recordings of therapy sessions as a basis of supervision, one has the advantage of comparing the process perspective of the supervisor (an external observer) with that of the therapist (a participant observer). Otherwise, supervision is limited to the therapist's view of process, which is not necessarily inferior or superior but is definitely different. For example, from the therapist's process perspective, the most robust indicators of favorable outcome, according to the research evidence, would be the patient's suitability, personal engagement, cooperation (versus resistance), openness (versus defensiveness), and positive feelings within and contribution to the therapeutic bond. From a supervisor's audiotape-based external process perspective, the most robust indicators of favorable outcome would be the therapist's skillfulness; sureness, or credibility; use of interpretation; focus on patient problems; and involvement in a mutually affirming relationship with the patient—in combination with the patient variables of suitability, cooperation, openness, positive contribution to and affirmation within the therapeutic bond, and experience of therapeutic realizations during sessions.

This is the guidance that the accumulated findings of psychotherapy research can begin to offer to practitioners of psychoanalytic therapy. As a knowledge base, it is probabilistic, applies to the average case rather than the individual case, and is subject to reservations such as the stipulation of "other things being equal." It does not offer certainty nor does it eliminate the need to use clinical judgment and insight in practical application. But it is the surest base of knowledge concerning psychotherapy we now have, and, as such, it cannot and should not be ignored.

REFERENCES

Ambühl, H. (1991). Die Aufnahmebereitschaft des Klienten als zentrales Bindeglied zwischen therapeutischer Tätigkeit und Therapieerfolg [Openness of clients as a central mediator between therapeutic intervention and therapeutic success]. In D. Schulte (Ed), *Therapeutische Entscheidungen* (pp. 71–87). Göttingen, Ger.: Hogrefe.

Ambühl, H. (1993). Was ist therapeutisch an Psychotherapie? Eine empirische Überprüfung der Annahmen im "Generic Model of Psychotherapy" [What is therapeutic about psychotherapy? An empirical test of the assumptions in the "Generic Model of Psychotherapy"]. *Zeitschrift für Klinische Psychologie, Psychopathologie, und Psychotherapie, 41,* 285–303.

Bergin, A. E., & Garfield, S. L. (Eds.) (in press). *Handbook of psychotherapy and behavior change* (4th ed.). New York: Wiley.

Beutler, L. E., & Clarkin, J. F. (1990). *Systematic treatment selection: Toward targeted therapeutic interventions.* New York: Brunner/Mazel.

Beutler, L. E., & Crago, M. (1991). *Psychotherapy research: An international review of programmatic studies.* Washington, DC: American Psychological Association.

Breuer, J., & Freud, S. (1955). Studies on hysteria. In J. Strachey (Ed. & Trans.), *The standard edition of the complete psychological works of Sigmund Freud* (Vol. 2). London: Hogarth Press. (Original work published 1895)

Dahl, H., Kächele, H., & Thomä, H. (Eds.). (1988). *Psychoanalytic process research strategies.* Berlin: Springer-Verlag.

Elkin, I. E. (in press). The NIMH Treatment of Depression Collaborative Research Program: Where we began and where we are. In A. E. Bergin & S. L. Garfield (Eds.), *Handbook of psychotherapy and behavior change* (4th ed.). New York: Wiley.

Frank, J. D., Hoehn-Saric, R., Imber, S. D., Liberman, B. L., & Stone, A. R. (1978). *Effective ingredients of successful psychotherapy.* New York: Brunner/Mazel.

Freud, S. (1958). On beginning the treatment. In J. Strachey (Ed. & Trans.), *The standard edition of the complete psychological works of Sigmund Freud* (Vol. 12., pp. 121–144). London: Hogarth Press. (Original work published 1913)

Freud, S. (1955). Psycho-analysis. In J. Strachey (Ed. & Trans.), *The standard edition of the complete psychological works of Sigmund Freud* (Vol. 18, pp. 235–254). London: Hogarth Press. (Original work published 1922)

Garfield, S. L. (1986). Research on client variables in psychotherapy. In S. L. Garfield & A. E. Bergin (Eds.), *Handbook of psychotherapy and behavior change* (3rd ed.). New York: Wiley.

Geertz, C. (1983). Centers, kings, and charisma: Reflections on the symbolics of power. In *Local knowledge: Further essays in interpretive anthropology.* New York: Basic Books.

Goldfried, M. R. (Ed.). (1982). *Converging themes in psychotherapy: Trends in psychodynamic, humanistic, and behavioral practice.* New York: Springer.

Gurman, A. S., Kniskern, D. P., & Pinsof, W. M. (1986). Research on marital and family therapies. In S. L. Garfield & A. E. Bergin (Eds.), *Handbook of psychotherapy and behavior change* (3rd ed.). New York: Wiley.

Henry, W. T., Schacht, T. E., & Strupp, H. H. (1990). Patient and therapist introject, interpersonal process, and differential psychotherapy outcome. *Journal of Consulting and Clinical Psychology, 58,* 768–774.

Howard, K., Kopta, M., Krause, M., & Orlinsky, D. (1986). The dose-effect relationship in psychotherapy. *American Psychologist, 41,* 149–164.

Kolden, G. G. (1991). The Generic Model of Psychotherapy: An empirical investigation of process and outcome relationships. *Psychotherapy Research, 1,* 62–73.

Kuhn, T. S. (1970). *The structure of scientific revolutions* (2nd ed.). Chicago: University of Chicago Press.

Laplanche, J. (1989). *New foundations for psychoanalysis.* Oxford, UK: Basil Blackwell.

Lietaer, G., Rombauts, J., & Van Balen, R. (Eds.). (1990). *Client-centered and experiential psychotherapy in the nineties.* Leuven, Belgium: Leuven University Press.

Luborsky, L., Crits-Christoph, P., Mintz, J., & Auerbach, A. (1988). *Who will benefit from psychotherapy: Predicting therapeutic outcomes.* New York: Basic Books.

Luborsky, L., & Spence, D. P. (1978). Quantitative research on psychoanalytic therapy. In S. L. Garfield & A. E. Bergin (Eds.), *Handbook of psychotherapy and behavior change* (2nd ed.). New York: Wiley.

Meier, C. A. (1967). *Ancient incubation and modern psychotherapy.* Evanston, IL: Northwestern University Press.

Meltzoff, J., & Kornreich, M. (1970). *Research in psychotherapy.* New York: Atherton Press.

Miller, N. E., Luborsky, L., Barber, J., & Docherty, J. (Eds.). (1993). *Psychodynamic treatment research.* New York: Basic Books.

Orlinsky, D. E. (in press) Learning from many masters: Toward a research-based integration of psychotherapy treatment models. *Der Psychotherapeut, 1, 1.*

Orlinsky, D. E., Grawe, K., & Parks, B. K. (in press). Process and outcome in psychotherapy—noch einmal. In A. E. Bergin & S. L. Garfield (Eds.), *Handbook of psychotherapy and behavior change* (4th ed.). New York: Wiley.

Orlinsky, D. E., & Howard, K. I. (1975). *Varieties of psychotherapeutic experience: Multivariate analyses of patients' and therapists' reports.* New York: Teachers College Press.

Orlinsky, D. E., & Howard, K. I. (1986). Process and outcome in psychotherapy. In S. L. Garfield & A. E. Bergin (Eds.), *Handbook of psychotherapy and behavior change* (3rd ed.). New York: Wiley.

Orlinsky, D. E., & Howard, K. I. (1987a). A generic model of psychotherapy. *Journal of Integrative and Eclectic Psychotherapy, 6,* 6–27.

Orlinsky, D. E., & Howard, K. I. (1987b). A generic model of process in psychotherapy. In W. Huber (Ed.), *Progress in psychotherapy research* . Louvain-la-Neuve, Belgium: Presses Universitaires de Louvain.

Orlinsky, D. E., & Howard, K. I. (in press). Unity and diversity among psychotherapies: A comparative perspective. In B. Bongar & L. E. Beutler (Eds.), *Foundations of psychotherapy: Theory, research, and practice* . New York: Oxford University Press.

Orlinsky D. E., & Russell, R. R. (in press). Tradition and change in psychotherapy research: Some reflections on the fourth generation. In R. R. Russell, (Ed.), *New Directions in Psychotherapy Research.* New York: Guilford.

Phillips, E. L. (1985). *Psychotherapy revised: New frontiers in research and practice.* Hillsdale, NJ: Erlbaum.

Pribram, K. H., & Gill, M. M. (1976). *Freud's "Project" re-assessed.* New York: Basic Books.

Rice, L. N., & Greenberg, L. S. (Eds.). (1984). *Patterns of change: Intensive analysis of psychotherapy process.* New York: Guilford Press.

Rogers, C. R., & Dymond, R. F. (Eds.). (1954). *Psychotherapy and personality change: Co-ordinated research studies in the client-centered approach.* Chicago: University of Chicago Press.

Safran, J. D., & Segal, Z. V. (1990). *Interpersonal process in cognitive therapy.* New York: Basic Books.

Schafer, R. (1976). *A new language for psychoanalysis.* New Haven, CT: Yale University Press.

Strupp, H. H., & Bloxom, A. L. (1973). Preparing lower class patients for group psychotherapy: Development and evaluation of a role-induction procedure. *Journal of Consulting and Clinical Psychology, 41,* 373–384.

Strupp, H. H., Fox, R. E., & Lessler, K. (1969). *Patients view their psychotherapy.* Baltimore: Johns Hopkins University Press.

Strupp, H. H., Hadley, S., & Gomes-Schwartz, B. (1977). *Psychotherapy for better or worse.* New York: Aronson.

Weber, M. (1978). The types of legitimate domination. In G. Roth & C. Wittich. (Eds.), *Economy and Society* (Vol. 1.). Berkeley, CA: University of California Press.

Winnicott, D. W. (1965). *The maturational process and the facilitating environment.* New York: International Universities Press.

CHAPTER 7

Developing a Working Marriage Between Psychotherapists and Psychotherapy Researchers: Identifying Shared Purposes

Robert Elliott and Cheryl Morrow-Bradley

THE TROUBLED RELATIONSHIP between researchers and therapists has been well documented in the literature (for example, Barlow, Hayes, & Nelson, 1984; Morrow-Bradley & Elliott, 1986). As in every troubled relationship, there are two sides to this rift: Researchers blame therapists for not utilizing research findings and for being biased, irresponsible, or antiscientific. On the other hand, therapists blame researchers for not researching common or clinically relevant treatments or populations (Morrow-Bradley & Elliott, 1986) and for being scientistic, boring, and irrelevant.

To the clinically trained ear, the strained relationship between therapists and researchers sounds like a troubled marriage in which there is a history of mutual blame, discounting, and self-justification. This clinical observation in turn raises the question of whether any accommodation is possible or whether it would be better for therapists and researchers to go their separate ways.

Our position on this issue will become obvious from a disclosure of our backgrounds: One of us (RE) is a therapy researcher who does some therapy, the other (CMB) a therapist who does some research. We have both tried, with varying success, to integrate practice and research in our work as researcher and therapist. Unfortunately, we have found at times that we were also at war with ourselves. On the one hand, we have been frustrated by the lack of usefulness of most therapy research, including our own; on the other hand, we have often felt at sea clinically and wished for more guidance from

We thank Denny Bradley and Janie Manford for their editorial assistance.

empirical research. As Jay Greenberg (this volume) points out, therapists and researchers live in different worlds. We would add that therapists and researchers live in different worlds even when they are the same person functioning at different times as therapist or researcher!

Furthermore, in our own scientific and clinical work we have found the gap between therapy research and practice to be counterproductive to our efforts to unravel the complexities of therapy. One of us is drawn to one of the most difficult issues in psychotherapy research, namely, understanding and integrating the multiple contexts and perspectives of the change process; the other is drawn to a particularly challenging clinical population, persons diagnosed with borderline personality disorder. We have a mutually shared purpose: to provide clinically useful research findings that will improve practice and provide better "road maps" for therapists. It is our view that when addressing these complex research and clinical problems, we need all the research and clinical resources we can gather.

We begin this chapter by reviewing our earlier work on practicing therapists' interests and criticisms for therapy research (we do this in the form of a critique of two recent therapy studies). Next, we move to the core of our argument, which is that therapists and researchers need each other in a number of ways, some of which have perhaps not previously been made explicit. We then illustrate our key argument with a series of "case studies," offering promising modes for research–practice dialogue. We conclude with a set of recommendations for further facilitating this dialogue. Thus, our position is to advocate constructive dialogue between two different but complementary views of the world in order to attain common purposes. Throughout, we comment on two chapters from this volume (by Kernberg and Clarkin and by J. Greenberg) and try to integrate some of their points into our argument.

An Evaluation of Two Psychotherapy Research Programs From the Perspective of Practicing Therapists

It seems logical to begin by reviewing our previous research on the therapy research versus practice split, a survey of almost 400 practicing psychotherapists (Morrow-Bradley & Elliott, 1986). In this study we asked a randomized sample of American Psychological Association Division 29 (Psychotherapy) members about their patterns of research utilization and the type of psychotherapy research they would find most helpful. Another aspect of our survey was a systematic evaluation of therapists' criticisms of current therapy, using a list derived from methodological writings on therapy research.

We documented a pattern of low utilization of research by therapists. We reported that therapists gained their most useful information from their own clinical work with clients. We also found that "the most useful psychotherapy research study would be a process–outcome study describing how the therapy was done and focusing on significant change moments and the therapeutic alliance. Therapists expressed less interest in more traditional comparative process or outcome studies or primarily theory-based research studies" (p. 192).

In this section we use the main findings of this survey to evaluate two recent practice-oriented psychotherapy research studies: Kernberg and Clarkin (this volume) and Elliott, Clark, Wexler, Kemeny, Brinkerhoff, and Mack (1990). We do this by taking the main recommendations and criticisms reported by the surveyed therapists and applying these as standards for evaluating the two studies. We have deliberately chosen one of our own studies for this purpose, not in order to congratulate ourselves but as an opportunity for self-reflection and critique. We believe that it is important for both therapists and researchers to think critically and reflectively about their work in order to improve upon it (cf. Schön, 1983).

Kernberg and Clarkin's study (this volume) involves the development and application of a psychodynamic form of treatment, the details of which they have organized in a manual, to clients broadly classified as suffering from borderline personality disorder. They use standardized outcome measures of psychological change and have included implementation checks to make sure that their therapists are following the treatment manual. Part of their research effort is the continued articulation of further aspects of their treatment and a corresponding refinement of their manual.

The study by Elliott et al. (1990) examined the impact of a manual-guided process-experiential treatment (Greenberg, Rice, & Elliott, 1993) applied to clients diagnosed with major depressive disorder. Impact was assessed at varying levels, including treatment outcome, immediate postsession impact, and client-identified significant change events within sessions. Specifically, clients were asked to identify the most helpful and hindering events in each session. Every four sessions, a researcher interviewed the client in order to obtain more in-depth information about the most helpful event in that session. The researchers also administered standard outcome measures (for example, Beck Depression Inventory, Hamilton Rating Scale for Depression) every eight sessions. Clients' descriptions of significant events were later content-analyzed.

Considering these two studies in light of the earlier survey, we note the following: Over 40% of the clinicians we surveyed (Morrow-Bradley & Elliott, 1986) wanted research on personality disorders or borderline disorders while about a third preferred research on neurotic or adjustment disorders. Kernberg and Clarkin have chosen to study borderline disorders while Elliott et al. (1990) chose to study major depressive disorders. Thus, both have chosen a diagnostic category that is seen as needing further study.

Adults seen in outpatient settings were the most preferred population of study. Thus, both research teams have addressed themselves to areas of psychotherapy research that a large number of practitioners would like to have studied. On the other hand, both of these studies are theory-based, a nonpreferred type of research, according to our survey.

In general, these two studies receive a mixed report when evaluated using the survey respondents' eight most frequently endorsed criticisms of psychotherapy research, listed in table 7.1. The most strongly endorsed of these criticisms was of research that "treats all therapists or all responses by therapists as interchangeable." While Kernberg and Clarkin say their approach allows for the personal style of their various therapists, they do not seem particularly interested in this factor or in how the personal style of the therapist may affect treatment. The approach of Elliott et al. examines the therapist responses that clients see as helpful or hindering but does not specifically compare therapists with each other. (Incidentally, other psychotherapy researchers have begun to take this criticism much more seriously in recent years, for example, Crits-Christoph et al., 1991, and Lambert, 1989.)

The next most popular criticism had to do with the absence of "practical, relevant and scientifically sound measures of psychological change due to therapy." Both the Kernberg and Clarkin and Elliott et al. research teams use a number of traditional outcome measures (standard personality inventories,

Table 7.1   Frequent Criticisms of Therapy Research

Research that treats all therapists or all responses by therapists as interchangeable obscures essential differences. (75% of informants)[a]

Practical, relevant, and scientifically sound measures of psychological change due to therapy often are unavailable. (68%)

Studies designed to try to incorporate the complexities of psychotherapy rarely are done. (67%)

In an effort to make studying psychotherapy more manageable, researchers often ignore important variables. (66%)

Often researchers focus on specific therapeutic techniques while ignoring the importance of the relationship between therapist and client. (66%)

Traditional research methodologies, those derived from the physical sciences, are not for the most part appropriate for the investigation of psychotherapy. (62%)

Psychotherapy researchers often use criteria that are either too global or too specific. (60%)

Clinically meaningful questions about psychotherapy often are not studied or selected. (54%)

Note. From "The Utilization of psychotherapy research by practicing psychotherapists" by C. Morrow-Bradley and R. Elliott, 1986, *American Psychologist, 41*, p. 193. Copyright 1986 by American Psychological Association. Reprinted by permission. [a]Endorsed as "true and needs to be corrected before psychotherapy research results could be more useful to me."

symptom checklists, and so on) while adding other measures to their outcome batteries. Thus, both studies apparently have adequate measures of psychological change.

The third most common criticism in the Morrow-Bradley and Elliott (1986) survey was that researchers rarely attempt to incorporate the complexities of psychotherapy into their studies (cf. Elliott & Anderson, in press). Elliott et al. appear to address this criticism more directly than Kernberg and Clarkin in that they allowed clients to describe a range of factors that may have been helpful or hindering in the psychotherapeutic process, as opposed to studying only global outcome. Nevertheless, neither study appears to even begin to address the intricacies of treatment.

The fourth most frequently endorsed criticism was similar in that it stated that researchers often ignore important variables in order to make their task more manageable. It is difficult to gauge this in the work of Kernberg and Clarkin, at least as reported in this volume. For their part, Elliott et al. appear to have looked at a wide range of variables; however, they then sacrifice some of the richness in the data by reducing significant events to broad categories. For example, they report that 38% of the helpful events involved enhanced self-awareness; it would have been much more enlightening for clinicians if they had provided examples of these self-awareness events and had described how they came about.

According to the fifth most common criticism, researchers often focus on specific techniques to the exclusion of the client–therapist relationship. We are certain that Kernberg and Clarkin view the therapeutic relationship as important, but they apparently have made no attempt to study it directly. Elliott et al. appear to have addressed this, but only indirectly, in that some categories and some scales appear to measure the therapeutic relationship (for example, "felt understood," "client becoming more involved in therapy").

The sixth criticism referred to problems brought about by applying inappropriate research methods from the physical sciences. On this score, both research studies appear to have combined traditional with more nontraditional methods; for example, both seem to be using quantitative outcome measurement as well as qualitative, or case study, methods.

A seventh criticism, which held that psychotherapy researchers often use criteria that are either too global or too specific, could be applied to both research teams. Kernberg and Clarkin globally measure patient change, apparently as a function of their theory-based, manual-supported treatment approach; on the other hand, they certainly cannot be criticized for being too specific. Elliott et al. also used a manual-supported (process-experiential) treatment approach, but they looked at the process of therapy and what seemed to be helpful or hindering from client and therapist perspectives. However, the broad categories they used to classify these experiences may also limit their clinical meaningfulness. (For example, there is little indication of what the client and therapist actually did in the significant events, information that might contribute to an understanding of their helpfulness.)

The eighth most frequent criticism was that psychotherapy researchers often ignore clinically meaningful questions about psychotherapy (cf. Spence, this volume). Obviously, both research teams have tackled meaningful and difficult questions in the psychotherapy field. Whether these researchers will be able to produce clinically useful answers to their research questions has yet to be determined.

While these two studies cannot be taken as a representation of all current psychotherapy research, they make it clear that contemporary psychotherapy research is capable of studying more clinically relevant issues. It is also apparent from these studies that therapy researchers still have much progress to make before achieving greater practical relevance. However, there is a deeper issue at stake: in spite of their mutual criticisms and frequent estrangement, researchers and therapists depend on and need each other more than has been admitted.

Researchers and Therapists Need Each Other

One possible approach to the research–practice gap in psychotherapy is to adopt the stance of the marital therapist who attempts to help the distressed partners to recognize and accept the fact that each lives in a different reality, to respect that reality, and to stop trying to change the other. In this section we argue that while the worlds of therapists and researchers may be very different, they are nevertheless inextricably bound to each other "for better or for worse." Whether they like it or not, therapy researchers and practitioners are mutually dependent on one another. They need each other for a number of purely practical reasons, which are discussed in the following paragraphs.

PRACTICE AS A SOURCE OF RESEARCH

Most of the major ideas in the field of psychotherapy have arisen out of extensive direct therapeutic contact with clients. These include psychoanalytic theory and treatment, cognitive and rational-emotive therapies, and experiential therapy interventions (that is, the use of gestalt therapy 2-chair dialogues to help clients enact and resolve internal conflicts).

These ideas have subsequently undergone a "translation" process in which they were first subjected to systematic qualitative/clinical observation and then further adapted so they could be measured quantitatively. The results of this scientific laundering process are many of the mainstays of therapy research over the past 30 years, including the following: therapist facilitative conditions (warmth, empathy, and genuineness; Rogers, 1957); therapeutic alliance (Bordin, 1979; Luborsky, 1977); core conflictual relationship themes (that is, client expresses a *wish* for closeness with others, but this is perceived as resulting in the *consequence* of his or her being taken advantage of; Luborsky & Crits-Christoph, 1990), and task analysis (example, systematic unfolding or reexperiencing of puzzling or problematic personal reactions; Rice & Sapiera, 1984).

Each of these lines of research contains a kernel of clinically relevant insight, directing the therapist's attention to potentially important therapeutic phenomena and in many instances suggesting or implying some form of guideline for therapist intervention. For example, Rogers's (1957) paper was the result of intensive study of hundreds of hours of taped therapy sessions. Subsequently, hundreds of studies were conducted on therapist facilitative conditions, and various methodological controversies followed (cf. Gurman, 1977; Lambert, DeJulio, & Stein, 1978). However, it is easy to forget that the original source of these constructs was the practice of psychotherapy, and it is highly unlikely that they would have developed outside of this context.

PRACTICE AS A JUSTIFICATION FOR PSYCHOTHERAPY RESEARCH

Psychotherapy research has involved both applied and basic research. Thus, some therapy researchers have found therapy to be a productive site for studying basic human processes, such as the organization of talk, cognitive–emotional schemes (that is, needs, fears, frames), and verbal/nonverbal modes of processing (for example, Dahl, Kächele, & Thomä, 1988; Labov & Fanshel, 1977). On the other hand, the majority of therapy researchers have seen themselves as carrying out work intended to improve the practice of psychotherapy (example, Elliott, 1983; Garfield & Bergin, 1986; Rice & Greenberg, 1984). This is especially the case with therapy outcome researchers and those who attempt to link pretherapy variables (for example, client personality disorder diagnosis) and therapy process (for example, therapeutic alliance) to outcome. If these researchers were told that there was no chance that any of their findings would improve any therapist's practice, they would either suffer a major disappointment or change research fields, or both. Also, The National Institute of Mental Health (NIMH) would certainly be less than enthusiastic about funding research whose potential for practical application was nil!

RESEARCH CAN JUSTIFY PRACTICE

In spite of the protests of organized psychology, managed care has already significantly altered the practice of psychotherapy in much of the United States. As a result, a large proportion of therapists are experiencing increasing restrictions on whom they can see, the length of treatment, and, in some cases, even the kind of treatment they are allowed to provide clients. Some, for example, Giles, Neims, and Prial (1993) are attempting to use existing psychotherapy research to justify managed care restrictions not only on the length of treatment but on the type of therapy that will be reimbursed (in this case, short-term cognitive-behavioral treatments).

However, psychotherapy research does not need to be a bludgeon for attacking psychodynamic and experiential therapies. Instead, recent meta-analytic reviews of outcome research on these treatments (for example, Crits-Christoph, 1992; Greenberg, Elliott, & Lietaer, 1994) can be called upon to support their efficacy, thus empowering therapists who follow these approaches. Therapists, particularly those of a noncognitive-behavioral persuasion, need researchers to help them fight this battle. We need more research examining the benefits of long-term treatment of serious disorders, in particular, borderline personality disorder. If insurance companies could be shown that there is a cost benefit, for example, in the form of fewer hospitalizations or of significant improvement in occupational/social functioning in persons with this diagnosis, they may be more willing to spend outpatient dollars.

RESEARCH CAN HELP THERAPISTS DO A BETTER JOB

As we and others have documented (Cohen, Sargent, & Sechrest, 1986; Morrow-Bradley & Elliott, 1986), practicing therapists report finding little of value in psychotherapy research. However, this does not mean that the influence has been nonexistent or that there is no potential for useful input from research. An alternative hypothesis is that much of the influence of research on practice has been indirect and not easily quantified. Also, psychotherapy research is still in its infancy and is concerned with understanding complex processes. We do not believe that therapists are interested in rejecting research findings that they can clearly see are relevant to their clinical work.

In regard to specifics, first, therapy research fosters in therapists (usually during their training) an attitude of thoughtful reflection about practice, which helps them evaluate both their own clinical experience and the research findings of others. If Kernberg and Clarkin could follow their therapists after training, it would be interesting to see what impact their participation in the research project described in their chapter of this volume has on their practice of psychotherapy.

Second, therapy research has helped to develop and clarify clinical observations, resulting in various "sensitizing concepts" (Strauss & Corbin, 1990) that are easily carried over into clinical practice. For example, Rogers's (1957) facilitative conditions (the use by therapists of accurate empathy, positive regard, and congruence) changed forever how we perceive the therapeutic process. At the same time, they also implied a set of guidelines (perhaps overgeneralized) for practicing therapy. In a similar fashion, Luborsky's core conflictual relationship theme research method (Luborsky & Crits-Christoph, 1990), which suggests the value of interpretations of recurrent conflict themes (Luborsky, 1984), is readily adapted as a helpful framework for contemporary dynamic therapists to use in listening to their clients' accounts of their interactions with other people.

Third, in our own experience we have found that research can facilitate practice. For example, Elliott's research team of experiential therapists has benefited particularly from three lines of research: (1) Rice and Greenberg's (1984) work on client "markers" for certain experiential interventions (example, two-chair work at client "splits" or conflicts; systematic "unfolding" or reexperiencing of the puzzling client reactions); (2) Luborsky's (1976) work on the predictive value of early indicators of therapeutic alliance; and (3) their own research on the varieties of immediate client reactions to therapist interventions (for example, insight, feeling understood, being misdirected; Caskey, Barker, & Elliott, 1984; Elliott, James, Reimschuessel, Cislo, & Sack, 1985). These last-mentioned studies have been helpful in providing direction and caution (that is, therapists sometimes need to inquire explicitly about client reactions, since these are often discrepant from the therapist's perceptions).

Psychotherapy researchers may also get an additional benefit from being able to experience directly the richness of their own primary data (that is, transcripts as well as client and therapist direct reports of therapy sessions) before they crunch it into scientifically acceptable but clinically dry and sometimes irrelevant statistics!

SUMMARY

Thus, while we believe that therapy research has often not been particularly useful for practicing therapists, therapy research can and does play a role in improving the practice of therapy, even though this is not always in direct or obvious ways. In our view, research and practice exist in a kind of dialogue with each other. This dialogue can be adversarial and unproductive, with each side devaluing, cutting off, or trying to dominate or change the other. Optimally, however, the dialogue can be challenging and mutually facilitative, with each side listening, stimulating, and collaborating with the other. In the next section, we offer a series of examples of positive research–practice interaction.

Case Studies in Researcher–Therapist Dialogue and Interaction

Researchers and therapists need each other, and there are a number of examples of how they can work together productively.

RESEARCH ON THERAPIST DIFFICULTIES

Shortly after we finished the research reported in Morrow-Bradley and Elliott (1986), one of us (RE) was offered the opportunity to carry out research with a group of practicing therapists (headed by Marcia and John Davis) in the British National Health Service who were also affiliated with the University of Warwick. After being presented with a list of our favorite research topics, these therapists were asked what they were interested in studying. Their answer was "None of the above." Instead, they wanted to study "therapist difficulties," that is, situations in therapy that created problems of various sorts. From the point of view of these practicing therapists, moments of difficulties were the times when they felt in greatest need of help from research; these were times when they most wanted to "turn to research." For starters, they wanted to know if other therapists also had trouble with the same situations, and they also wanted to know what other therapists did about these difficulties.

Starting with this interest, this therapist–researcher team began by studying themselves, with each person writing down descriptions of a number of difficulties he or she had encountered. These descriptions were then sorted by all members of the team, and a taxonomy of therapist difficulties was agreed upon. This taxonomy included the following: Incompetent, Damaging, Puzzled, Threatened, Out of Rapport, Personal Issues, Painful Reality/Ethical Dilemma, Stuck, and Thwarted (Davis et al., 1987). For example, if a therapist felt that therapy was at an unresolvable impasse, this would be classified as Stuck; if a therapist felt it was necessary in some way to protect himself or herself from the client, this would be classified as Threatened; finally, if a therapist felt that he or she was injuring the client, this would be classified as Damaging.

The therapist–researcher team next carried out a survey of therapist difficulties in a broad sample of psychotherapists working in the British National Health Service. They then used their data to develop a taxonomy of coping strategies used by therapists for dealing with difficulties (Schröder, Binns, Davis, Elliott, Francis, & Kelman, 1987), including Turns to Self (for example, by managing one's own feelings), Turns to Patient (for example, by inviting collaboration), Turns to Other (for example, seeking consultation or education), Turns to Practice (for example, through interpretation or some other technical intervention or through change of therapeutic tactic), Turns Away

From Difficulty (that is, avoids), Turns Against Patient (for example, blames or persecutes patient), and Turns Away From Patient (example, considers terminating patient). Among other things, they found that therapists were most likely to feel threatened with borderline clients and that the coping strategy Turns Away From Patient was most likely with the Out of Rapport, Stuck, and Thwarted forms of difficulty (Binns et al., 1989).

Currently, questionnaire versions of the difficulties and coping strategies taxonomies are being used as part of a large-scale international study on the personal and professional development of therapists over time. One of the goals of this research is to see if difficulties and coping strategies change across different levels of therapist experience (Orlinsky et al., 1991).

SYSTEMATIC CASE STUDIES IN THE TRAINING/RESEARCH CLINIC

A third model for research–practice dialogue is to encourage therapists-in-training to carry out "systematic case studies" on their own cases. A systematic case study is a careful investigation of a particular treatment case, using a variety of nonexperimental research methods (Elliott, 1983). Kernberg and Clarkin's description of involving trainees in research on their own cases also illustrates this approach.

In the systematic case study, the researcher typically addresses questions such as the following:

1) *Client change:* "Is this client better?"; "In what ways has the client changed?"; "When did change occur?"
2) *Therapy process:* "What did the client and therapist typically do or experience in therapy?"; "How much do client and therapist agree with each other about what happened?"; "Did these processes change over time?"
3) *Change processes:* "What processes in the therapy were effective or helpful?"; "Did the therapy help the client get better?"

These are questions about which therapists have reason to be interested, and, in fact, such questions may be addressed with a range of research measures and procedures, involving varying commitments of time and effort (see Barker, Pistrang, & Elliott, in press). For example, client change can be measured by beginning with one well-chosen change measure, administered before and after therapy; to this can be added an individualized change measure, such as the Personal Questionnaire, which addresses a set of target complaints that are rated on a regular basis throughout therapy (Phillips, 1986).

Similarly, therapy process can be assessed simply by process notes or periodic relationship measures (for example, the Penn Helping Alliance Questionnaire by Alexander & Luborsky, 1986), to which can be added weekly client self-report measures, such as the Therapy Session Report (Orlinsky & Howard, 1986).

Finally, change processes or effective ingredients can be measured by asking clients to rate helpful factors on a posttreatment questionnaire (for example, Sloane, Staples, Whipple, & Cristol, 1977) or to write descriptions of what was most helpful after each session (for example, on the Helpful Aspects of Therapy form; Llewelyn, Elliott, Shapiro, Firth, & Hardy, 1988).

Parry, Shapiro, and Firth (1986) present an excellent example of a systematic case study illustrating a number of these possibilities. Therapist-researchers can strengthen the credibility and internal validity (causal explanatory power) of their systematic case studies by incorporating the design features described by Kazdin (1981), for example, using standardized change measures and assessing client symptoms prior to therapy and repeatedly over time. However, the ultimate strength of systematic case studies is their potential for linking clinical practice and research in nonbehavioral treatments. They thus provide an alternative to the experimental single-case designs favored by behavioral therapists, designs that do not readily lend themselves to dynamic or experiential treatments.

RESEARCHER–THERAPIST DIALOGUE IN THE ANALYSIS OF SIGNIFICANT EVENTS

Elliott and Shapiro (1992) present another example of how researchers and therapists can work together. In their study the researcher asked the client to identify a significant change event in a session; client and therapist were then interviewed about the event. Next, the researcher carried out his own analysis of the event, using the Comprehensive Process Analysis method (Elliott, 1989). Following this, the researcher organized the client and therapist material into the same framework and carefully integrated the three different analyses into a single version. He then gave this integrated analysis to the therapist for correction. Finally, after therapist and researcher had agreed on the analysis, the therapist wrote a commentary on the process. A portion of this commentary is worth quoting here:

> From the point of view of the interface between research and clinical practice, this analysis of contrasting perspectives can be highly educational for the therapist. The data allow for the corroboration and revision of therapist views. . . . In effect, taking part in this research was for the therapist like receiving supervision from the client and research colleagues. The therapist was required to make explicit his rationales and purposes, and to have these checked out against the experiences of the client and the sense made of the process by observers. Like all good supervision, this process is often challenging and stressful, but can be very useful for continued learning, particularly if the validity of the therapist perspective is recognized and respected. (pp. 183–184)

This approach seems to take seriously the importance of considering different perspectives on the therapy process, a point emphasized by Jay Greenberg (this volume) and others (for example, Orlinsky & Howard, 1986).

Recommendations for Promoting Facilitative Dialogue in the Therapist–Researcher Marriage

As our examples illustrate, we believe that what is needed is an opening up of the dialogue between research and practice in psychotherapy. The implications of our discussion can be presented in the form of suggestions, which are the subject of the following paragraphs.

DETERMINE THERAPISTS' INTERESTS

Researchers who want their research to be attended to by therapists should find out what therapists are interested in knowing about. As noted earlier, Morrow-Bradley and Elliott (1986) have reported some of these needs and wishes. In addition, it would be important to study what the therapists are interested in versus what researchers are interested in, as illustrated by the research on therapist difficulties described in the previous section.

CONDUCT MORE FRONTLINE RESEARCH

More frontline research is needed, focusing on therapy as it is actually practiced in everyday clinical work. For example, in reviewing research on treatment of posttraumatic stress disorder (PTSD), Blake, Abueg, and Woodward (1993), note that the current research does not reflect the actual practice of the great majority of experienced therapists working with PTSD populations; as those authors note, most practitioners treat PTSD with eclectic or psychodynamically oriented treatments unrepresented in the research literature. Rather than berating therapists for using unproven treatments (cf. Giles et al., 1993), Blake et al. (1993) argue that researchers should be studying these commonly used treatments. Just because it is difficult to study therapies as they occur in their "natural state" and complexity does not mean it is not worthwhile to study them. In fact, we have found the opposite to be the case.

Similarly, Weisz, Weiss, and Donenberg (1992) argue that the bulk of research on therapeutic interventions with children does not reflect the typical practice situation, in which broadly trained, loosely supervised therapists carry large caseloads of referred clients. In contrast, research on the treatment of children typically involves specially trained, closely supervised therapists with small caseloads of specially recruited clients. The ecological validity of such research is highly questionable (cf. Shapiro & Shapiro, 1983).

ADDRESS PHILOSOPHY OF SCIENCE ISSUES

Philosophy of science issues need to be addressed as part of fostering better communication between researchers and therapists. One obstacle to more productive dialogue stems from differences between styles of research and the criteria used for evaluating research. Thus, one way to address the researcher–therapist gap would be to broaden our vision of science to include both the traditional, experimental, "received view" research and qualitative, "new paradigm," research (for example, interpretive, hermeneutic, or critical). These emerging genres of therapy research highlight the multiperspectival nature of the therapeutic process, focusing on questions of meaning, definition, and interpretation. They also involve a more interactive, equalitarian relationship between researchers and those they study. Also, in these approaches, the researcher collects and analyzes data in a more discovery-oriented, open-ended manner (Mahrer, 1988; Patton, 1990; Strauss & Corbin, 1990; Toukmanian & Rennie, 1992).

Jay Greenberg hints at this issue in his discussion of truth criteria for psychoanalytic interpretations. We do not have space for a discussion of the emerging alternative ways of thinking about the foundations of scientific research in psychology and of the associated new qualitative and interpretative approaches to doing research (see Packer & Addison, 1989; Polkinghorne, 1983). However, it is our view that the new, more flexible approaches to research on psychotherapy can go a long way toward humanizing clinical research and bringing it closer to the therapist's perspective (Barker, Pistrang, & Elliott, in press). In fact, two of the main journals that publish psychotherapy research (*Journal of Consulting and Clinical Psychology* and *Journal of Counseling Psychology*) have recently adopted a set of review criteria specific to qualitative research (Elliott, 1992).

ENCOURAGE THERAPISTS TO DO RESEARCH (AND RESEARCHERS TO DO THERAPY)

Therapy research ideally should be carried out by persons who also do therapy. When the researcher is also a therapist, he or she is more likely to experience the discrepancy between research and practice as an internal conflict and thus be more motivated to pay attention to each side of this conflict.

MAINTAIN AN OPENNESS TO ALL PERSPECTIVES

In his chapter, Jay Greenberg brings up a major point about life "in the trenches" for clinicians. "Not only is it messy down here," he says, "it is *sub-*

tle." Good psychotherapy research needs to examine qualitative as well as quantitative data; and when summarizing mountains of data, it is important not to lose the essence and richness of the information collected. As noted earlier, Greenberg and others suggest that we look at psychotherapy process and outcome from varying perspectives, since all have a grain of truth. Certainly, client and therapist raters of psychotherapy process, and possibly supervisors, bring unique and valuable information to the process of understanding psychotherapy. The problem is to focus the information so that one does not lose sight of the forest of therapy in the large number of individual trees.

RECOGNIZE LIMITS OF THEORY-GUIDED RESEARCH

Theory-guided research, such as that advocated by Luborsky, Barber, and Crits-Christoph (1990), Rice and Greenberg (1984), Weiss, Sampson, et al. (1986) and others, can help maintain the focus on clinically meaningful patterns. However, theory-bound research may provide little useful information for practitioners who do not share the researchers' theoretical perspective; such research may also be limited if the theory is developed at a high level of abstraction and therefore removed from the immediate process of treatment and observable or measurable behaviors or experiences. We believe that it would be quite valuable to develop data-based theories of treatment or aspects of treatment. This could include models of what is typically helpful or hindering in specific clinical populations. One of us (CMB) is currently carrying out research aimed at developing a theory of treatment for borderline personality disorder that is based on clients' experiences of significantly helpful and hindering events in their treatment. This is accomplished by having the client fill out a Helpful Aspects of Therapy questionnaire (Llewelyn et al., 1988) after each session. Clients are also asked after each session to report on how they feel about themselves, their therapist, and various aspects of their treatment, including the therapeutic relationship. For example, a key repeating helpful theme found in the significant events data is the therapist's perceived ability to directly express caring or protectiveness of the client (such as when the therapist becomes angry on the client's behalf).

In addition, theory-building research might focus on particular kinds of change events in treatment (for example, Greenberg, Rice, & Elliott, 1993 Rhodes & Greenberg, this volume), an approach that may lend some observable and measurable criteria to help delineate what, in particular, works to help clients change in a particular treatment approach. In either case, we believe that research that attempts to build theory that is systematically grounded in the actual therapeutic process has the best chance of making itself useful to practicing therapists.

Conclusion

From our perspective, it is ultimately not the gap between researchers and therapists that is the problem but the failure to carry on a mutually challenging and facilitating dialogue. To return to our marriage metaphor, difference and conflict are part of every important relationship. It is neither possible nor healthy to avoid or cover over real differences and conflicts; instead, the art of relationship is using differences to arrive at greater truth and effectiveness in the form of "unforced consensus through open dialogue" (Gadamer, 1979). This is what we believe is needed in this situation as well. We believe that the field will be better served to the extent that researchers can be persuaded that they will be better researchers if they make greater use of their clinical skills and therapists come to see how they may become better therapists through a greater involvement in research (Elliott, Stiles, & Shapiro, 1993). As therapists and researchers, we need to help each other reach our common purpose of understanding and helping clients improve their lives. To do so, we need to build on each other's strengths and mitigate each other's weaknesses, blending our knowledge to create an end product that has clinical meaning and utility.

REFERENCES

Alexander, L. B., & Luborsky, L. (1986). The Penn Helping Alliance Scales. In L. Greenberg & W. Pinsof (Eds.), *The psychotherapeutic process* (pp. 325–366). New York: Guilford Press.

Barker, C., Pistrang, N., & Elliott, R. (in press). *Research methods in clinical and counseling psychology.* Chichester, U.K.: Wiley.

Barlow, D. H., Hayes, S. C., & Nelson, R. O. (Eds.). (1984). *The scientist practitioner: Research and accountability in clinical and educational settings.* New York: Pergamon Press.

Binns, M., Davis, J. D., Davis, M. L., Elliott, R., Francis, V. M., Kelman, J. E., & Schröder, T. A. (1989, April). *A survey of therapist difficulties and coping strategies.* Paper presented at meeting of British Society for Psychotherapy Research, Ravenscar, North York, U.K.

Blake, D. D., Abueg, F.R., & Woodward, S. H. (1993). Treatment efficacy in posttraumatic stress disorder. In T. R. Giles (Ed.), *Handbook of effective psychotherapy* (pp. 195–226). New York: Plenum.

Bordin, E. S. (1979). The generalizability of the psychoanalytic concept of working alliance. *Psychotherapy: Theory, Research and Practice, 16,* 252–260.

Caskey, N., Barker, C., & Elliott, R. (1984). Dual perspectives: Clients' and therapists' perceptions of therapist responses. *British Journal of Clinical Psychology, 23,* 281–290.

Cohen, L. H., Sargent, M. M., & Sechrest, L. B. (1986). Use of psychotherapy research by professional psychologists. *American Psychologist, 41*, 198–206.

Crits-Christoph, P. (1992). The efficacy of brief dynamic psychotherapy: A meta-analysis. *American Journal of Psychiatry, 149*, 151–158.

Crits-Christoph, P., Baranackie, K., Kurcias, J. S., Beck, A. T., Carroll, K., Perry, K., Luborsky, L., McLellan, A. T., Woody, G. E., Thompson, L., Gallagher, D., & Zitrin, C. (1991). Meta-analysis of therapist effects in psychotherapy outcome studies. *Psychotherapy, 1*, 81–91.

Dahl, H., Kächele, H., & Thomä, H. (Eds.). (1988). *Psychoanalytic process research strategies*. New York: Springer-Verlag.

Davis, J. D., Elliott, R., Davis, M. L., Binns, M., Francis, V. M., Kelman, J., & Schroeder, T. (1987). Development of a taxonomy of therapist difficulties: Initial report. *British Journal of Medical Psychology, 60*, 109–119.

Elliott, R. (1983). Fitting process research to the practicing psychotherapist. *Psychotherapy: Theory, Research & Practice, 20*, 47–55.

Elliott, R. (1989). Comprehensive process analysis: Understanding the change process in significant therapy events. In M. Packer & R. B. Addison (Eds.), *Entering the circle: Hermeneutic investigation in psychology* (pp. 165–184). Albany, NY: State University of New York Press.

Elliott, R. (1992). *Proposed criteria for evaluating qualitative research*. Unpublished manuscript, University of Toledo, Department of Psychology.

Elliot, R., & Anderson, C. (in press). Simplicity and complexity in psychotherapy research. In R. L. Russell (Ed.), *Psychotherapy research: Assessing and redirecting the tradition*. New York: Plenum.

Elliott, R., Clark, C., Wexler, M., Kemeny, V., Brinkerhoff, J., & Mack, C. (1990). The impact of experiential therapy of depression: Initial results. In G. Lietaer, J. Rombauts, & R. Van Balen (Eds.), *Client-centered and experiential psychotherapy towards the nineties* (pp. 549–577). Leuven, Belgium: Leuven University Press.

Elliott, R., James, E., Reimschuessel, C., Cislo, D., & Sack, N. (1985). Significant events and the analysis of immediate therapeutic impacts. *Psychotherapy, 22*, 620–630.

Elliott, R., & Shapiro, D. A. (1992). Clients and therapists as analysts of significant events. In S. G. Toukmanian & D. L. Rennie (Eds.), *Two perspectives on psychotherapeutic change: Theory-guided and phenomenological research strategies* (pp. 163–186). Newberry Park, CA: Sage.

Elliott, R., Stiles, W. B., & Shapiro, D. A. (1993). Are some psychotherapies more equivalent than others? In T. R. Giles (Ed.), *Handbook of effective psychotherapy* (pp. 455–479). New York: Plenum.

Gadamer, H. G. (1979). *Truth and method*. London: Sheed & Ward.

Garfield, S. L., & Bergin, A. E. (Eds.). (1986). *Handbook of psychotherapy and behavior change* (3rd ed.). New York: Wiley.

Giles, T. R., Neims, D. M., & Prial, E. M. (1993). The relative efficacy of prescriptive techniques. In T. R. Giles (Ed.), *Handbook of effective psychotherapy* (pp. 21–39). New York: Plenum.

Greenberg, L. S., Elliott, R., & Lietaer, G. (1994). Research on humanistic and experiential psychotherapies. In A. E. Bergin & S. L. Garfield (Eds.), *Handbook of psychotherapy and behavior change* (4th ed.) (pp. 509–539). New York: Wiley.

Greenberg, L. S., Rice, L. N., & Elliott, R. (1993). *Facilitating emotional change.* New York: Guilford Press.

Gurman, A. S. (1977). The patient's perception of the therapeutic relationship. In A. S. Gurman & A. M. Razin (Eds.), *Effective psychotherapy: A handbook of research* (pp. 503–543). New York: Pergamon Press.

Kazdin, A. E. (1981). Drawing valid inferences from case studies. *Journal of Consulting and Clinical Psychology, 49,* 183–192.

Labov, W., & Fanshel, D. (1977). *Therapeutic discourse.* New York: Academic Press.

Lambert, M. J. (1989). The individual therapist's contribution to psychotherapy process and outcome. *Clinical Psychology Review, 9,* 469–486.

Lambert, M. J., DeJulio, S. J., & Stein, D. M. (1978). Therapist interpersonal skills: Process, outcome, methodological considerations, and recommendations for future research. *Psychological Bulletin, 85,* 467–489.

Llewelyn, S. P., Elliott, R., Shapiro, D. A., Firth, J., & Hardy, G. (1988). Client perceptions of significant events in prescriptive and exploratory periods of individual therapy. *British Journal of Clinical Psychology, 27,* 105–114.

Luborsky, L. (1976). Helping alliances in psychotherapy. In J. L. Claghorn (Ed.), *Successful psychotherapy* (pp. 92–116). New York: Brunner/Mazel.

Luborsky, L. (1977). Measuring a pervasive psychic structure in psychotherapy: The core conflictual relationship theme. In N. Freedman (Ed.), *Communicative structures and psychic structures* (pp. 367–395). New York: Plenum.

Luborsky, L. (1984). *Principles of psychoanalytic psychotherapy: A manual for supportive-expressive treatment.* New York: Basic Books.

Luborsky, L., Barber, J. P., & Crits-Christoph, P. (1990). Theory-based research for understanding the process of dynamic psychotherapy. *Journal of Consulting and Clinical Psychology, 58,* 281–287.

Luborsky, L., & Crits-Christoph, P. (1990). *Understanding transference: The CCRT method.* New York: Basic Books.

Mahrer, A. R. (1988). Discovery-oriented psychotherapy research: Rationale, aims, and methods. *American Psychologist, 43,* 694–702.

Morrow-Bradley, C., & Elliott, R. (1986). The utilization of psychotherapy research by practicing psychotherapists. *American Psychologist, 41,* 188–197.

Orlinsky, D., Aapro, N., Backfield, J., Dazord, A., Geller, J., Rhodes, R., & the Collaborative Research Network (1991, October). *The development of a psychotherapist's core questionnaire: A new research instrument and its rationale.* Workshop presented at meeting of North American Society for Psychotherapy Research, Panama City, FL.

Orlinsky, D. E., & Howard, K. I. (1986). The psychological interior of psychotherapy: Explorations with the Therapy Session Reports. In L. Greenberg & W. Pinsof (Eds.), *The psychotherapeutic process* (pp. 477–501). New York: Guilford Press.

Packer, M. J., & Addison, R. B. (Eds.). (1989). *Entering the circle: Hermeneutic investigation in psychology*. Albany, NY: State University of New York Press.

Parry, G., Shapiro, D. A., & Firth, J. (1986). The case of the anxious executive: A study from the research clinic. *British Journal of Medical Psychology, 59,* 221–233.

Patton, M. Q. (1990). *Qualitative evaluation and research methods* (2nd ed.). Beverly Hills, CA: Sage.

Phillips, J. P. N. (1986). Shapiro Personal Questionnaire and generalized personal questionnaire techniques: A repeated measures individualized outcome measurement. In L. S. Greenberg & W. M. Pinsof (Eds.), *The psychotherapeutic process: A research handbook* (pp. 557–590). New York: Guilford Press.

Polkinghorne, D. (1983). *Methodology for the human sciences*. Albany, NY: State University of New York Press.

Rice, L. N., & Greenberg, L. (Eds.). (1984). *Patterns of change*. New York: Guilford Press.

Rice, L. N., & Sapiera, E. P. (1984). Task analysis and the resolution of problematic reactions. In L. N. Rice & L. S. Greenberg (Eds.), *Patterns of change* (pp. 29–66). New York: Guilford Press.

Rogers, C. R. (1957). The necessary and sufficient conditions of therapeutic personality change. *Journal of Consulting Psychology, 21,* 95–103.

Schön, D. (1983). *The reflection practitioner: How professionals think in action*. New York: Basic Books.

Schröder, T., Binns, M., Davis, J. D., Elliott, R., Francis, V. M., & Kelman, J. E. (1987, June). *A taxonomy of therapist coping strategies*. Paper presented at meeting of Society for Psychotherapy Research, Ulm, West Germany.

Shapiro, D. A., & Shapiro, D. (1983). Comparative therapy outcome research: Methodological implications of meta-analysis. *Journal of Consulting and Clinical Psychology, 51,* 42–53.

Sloane, R. B., Staples, F. R., Whipple, K., & Cristol, A. H. (1977). Patients' attitudes toward behavior therapy and psychotherapy. *American Journal of Psychiatry, 134,* 134–137.

Strauss, A. L., & Corbin, J. (1990). *Basics of qualitative research: Grounded theory procedures and techniques*. Beverly Hills, CA: Sage.

Toukmanian, S., & Rennie, D. L. (Eds.). (1992). *Psychotherapy process research: Paradigmatic and narrative approaches*. Newbury Park, CA: Sage.

Weiss, J., Sampson, H., & the Mount Zion Psychotherapy Research Group. (1986). *The psychoanalytic process: Theory, clinical observation and empirical research*. New York: Guilford Press.

Weisz, J. R., Weiss, B., & Donenberg, G. R. (1992). The lab versus the clinic: Effects of child and adolescent psychotherapy. *American Psychologist, 47,* 1578–1585.

CHAPTER 8

Standardization of Intervention: The Tie That Binds Psychotherapy Research and Practice

Donald J. Kiesler

OVER THE YEARS a widely voiced complaint of practicing clinicians has been that psychotherapy research is of little use to them (for example, Elliott, 1983; Kupfersmid, 1988; Luborsky, 1972; Orlinsky & Howard, 1978; Parloff, 1980; Strupp, 1989). When clinical psychologists are asked to rank order the usefulness to their practice of various sources of information, research publications are generally rated at the bottom of the scale (Cohen, 1979; Cohen, Sargent, & Sechrest, 1986; Morrow-Bradley & Elliott, 1986).

The consensus, then, seems to be that few worthwhile research findings can be applied to the clinical setting, that is, that little psychotherapy research is relevant to routine clinical practice. This conclusion seldom fails to frustrate and upset psychotherapy researchers. Has the mountain indeed produced a mouse?

My belief is that all parties have failed to appreciate that the reality cannot often be otherwise! Psychotherapeutic practice always will take the lead, with theory and research following. The hallmark role of research is *not* to innovate, *not* to discover exciting new therapeutic techniques or interventions, *not* to dramatize new learnings via enthralling clinical anecdotes. The researcher's task is of much less front-page interest. The researcher systematizes, standardizes, and operationalizes available techniques; validates promising interventions that have emerged from clinical theory and practice; and attempts to isolate and validate the essential ingredients of the change process. Seldom, if ever, can studies offer new clinical discoveries or settle theoretical controversies. In short, psychotherapy research always "plays catch-up" to psychotherapy practice.

Also, it is often the case that available research findings need to be translated and integrated to various degrees before they can appreciably affect the practicing clinician. As Kernberg and Clarkin (this volume) state: "The body of clinical research is useful to clinicians only if it is integrated. This integration must involve clinical judgment; that is, clinicians and researchers alike must contribute to this integration."

Having stated these provisos, I nevertheless conclude that psychotherapy research can contribute significantly to clinical practice. Havens (this volume) creatively applies to his clinical cases a methodological framework (the "change event") first articulated by a clinical researcher (Greenberg, 1986; Rice & Greenberg, 1984). In doing so, Havens compellingly illustrates how a methodological paradigm can guide the clinician, in this case through the very systematic process of (1) identification of adverse patient states (client "markers") that surface during sessions, (2) administration of interventions designed to ameliorate these states, and (3) administration of measures designed to show positive client changes away from the original adverse state (toward resolution of the patient's affective problem). It is difficult to see how any reader could not appreciate the conceptual clarity, empathic head start, and interventive efficiency that have been brought to bear by Havens through his clinical application of this research-derived methodological focus. What this "patterns of change" approach offers, and Havens demonstrates, is a clearly innovative model of single-case analysis for both psychotherapy research and practice that can by itself span the apparent gulf between researcher and clinician.

Kernberg and Clarkin (this volume) remind us that one cannot find "all-good guys" or "all-bad guys" when discussing clinical research, only individuals pursuing the constantly evolving question of how to "integrate research and its relevant results into clinical practice for the optimal care of the patient." Kernberg and Clarkin outline, for borderline personality disorder patients, their "differential therapeutics" paradigm, which concentrates on the "application of principles derived from research and clinical experience in matching the individual patient to the most efficacious treatment." They cogently argue, and their training/research team illustrates, that "our field can only progress if patient care is advanced by active research, which in turn will only be as good as the clinical experience upon which it is based. . . . The process of integration, which can only be carried out within the individual, is fostered by a training experience that exposes the individual to both research and clinical work."

Thus far in our discussion, then, it seems that the answer to whether psychotherapy research findings have any relevance to the practicing clinician is a relative one, one that depends crucially upon the findings and the particular clinician. In the remainder of this chapter, the thesis I want to develop is much bolder, namely, that it is no longer valid to assert that psychotherapy research has little, if anything, to provide the clinical practitioner. It is my view that any person continuing to make the claim of irrelevance can be doing so only in ignorance of a major recent development in psychotherapy research.

Psychotherapy Treatment Manuals

A major revolution in the relationship between psychotherapy research and practice occurred when researchers began to standardize and operationalize the psychotherapy treatments that were to be evaluated in large-scale clinical trials and comparative outcome studies. The position crystallized that research on the efficacy of a particular psychotherapy or on the relative benefits of different types of psychotherapy needed to include at a minimum the following three empirical components: (1) a definitive description of the principles and techniques of each form of psychotherapy; (2) a clear statement of the operations the therapist is supposed to perform (presenting each technique as concretely as possible, as well as providing examples of each); and (3) a measure of the degree to which the therapist conforms to the techniques in his or her experimental therapy sessions.

These three basic requirements came to constitute the three essential components of a psychotherapy treatment manual (Luborsky, 1984; Luborsky & DeRubeis, 1984; Luborsky, Woody, McLellan, O'Brian, & Rosenzweig, 1982). This treatment manual requirement, imposed as a routine design demand, chiseled permanently into the edifice of psychotherapy outcome research the basic scientific canon of standardization. What was being evaluated was no longer some vaguely specified psychotherapy but, for example, cognitive therapy for depressives as operationalized ("manualized") by Beck, Rush, Shaw, and Emery (1979).

Since their appearance during the late 1970s, treatment manuals have come to be routinely utilized in clinical trials and comparative studies of psychotherapy. By far the largest and best-known study using these manuals is the National Institute of Mental Health (NIMH) Collaborative Study of Depression (DeRubeis, Hollon, Evans, & Bemis, 1982; Elkin, Parloff, Hadley, & Autry, 1985), which compared interpersonal psychotherapy (Klerman, Weissman, Rounsaville, & Chevron, 1984), cognitive-behavioral psychotherapy (Beck, Rush, Shaw, & Emery, 1979), and psychopharmacotherapy.

What has become abundantly established since their introduction is that routine use of treatment manuals in psychotherapy research (1) provides for more objective comparisons of psychotherapies, revealing the ways in which psychotherapies are distinct from each other or overlap; (2) offers more precise measurement of the degree to which each therapist provides what is recommended in the manual, the level of conformity perhaps reflecting the therapist's skill and perhaps also predicting differential outcomes of the psychotherapy; and (3) facilitates improved training of therapists in the specific form of psychotherapy. By training participating therapists in comparative efficacy studies to use manuals and then rating them on manual-based categories, it is possible to measure what is actually delivered, both by type of treatment and by individual therapists providing the treatment.

The manual format has been found to be useful also in the more general training of practicing therapists. Besides its obvious benefit to novice therapists, a manual helps experienced therapists to define their interventions and improve their skills and can serve as a resource during supervision. Manuals are written with special empathy for the therapist's task through their delineation of the principles the therapist should follow in understanding the patient's communications. They provide concise rationale and definitions, clinical guidelines, and case illustrations for the training of therapists in the given interventions. If the clinician wants additional precision, the manuals have available as companion research material coding systems that were developed to provide experimental checks on the integrity with which individual clinicians learned and applied the particular psychotherapeutic treatment.

Kernberg and Clarkin describe in the present volume their use of a manual for the psychotherapeutic treatment for borderline patients (Kernberg, Selzer, Koenigsberg, Carr, & Appelbaum, 1989) and elsewhere detail its application in a preliminary clinical trials study (Clarkin et al., 1992). Simultaneous availability of a manual-based cognitive-behavioral treatment for borderlines (Linehan, 1984) will eventually permit a study comparing the relative efficacies of the two treatment approaches. Importantly, any practicing clinician seeking relevant psychotherapeutic approaches for borderline patients can find a mine of clinical wisdom and procedure systematized in either of these treatment manuals.

In sum, one of the major contributions that psychotherapy research already offers, and will continue to offer, to practicing clinicians is a growing armamentarium of treatment manuals (and companion coding systems) that standardize and operationalize the various psychotherapeutic treatments that have been developed for distinct patient disorders or groups.

Further, as robust research findings from clinical trials and comparative treatment studies using these treatment manuals begin to accumulate, researchers will be able to make more confident recommendations regarding the treatment of choice for particular disorders. For example, based on the findings of the NIMH Collaborative Study of Depression, researchers tentatively can recommend to clinicians working with major depressive (as defined by the American Psychiatric Association's [1987] *DSM-III-R*) patients that psychotherapy is more effective on a long-term basis than antidepressant medication and that either the cognitive behavior therapy of Beck et al.

(1979) or the interpersonal psychotherapy of Klerman et al. (1984) will serve nicely as the psychotherapy of choice.

Stage Models of Psychotherapy

It is important to realize that standardization of psychotherapeutic treatment can occur at all levels—"macro" to "micro"—of the temporal course of psychotherapy. The treatment manuals (Luborsky, 1984; Luborsky & DeRubeis, 1984) discussed so far specify the treatment at its most "macro" level by defining the rules and interventions that obtain from the first to the terminal session of psychotherapy. Manuals define at the most general level the therapist techniques or operations that may (and may not) occur at any time during the therapy sessions.

As Greenberg (1986) notes, however, the real task

> of describing what is actually occurring in a particular therapy remains unaddressed by manual-guided research. Manuals do not provide sufficient control of the variables affecting treatment delivery nor do they allow any statement as to the nature of the active ingredients of the treatment. Although the manuals specify the components, they do not sequence or prioritize these components. Nor do they provide adequate descriptions of the complex, multidimensional variables involved in the therapist behaviors which are needed to describe not only the type but also the manner and the quality of the behaviors. (p. 727)

Fortunately, a more intermediate level of standardization can be offered that addresses some of these deficiencies of treatment manuals by carefully conceptualizing the separate temporal chunks in which a set of interventions occur. Cashdan (1973), for example, proposes a general process-stage model in which process consists of a series of stages each of which is composed of a set of therapist rules and techniques along with a predicted behavioral shift in the patient.

In Cashdan's framework, a psychotherapeutic treatment might consist, say, of three stages: a first set of interviews during which the therapist's goal is to establish a therapeutic bond with the patient, a second set in which the therapist's goal is to frustrate the patient's maladaptive interpersonal behaviors during the session, and a final set during which the goal is to explore the benefits of new interpersonal behaviors both with the therapist and with significant others. In line with Cashdan's model, each of the three stages needs to be carefully defined as consisting of a set of therapist rules and techniques along with an associated behavioral shift in the patient. (Rules are principles that govern the therapist's behavioral responses; techniques are the concrete responses of the therapist.)

Examples of specific interpersonal process-stage models proposed for therapy can be found in Anchin and Kiesler (1982) and Cashdan (1988). A proto-typical operational translation of a process-stage model for patients with dysthymia can be found in McCullough (1984) and McCullough and Carr (1987). Interestingly, one can find in Kernberg and Clarkin's chapter in the present volume, the rudimentary beginnings of an intermediate level stage model within their treatment for borderline patients. They note that treatment response tends to involve, first, "some change in the impulsive behavior," which is followed by "some control of affect modulation" and then "gradual change in identity formation." Should Kernberg and Clarkin decide to adopt Cashdan's stage model, their manual-based treatment could be systematically modified to incorporate the three-step order of change into a formal three-stage process model of treatment.

Standardized Intervention Modules

We obviously can move to more micro levels of intervention than stages, to interventions that might be identified and defined within the context of a single session. The techniques (therapist operations) defined globally in treatment manuals, and defined in more detail in stage models, are actually applied by therapists during particular instances within individual psychotherapy sessions. As part of an overall treatment package, therapist-initiated miniature interventions are plugged in at various appropriate moments of therapy sessions.

At a highly "micro" unit of analysis, a standardization of intervention is possible that is similar to what would be required of an "intervention module" (Hudgins & Kiesler, 1987). An intervention module refers to

> an independent, functionally organized unit of therapy activity (1) which is initiated by the therapist upon identification within the session of a specific deficient experiential and/or behavioral state of the patient, (2) which consists of a specifiable optimal sequence of therapist actions and patient reactions, (3) for which sequence the start-and-stop points can be clearly demarcated, and (4) which has as its objective a facilitative amelioration, over the start-to-stop period, of the patient's originally identified specific deficient functioning. (Hudgins & Kiesler, 1987, p. 246)

Examples of intervention modules are empty-chair dialogues, systematic situational analyses, behavioral rehearsals, role enactments, imagery explorations, and metacommunicative feedback. Successful application of any one of these modules may require part of a session or the entire session but no more than one or two therapy sessions.

Hudgins and Kiesler (1987) evaluated the effectiveness of the intervention module of "psychodramatic doubling," which they have elaborated in a manual (Hudgins & Kiesler, 1984). The intervention is a modification for individual psychotherapy of Moreno and Moreno's (1969) use of a "double" or group member who is asked by the leader to adopt the nonverbal posture of a second "protagonist" group member. In line with Cashdan's (1973) process-stage model, the intervention module of doubling was standardized by Hudgins and Kiesler (1984) in the form of three separate stages, each associated with rules for therapist behavior as well as specific behavioral criteria that defined expected behavioral shifts or improvements in the patient. In Stage 1 the therapist's focus is exclusively intrapsychic, with the therapist serving as a catalyst to stimulate the patient's awareness of personal thoughts, feelings, action tendencies, and nonverbal behaviors. Therapist rules include speaking in the first person singular, mirroring the patient's nonverbal behaviors, and targeting intrapsychic awareness. Stage 2 focuses on sharpening and accenting the patient's covert interpersonal experience as the patient dialogues with an imagined significant other in an empty chair. Therapist rules for Stage 1 continue except that interpersonal thoughts, feelings, and so on are now the target of therapist verbalizations. Stage 3 returns to an intrapsychic focus to assist the patient in creating and expanding the meaning of experiences clarified in the previous stages. It consists of a modified version of Gendlin's (1981) "focusing" instruction and is designed to facilitate symbolization of cognitive meanings as they emerge from the experiential felt meanings elicited in the previous stages.

Hudgins and Kiesler (1987) found unusually consistent confirmation of the effectiveness of the doubling intervention module when they administered it to subjects in a simulated therapy situation. The doubling intervention was found to be significantly more effective in increasing experiential self-disclosure over the course of the session than was a standard intake interview stance using open-ended questions and tracking/reflective statements. Furthermore, plottings of each subject's profile of disclosure over the three stages showed remarkable mirroring of the group profile.

Interestingly, in the present volume we can find examples of this micro level of intervention standardization in Havens's chapter, which exemplifies the power of Greenberg's (1986) "change event" paradigm in routine psychotherapeutic practice. The reader will note that throughout his chapter, Havens implicitly articulates an intervention manual designed to guide the therapist's optimal response to each of the seven instances of therapy impasse. In each case the recommended intervention is in "three parts: [therapist's] physical position, content of [therapist's] speech, and emotional force of the intervenor."

Conclusion

I hope I have illuminated how standardization of therapeutic intervention can significantly enhance communication and dialogue between clinician and researcher. It should be abundantly clear that therapist interventions come in different sizes. We have encountered standardization of psychotherapy treatment at various analytic levels all the way from macro to micro, that is, from treatment manuals that globally define the ingredients of a total treatment package, through stage models that define these ingredients as successively occurring in chunks over the temporal course of therapy, to intervention modules ("change events" and the like) that standardize miniature interventions that can transpire within a single session.

It seems quite easy for clinician and researcher to understand and learn from each other once this single routine methodological prerequisite is mutually accepted, that is, that we operationalize and standardize for each other our interventions of interest. Operationalized intervention manuals, from macro to micro levels, dramatically facilitate communication and dialogue between psychotherapy practitioners and researchers. Through use of these manuals one can not only standardize treatment but also directly train and supervise therapists.

Our intervention manuals, and the coding systems that accompany them, provide a common language for technique and intervention and directly reflect what Pinsof (1981) named the principle of "reconstructivity," that is, the ability of a psychotherapy coding system to permit clinically meaningful reconstruction of therapeutic process and events from the specific code data. To the extent that a given method or measure is reconstructive, the boundaries between research and practice/training are removed. With high reconstructivity, our process measures can not only be useful for research but can also serve as standardized tools for training and therapy.

Our shared goal, as clinicians and researchers, is to understand important or critical patient-change events that can be observed in the psychotherapy session itself. Heuristic psychotherapy research

> attempts to identify and measure the more proximal patient-change events that occur in the therapy sessions themselves as well as the therapist activity and other transactional events that are contributory to these specific patient behavioral shifts. It further attempts to conceptualize and measure the hookups of specific in-session patient shifts (a) to concurrent extra-therapy patient shifts and (b) to later both in-session and extra-therapy patient changes. The cumulative empirical charting of these successive stages of events and their network of interrelationships throughout the entire therapy course and follow-up periods represents a comprehensive explanation of the process-outcome of a particular therapy case. (Kiesler, 1983, p. 4)

In conclusion, recent standardization of psychotherapeutic intervention has led to an armamentarium of well-developed manuals of the psychotherapy change process that are available to us all as we pursue the goal of a more meaningful and comprehensive understanding of psychotherapy. These manuals will continue to permit both robust empirical answers through efficacy studies and an evolving operational language that can form the common basis for theory, research, and training in psychotherapy. Most of all, they have begun the process of tearing down the mythical "iron curtains" that have been arbitrarily hung between the purposes and activities of clinical researchers and practitioners.

REFERENCES

American Psychiatric Association. (1987). *Diagnostic and statistical manual of mental disorders* (3rd ed., rev.). Washington, DC: Author.

Anchin, J. C., & Kiesler, D. J. (Eds.). (1982). *Handbook of interpersonal psychotherapy.* Elmsford, NY: Pergamon Press.

Beck, A. T., Rush, A. J., Shaw, B. F., & Emery, G. (1979). *Cognitive therapy of depression.* New York: Guilford Press

Cashdan, S. (1973). *Interactional psychotherapy: Stages and strategies in behavior change.* New York: Grune & Stratton.

Cashdan, S. (1988). *Object relations therapy: Using the relationship.* New York: Norton.

Clarkin, J. F., Koenigsberg, H., Yeomans, F., Selzer, M., Kernberg, P., & Kernberg, O. F. (1992). Psychodynamic psychotherapy of the borderline patient. In J. F. Clarkin, E. Marziali, & H. Munroe-Blum (Eds.), *Borderline personality disorder: Clinical and empirical perspectives.* New York: Guilford Press.

Cohen, L. (1979). The research readership and information source reliance of clinical psychologists. *Professional Psychology, 10,* 780–785.

Cohen. L., Sargent, M., & Sechrest, L. (1986). Use of psychotherapy research by professional psychologists. *American Psychologist, 41,* 198–206.

DeRubeis, R., Hollon, S., Evans, M., & Bemis, K. (1982). Can psychotherapies for depression be discriminated? A systematic investigation of cognitive therapy and interpersonal therapy. *Journal of Consulting and Clinical Psychology, 50,* 744–756.

Elkin, I., Parloff, M. B., Hadley, S. W., & Autry, J. H. (1985). NIMH Treatment of Depression Collaborative Research Program: Background and research plan. *Archives of General Psychiatry, 42,* 305–316.

Elliott, R. (1983). Fitting process research to the practicing psychotherapist. *Psychotherapy: Theory, Research and Practice, 20,* 47–55.

Gendlin, E. T. (1981). *Focusing.* New York: Bantam Books.

Greenberg, L. S. (1986). Research strategies. In L. S. Greenberg & W. M. Pinsof (Eds.), *The psychotherapeutic process: A research handbook* (pp. 707–734). New York: Guilford Press.

Hudgins, M. K., & Kiesler, D. J. (1984). *Instructional manual for doubling in individual psychotherapy*. Richmond, VA: Virginia Commonwealth University.

Hudgins, M. K., & Kiesler, D. J. (1987). Individual experiential psychotherapy: An analogue validation of the intervention module of psychodramatic doubling. *Psychotherapy, 24,* 245–255.

Kernberg, O., Selzer, M., Koenigsberg, H., Carr, A., & Appelbaum, A. (1989). *Psychodynamic psychotherapy of borderline patients*. New York: Basic Books.

Kiesler, D. J. (1983). *The paradigm shift in psychotherapy process research*. Summary discussant paper presented at the NIMH Workshop on Psychotherapy Process Research, Bethesda, MD.

Klerman, G. L., Weissman, M. M., Rounsaville, B. J., & Chevron, E. S. (1984). *Interpersonal psychotherapy of depression*. New York: Basic Books.

Kupfersmid, J. (1988). Improving what is published: A model in search of an editor. *American Psychologist, 43,* 635–642.

Linehan, M. M. (1984). *Dialectical behavior therapy for treatment of parasuicidal women: Treatment manual*. Unpublished manuscript, University of Washington, Seattle.

Luborsky, L. (1972). Research cannot yet influence clinical practice. In A. E. Bergin & H. H. Strupp (Eds.), *Changing frontiers in the science of psychotherapy* (pp. 120–127). Chicago, IL: Aldine.

Luborsky, L. (1984). *Principles of psychoanalytic psychotherapy*. New York: Basic Books.

Luborsky, L., & DeRubeis, R. J. (1984). The use of psychotherapy treatment manuals: A small revolution in psychotherapy research style. *Clinical Psychology Review, 4,* 5–14.

Luborsky, L., Woody, G., McLellan, A., O'Brian, C., & Rosenzweig, J. (1982). Can independent judges recognize different psychotherapies? An experience with manual guided therapies. *Journal of Consulting and Clinical Psychology, 50,* 49–62.

McCullough, J. P. (1984). Cognitive-behavioral analysis system of psychotherapy: An interactional treatment approach for dysthymic disorder. *Psychiatry, 47,* 234–250.

McCullough, J. P., & Carr, K. F. (1987). Stage process design: A predictive confirmation structure for the single case. *Psychotherapy, 24,* 759–768.

Moreno, J. L., & Moreno, Z. T. (1969). *Psychodrama: Action therapy and principles of practice*. Beacon, NY: Beacon House Press.

Morrow-Bradley, C., & Elliott, R. (1986). Utilization of psychotherapy research by practicing psychotherapists. *American Psychologist, 41,* 188–197.

Orlinsky, D., & Howard, K. (1978). The relation of process to outcome in psychotherapy. In S. L. Garfield & A. E. Bergin (Eds.), *Handbook of psychotherapy and behavior change: An empirical analysis* (2nd ed., pp. 283–330). New York: Wiley.

Parloff, M. B. (1980). Psychotherapy and research: An anaclitic depression. *Psychiatry, 43,* 279–293.

Pinsof, W. M. (1981). Family therapy process research. In A. Gurman & D. Kniskern (Eds.), *Handbook of family therapy* (pp. 699–741). New York: Brunner/Mazel.

Rice, L. N., & Greenberg, L. S. (Eds.). (1984). *Patterns of change: Intensive analysis of psychotherapy process.* New York: Guilford Press.

Strupp, H. H. (1989). Psychotherapy: Can the practitioner learn from the researcher? *American Psychologist, 44,* 717–724.

CHAPTER 9

Views of the Chasm Between Psychotherapy Research and Practice

William B. Stiles

I N THEIR CHAPTERS of this volume describing their views of the chasm between research and practice, Marshall Edelson and Jay Greenberg have posed some challenging questions and advanced some intriguing suggestions. In my response, I consider these issues from two of my own viewpoints.

In brief, I suggest, from a traditional hypothesis-testing viewpoint, research should not be expected to contribute to clinical practice except negatively, by discrediting approaches that fail to fulfill their claims. On the other hand, if research encompasses interpretive, qualitative approaches, then clinical practice, properly reported, *is* research.

Hypothesis-Testing Research Consumes Practitioners' Ideas

From a traditional hypothesis-testing viewpoint, psychotherapy researchers may be considered more accurately as consumers of practitioners' ideas than as producers of new ideas for practice (Stiles, 1992). Hypothesis-testing research works by discrediting ideas, and in psychotherapy research these ideas are derived primarily from clinical theories and clinical lore.

This chapter was written while the author was a Visiting Fellow at the MRC/ESRC Social and Applied Psychology Unit, University of Sheffield, Sheffield, United Kingdom, supported in part by Senior International Fellowship number 1 F06 TW01808-01 from the Fogarty International Center of the National Institutes of Health.

A traditional scientific study can only falsify or fail to falsify the ideas that guided it. According to Popper's (1934/1959) familiar argument, the failure of a prediction logically disconfirms the theory, by *modus tolens*. Research "support" for a theory amounts to affirming the consequent, a classical logical fallacy; other theories could have predicted the same result.

Critics from Kuhn (1970) to Meehl (1990) have pointed out that the Popperian account is overly simplistic and misleading. For a variety of reasons, scientific theories are seldom, if ever, vulnerable to definitive disconfirmation, and the central tenets of theories (paradigms, research programs) are rarely tested directly. Nevertheless, even the critics agree that the logic of scientific studies is to discredit ideas rather than to produce them. Research results occasionally suggest new ideas, but these are by-products.

Understanding psychotherapy research as quality control on theories helps explain why surveys show that most practitioners ignore psychotherapy research reports, finding them narrow and tedious overemphasizing methodology and statistics (Cohen, Sargent, & Sechrest, 1986; Morrow-Bradley & Elliott, 1986; Raush, 1974). Traditional hypothesis-testing research (including process as well as outcome research and correlational studies as well as clinical trials and experimental designs) involves deriving some testable consequence from a clinical theory and measuring the relevant variables. At best, a study's hypothesis is a narrow, focused fragment of an existing theory. Reports of the research manipulations and measurements are necessarily technical and detailed, so that other researchers can assess whether the results indeed bear on the theory. Thus, it is not surprising that research reports offer practitioners little that is new and much that is only tangentially relevant to their practice.

Hypothesis testing can influence professional practice in the long run, as discredited ideas (for example, that bottle feeding causes neurosis) are weeded out. However, in the century since Freud began using the talking cure, psychotherapy practitioners and theorists have produced ideas far faster than researchers can consume them. Although hundreds of therapies have been described and implemented (Herink, 1980; Karasu, 1986), relatively few of their processes and outcomes have been rigorously researched.

In summary, critics who call for psychotherapy research that directly enriches practice may expect too much. Researchers may look to practitioners in deciding which hypotheses to test but need not feel compelled to generate new ideas for practice.

MARSHALL EDELSON'S CHAPTER FROM THE HYPOTHESIS-TESTING VIEWPOINT

Even though Edelson criticizes psychotherapy research, the position taken in his chapter is, I think, surprisingly consonant with the hypothesis-testing view. In the first few pages he underlines the different perspectives and purposes of practitioners and researchers, suggesting, for example, (1) that therapists are interested in the particulars of cases whereas researchers are interested in principles and generalities and (2) that evidence of a treatment's absolute or relative effectiveness or ineffectiveness (the expectable result of psychotherapy outcome research) is useful primarily at a policy level and offers little day-to-day help to a psychotherapist who is already engaged in treating a particular patient. He seems to concur that critics ask more of hypothesis-testing research than it can deliver and that psychotherapists should not expect to find practical help in psychotherapy research journals.

As the chapter proceeds, Edelson joins forces with the researchers. Enacting the view of practitioners as producers of psychotherapy research ideas (for researchers to consume), he points to several interesting phenomena, which I think, can be starting points for psychological research and theory. He focuses attention on the therapist's internal processes, highlighting (1) the important role of the therapist's being reminded of something by the patient's words or actions; (2) the content of such memories as being stories or scenes rather than theories or general techniques;[1] and (3) the source of the memories as being not scientific findings but personal experience—as a therapist, apprentice, friend, husband, father, and child—and works of art, movies, plays, and novels. "What determines that you will be reminded of this particular rather than that particular by what your patient says?" he asks. "Why are you reminded of one scene or event whereas another psychotherapist who hears an account of what the patient said will be reminded of some other scene or event? . . . Where, oh where, is *that* psychotherapy research?" (p.68).

Perhaps even more importantly, Edelson proposes a coherent theory of the therapeutic process. Briefly, patients' stories and actions are considered as versions of an unconscious master story, endlessly (and problematically) repeated, in which the patient attempts (unconsciously and unsuccessfully) to fulfill an old wish or improve a previously adverse or painful outcome. The therapist follows these stories wherever they lead, looking for similarities in the patient's productions. Eventually, having understood the story with the therapist's help, the patient is empowered to escape its grip.

Edelson's master story theory, like most psychotherapy theories, was drawn from its author's clinical practice. It could be a rich source of hypothe-

---

[1]Of course, Edelson is a mature and skilled therapist, and, like any skilled worker, his use of fundamental principles is automatic. He no longer needs to rehearse consciously the psychoanalytic precepts on which his interventions are based. Indeed, his performance might deteriorate if he were to focus his attention on such details, like a skilled typist focusing on finger movements. But no doubt he could reconstruct reasons for a particular action if he were asked to do so. The general theories are incorporated within his framework of action, as Edelson acknowledges when he later points out that his whole approach is subordinate to a psychodynamic view of the therapeutic enterprise.

ses for research. Recognizing this potential, Edelson goes on to list some of the puzzles that a researcher would have to solve: how to define the central concept of story, how to locate stories within a transcript, how to identify repeated instances of a particular story reliably, how to classify stories that have been identified, and so forth.

Thus, far from being revolutionary in kind, Edelson's contribution follows the typical pattern of drawing on clinical practitioners' experience to enrich theory and research. Further, as Edelson points out, the master story theory is not an isolated idea but one that is well rooted in the psychodynamic tradition.

Indeed, the master story theory very strongly recalls the research of Teller and Dahl (1986; Dahl, 1988), who use the term *frame* to describe the basic plot line that patients repeatedly tell and enact. These researchers have made substantial progress on some of the puzzles that Edelson identifies, such as defining stories (frames), locating them in transcripts, and identifying repeated instances. Teller and Dahl would probably appreciate an acknowledgment of their precedence, but I think there is credit enough to go around. The master story version includes details that enrich the frame conception, and the theoretical convergence helps convince me that this line of research is worth following.

But, of course, hypothesis-testing research will only assess whether the theory fits with systematic observation. At best, such research can only fail to falsify this approach; it will not contribute new ideas for clinical application. The theory, which may usefully focus therapists' attention on patients' stories, already exists. Success in research—solving the technical puzzles (for example, finding reliably identifiable repetitions of master stories)—may help clinicians retain their confidence in the theory, but it won't solve the clinical puzzles. Practitioners would still have to work to figure out the next patient's master story.

It may be that Edelson's objection to psychotherapy research boils down to researchers not studying the theory that he happens to use. If so, Teller and Dahl's (1986; Dahl, 1988) research should be a counterexample for him. But probably his objection will not be so easily overcome. I suspect that the details of, for example, the procedures and statistics needed to show that repetitions of stories can be reliably identified in session transcripts, which are essential in reports of research on this theory, would be of little direct use or interest to practicing clinicians, unless they happen to be theorists or researchers as well. That is, practitioners would find reports of hypothesis-testing research on Edelson's theory just as tedious and overdetailed and irrelevant to their practice as they find reports of research on other clinical theories.

Greenberg's chapter offers a more profound challenge to hypothesis-testing research, according to my reading of it. Greenberg tells a partly imaginary story of a transference interpretation by a therapist to a patient ("You want me to be the mad scientist. . . "), which is subsumed and reinterpreted as counter-transference by a supervisor, which reinterpretation is in turn subsumed and reinterpreted as parallel process (therapist is to patient as supervisor is to ther-apist) by a consultant. The story is one of constantly shifting frames of refer-ence. The interpretation changes as the evidence from different perspectives rolls in. What is constructed is not a theory but a progression of theories.

Although it is imaginary, Greenberg's story has great plausibility for me as a clinician and, I suspect, for other clinicians. To respond to Greenberg, I need to summarize an alternative to the hypothesis-testing view of research.

The Qualitative Alternative

Qualitative, interpretive research represents a contrasting viewpoint (Stiles, 1990, 1993). It offers an alternative approach to formulating trustworthy statements about the world of observation, which I consider to be the aim of science. I think it can help bridge—or even close—the chasm between psy-chotherapy research and practice. The qualitative alternative encompasses traditional hypothesis testing but extends beyond it in ways that include the following:

1. In qualitative research, results tend to be expressed in words rather than exclusively in numbers. Dialogues, narratives, and so forth, are pre-sented and analyzed without being coded or rated or otherwise reduced to numbers.

2. Qualitative research often uses empathy as a legitimate observation strategy. Whereas traditional psychological research counts people's ex-ternally observable behavior as data, qualitative research additionally uses the investigator's understanding of their experience. Thus, qualita-tive research encompasses meanings, including the purposes and signifi-cance that people attach to what they say or do.

3. Qualitative research is typically interpreted and reported contextu-ally. Events are understood and reported in their unique context, rather than isolated. This represents an acknowledgment that no two things are exactly alike.

4. Qualitative research recognizes what I call the polydimensionality of experience. Variation in human experience is not confined to just a few dimensions. Every experience and every descriptor of experience can be considered as a new dimension.

5. Qualitative research admits nonlinear causality. Systems that incorporate feedback (that is, nonlinear systems) often behave unpredictably, or chaotically (Gleick, 1987; Prigogene & Stengers, 1984). Even though such a system is completely deterministic, predicting its behavior more than a few steps in advance may be impossible due to sensitive dependence on initial conditions. Trivial differences in starting points can be compounded and can lead to enormous differences in outcomes. In psychotherapy, for example, therapists continually adjust their behavior in light of what seems to be working. If the client doesn't give an intelligible answer, the therapist asks the question again or puts it a different way. In this sort of interaction a seemingly minor event—the phrasing of some intervention, perhaps—can initiate an unexpected chain of reactions with unpredictable results.

Because it is linguistic, empathic, contextual, polydimensional, and nonlinear, qualitative research adopts a more tentative epistemology than that of hypothesis-testing research. It shifts the goal of quality control from the truth of statements to understanding by people. It does this by revealing rather than avoiding personal involvement in the process of observing and interpreting and by evaluating interpretations according to their impact on people.

EVALUATING QUALITATIVE RESEARCH

The interpretive approach assumes that objectivity is impossible because scientific observers and authors are always people. Because observations cannot be detached from the people who make them, understanding the observations entails understanding the observers, including their personal and political views as well as the theory they are using. Therefore, far from advocating impersonality and detachment, an emerging canon of good practice asks investigators to disclose their initial orientation, expectations, and preconceptions; their social and cultural context; and their internal processes during the investigation. Good practice further recommends immersion in the data (through personal contact with participants or intimate familiarity with a text, prolonged engagement, persistent observation, and discussion of preliminary interpretations with other investigators and by actively seeking disconfirming data and checking participants' reactions) and systematic grounding of interpretations (explicit procedures for linking relatively abstract interpretations with relatively concrete observations).

The epistemological shift of emphasis from the truth of statements to understanding by people has fostered alternative criteria for evaluating the validity of interpretations. These criteria, which I have compiled from others' writings (Stiles, 1990, 1993), can be cross-classified (1) by whose understand-

Table 9.1   Typology of Validity in Qualitative Research

	Type of impact	
People impacted	Fit or agreement	Change or growth
Readers (consumers)	Coherence	Self-evidence; Uncovering
Participants	Testimonial validity	Catalytic validity
Investigators and the theory	Consensus; Replication	Reflexive validity

ing is considered (the reader's, the participant's, or the investigator's) and (2) by whether the impact is one of simple fit or agreement with preconceptions versus change or growth in understanding (table 9.1). Impacts on readers include coherence (internal consistency, comprehensiveness of the elements and their interrelations, usefulness in encompassing new elements and rival interpretations) and uncovering (whether the interpretation solves the problem that motivated the inquiry), or self-evidence (whether it feels right in the context of all of the reader's other beliefs). Impacts on participants included testimonial validity (whether participants allude, directly or indirectly, to being seen and understood; whether their reactions, favorable or not, are consistent with the interpretation's motifs) and catalytic validity (whether participants are impelled to reveal fresh and deeper material; the degree to which the research process reorients, focuses, and energizes participants; whether they are empowered to take more control of their lives). Impacts on investigators and the guiding theory include consensus (agreement with an interpretation by multiple investigators who were familiar with the raw data), or replication (whether an interpretation fits two or more independent sets of observations), and reflexive validity (whether the theory and the investigators' beliefs are changed by the data and the interpretation).

An overriding principle is triangulation, which simply means assessing convergence of information from multiple data sources, multiple methods, multiple theories, and multiple validity criteria. Each of the validity types (table 9.1) is subject to distortion; no one of them alone can ensure that an interpretation is trustworthy. However, other things being equal, each one can add a measure of confidence, so that interpretations that meet several or many of them are more trustworthy than interpretations that do not.

Evaluating validity by growth or change in people's ideas (the right-hand column of table 9.1) implies that interpretation is in a dialectical relationship with observation. In traversing the "hermeneutic circle" (Packer & Addison, 1989), an interpretation, being applied to observations and then being reviewed through them, should change. New ideas emerge from a living theory, as it encounters new data and is acted upon by new minds.

ALTERNATIVE FORMS OF DISCOURSE

The epistemological shift supports a rhetorical one. Qualitative research in psychology has moved beyond the traditional restriction to didactic discourse into hermeneutic and narrative forms.

Didactic discourse reflects a search for general truth using logic (Bruner, 1986). It advances lawlike generalizations, however qualified and hedged.

Hermeneutic discourse is superficially similar to didactic discourse, but with an important difference: each interpretation is offered not as a candidate final account but as a step in a continuing cycle of reframing. When didactic accounts change, the revision is advanced as a closer approximation to the truth; hermeneutic interpretation makes no such claim because it recognizes no possibility of unchanging truth (Packer & Addison, 1989; Woolfolk, Sass, & Messer, 1988). This discourse assumes that multiple viewpoints can be informative and enriching. Systematic evaluation of each succeeding alternative is important, and while it may sometimes be possible to decide between alternatives by triangulation, this does not imply movement toward a final answer.

Narrative discourse reflects a search for meaningful connections (for example, causal, temporal, correspondence) between specific events (Bruner, 1986). A story has a point. It constructs reality according to some internal logic. Events have to be sorted and made intelligible. Details have to be sacrificed, selected, emphasized, sequenced, viewed from different angles. A story without an underlying interpretation is a mere chronicle of events (cf. Mitchell, 1981; Robinson & Hawpe, 1986; White, 1980). Thus, the point of a story can be considered as a latent theoretical assertion.

Narratives offer an alternative to science's usual connotation-stripping path for saying the same thing to everybody (cf. Howard, 1991; Russell, 1991; Vitz, 1990). One familiar version, the case study method, has long been a principal form for scientific discourse in fields from anthropology to surgery. Stories can record the possibilities and limits of what people may do, even when we cannot predict what they will do. They enable us to prepare for a range of eventualities. Stories about therapy can build a repertoire of demonstrated process–outcome relationships—scenarios that permit recognition of similar situations as they arise during interviews, along with actions that may be effective in those situations.

Narratives seem well adapted for reporting qualitative research (Mishler, 1986; Polkinghorne, 1988). Stories are linguistic. They facilitate empathy with the protagonist (Bruner, 1986, 1987), creating and enriching the meaning of statements through the empathic response of putting oneself in the role of the other (Gusfield, 1990). Stories supply their own context; we do not have to specify the conditions under which they will hold. And by tracing a causal path from initial conditions to their unpredicted consequences in a particular case, stories can deal with nonlinear causality, that is, with behavior that is deterministic but unpredictable in the long term. As a form for presenting interpretations, stories are inherently tentative; they apply an interpretation to a single case and leave the generalizing to the reader.

Commerce between story and theory can flow both ways. We can illustrate a theory, and thus explain it to someone, by telling a story. Conversely, we can extract a latent theory from a story or a collection of similar stories by identifying themes—what Martin (1982) calls a script and what Dahl (1988) calls a frame and what Edelson (this volume) calls a master story—a skeletal structure that specifies the common elements.

Having the intention to extract their theory from a story allows narrative-based researchers a starting point that is radically different from that of hypothesis-testing researchers. Good practice requires qualitative (or perhaps all) investigators to disclose their expectations and preconceptions, but these serve as orientation for the reader, not necessarily as hypotheses to be tested. Instead, narrative research may start with unanalyzed stories (interviews, conversations). The absence of explicit hypotheses (and hence of the possibility of falsification) can be a source of consternation to journal editors and reviewers used to hypothesis-testing research.

JAY GREENBERG'S CHAPTER FROM THE INTERPRETIVE VIEWPOINT

Greenberg's story is imaginary, so it cannot be evaluated for good practice. If it concerned observations, however, it would illustrate some features of qualitative research.

The chapter uses both narrative and hermeneutic discourse. The narrative case history would demonstrate how the information available to different perspectives leads to incompatible but coherent and plausible accounts of common, agreed-upon observations (for example, that the patient reported substantial improvement following the interpretation). The narrative is not just a suggestion for research but could be considered as research itself from a qualitative viewpoint.

The shifting reinterpretations, which subsume each other but do not lead to a final account, illustrate hermeneutic discourse. Qualitative research's tentative epistemology makes it unnecessary to decide which of the accounts is the right one. Many others are possible—and these may emerge as new data are gathered—and each may suggest further empirical investigations.

Greenberg's chapter's last few pages forcefully articulate the hermeneutic position. For example:

> Research, precisely because it approaches the issues from a novel perspective, will always be a part of the debate. But I don't think that its role is to confirm or

to disconfirm hypotheses. In this sense, perhaps, psychotherapy research is fundamentally different by design and in intent than research in the hard sciences.

After making allowances, Greenberg's account can be evaluated using the validity criteria cross-classified in table 9.1. As I said earlier, for me as a reader, each of the three interpretations seem coherent. For me, the more general discussion further uncovered a deep similarity between clinical thinking, familiar from my own work as a therapist, and the thinking I have more recently come to recognize is needed in qualitative research. The imaginary participants in Greenberg's story all testified to the fit of the interpretations (or reinterpretations) with their own experience. Further, the recipients of the interpretations—the patient, the therapist, and the supervisor—all subsequently changed their behavior in seemingly productive ways, supporting the interpretations' catalytic validity. (Of course, it is much easier to arrange this in an imaginary story than in a report of observations of people.)

My mock evaluation breaks down in trying to assess how the research affected the researcher and the theory (see table 9.1) because there were no observations actually considered. It does not make sense to ask whether there was researcher consensus about how the observations were interpreted or whether they reflexively changed the investigator's preconceptions. We cannot use the response to observations to tell if this account is permeable or if it represents the author's unalterable prejudices.

In summary, I think Greenberg's chapter would qualify as qualitative research if he had interviewed the participants instead of imagining them.

MARSHALL EDELSON'S CHAPTER FROM THE INTERPRETIVE VIEWPOINT

As I suggested earlier, I think the position taken in Edelson's chapter resonates more with hypothesis-testing than with interpretive research, consistent with Edelson's "stubborn opposition to the hermeneutic stance." Nevertheless, there are many hints—perhaps even wishes—favoring a qualitative alternative. For example, there is a clear affinity with the qualitative approach's recognition of context and uniqueness in Edelson's emphasis on the particularities of clinical practice, as contrasted with the controlled generalizations of traditional research, and in his admission of being "leery of anything that promotes reliance on formulas" (p. 81). There are many echos of the hermeneutic stance, as in his early discussion of why clinicians can't agree on what counts as an observation and in his recommendation to make more than one inference from clinical material. There are direct parallels between criteria considered in his closing discussion of the credibility and accuracy of psychoanalytic interpretations and those discussed by other authors for assessing the accuracy of interpretations of qualitative data (for example, consilience is equivalent to triangulation; abduction is similar to self-evidence; "the patient's response to my communication tells me more than I knew before, surprises me, adds a new twist to the story" [p.86] is an example of catalytic validity).

More central, though, is the role of narrative in Edelson's thinking. Stories are the target of attention, but in a qualitative approach they could also be the means of attending and describing. Perhaps this is recognized in Edelson's recommending rigorous case studies for testing hypotheses. This recommendation has several levels. The point that narrative evidence, as a counterexample, can discredit a theoretical proposition (something close to Popperian falsification) is well taken. But surely narratives' constructive impact—their ability to transmit and suggest new ideas—goes well beyond their ability to count for or against some hypothesis. As argued earlier, stories carry their own theories, which may incorporate a general viewpoint and go beyond this into subtle and complex particulars. Edelson's story of the patient who arrived late, for example, is embedded within a broader psychoanalytic view of therapy (a behavioral therapist would be unlikely to tell this story), and it embodies a subtle theory of being governed by master stories. It goes well beyond Edelson's didactic presentation in furthering readers' understanding.

Closing Comment

What do practitioners want? The demand that psychotherapy research should inform the details of clinical practice often seems rooted in a view of psychotherapists as technicians who follow scientifically approved formulas. However, because psychotherapy, like all human interaction, is responsive—and hence nonlinear and technically chaotic—prediction and control at the level of particular interventions seem exceedingly unlikely. This places severe limits on the specificity of recommendations that can be usefully investigated by hypothesis-testing research. Testing the efficacy of a detailed session script, for example, would be pointless because the probability that an appropriate occasion would arise is infinitesimally small. At best, hypothesis-testing research might support (that is, fail to falsify) abstract descriptions of responsive procedures for interacting with clients.

On the other hand, interpretive research could provide a repertoire of possibilities. The more tentative epistemology and varied discourse (narrative and hermeneutic as well as didactic) cannot provide a technician's sense of certainty but may be more satisfying to professional practitioners.

REFERENCES

Bruner, J. (1986). *Actual minds, possible worlds.* Cambridge, MA: Harvard University Press.

Bruner, J. (1987). Life as narrative. *Social Research, 54,* 11–32.

Cohen, L. H., Sargent, M. M., & Sechrest, L. B. (1986). Use of psychotherapy research by professional psychologists. *American Psychologist, 41,* 198–206.

Dahl, H. (1988). Frames of mind. In H. Dahl, H. Kachele, & H. Thoma (Eds.), *Psychoanalytic research strategies* (pp. 51–66). New York: Springer-Verlag.

Gleick, J. (1987). *Chaos: Making a new science.* New York: Penguin.

Gusfield, J. R. (1990). Two genres of sociology: A literary analysis of *The American Occupational Structure* and *Talley's Corner.* In A. Hunter (Ed.), *The rhetoric of social research: Understood and believed* (pp. 62–96). New Brunswick, NJ: Rutgers University Press.

Herink, R. (Ed.). (1980). *The psychotherapy handbook.* New York: Meridan.

Howard, G. S. (1991). Culture tales: A narrative approach to thinking, cross-cultural psychology, and psychotherapy. *American Psychologist, 46,* 187–197.

Karasu, T. B. (1986). The specificity versus nonspecificity dilemma: Toward identifying therapeutic change agents. *American Journal of Psychiatry, 143,* 687–695.

Kuhn, T. S. (1970). *The structure of scientific revolutions.* Chicago: University of Chicago Press.

Martin, J. (1982). Stories and scripts in organizational settings. In A. Hastorf & A. Isen (Eds.), *Cognitive social psychology* . New York: Elsevier.

Meehl, P. E. (1990). Appraising and amending theories: The strategy of Lakatosian defense and two principles that warrant it. *Psychological Inquiry, 1,* 108–141.

Mishler, E. G. (1986). *Research interviewing: Context and narrative.* Cambridge, MA: Harvard University Press.

Mitchell, W. J. T. (Ed.). (1981). *On narrative.* Chicago: University of Chicago Press.

Morrow-Bradley, C., & Elliott, R. (1986). Utilization of psychotherapy research by practicing psychotherapists. *American Psychologist, 41,* 188–197.

Packer, M. J., & Addison, R. B. (1989). Introduction. In M. J. Packer & R. B. Addison (Eds.), *Entering the circle: Hermeneutic investigation in psychology* (pp. 13–36). Albany, NY: State University of New York Press.

Polkinghorne, D. E. (1988). *Narrative knowing and human sciences.* Albany: State University of New York Press.

Popper, K. (1959). *The logic of scientific discovery.* New York: Basic Books (Original work published 1934)

Prigogene, I., & Stengers, I. (1984). *Order out of chaos: Man's new dialogue with nature.* New York: Bantam.

Raush, H. L. (1974). Research, practice, and accountability. *American Psychologist, 29,* 678–681.

Robinson, J. A., & Hawpe, L. (1986). Narrative thinking as a heuristic process. In T. R. Sarbin (Ed.), *Narrative psychology: The storied nature of human conduct* (pp. 111–125). New York: Praeger.

Russell, R. L. (1991). Narrative in views of humanity, science, and action: Lessons for cognitive therapy. *Journal of Cognitive Psychotherapy, 5,* 241–256.

Stiles, W. B. (1990). *Narrative in psychological research*. Occasional Papers in Psychology: Visiting Fellowship Series 1. (Department of Psychology, Massey University, Palmerston North, New Zealand).

Stiles, W. B. (1992). Producers and consumers of psychotherapy research ideas. *Journal of Psychotherapy Practice and Research, 1*, 305–307.

Stiles, W. B. (1993). Quality control in qualitative research. *Clinical Psychology Review, 13*, 593–618.

Teller, V., & Dahl, H. (1986). The microstructure of free association. *Journal of the American Psychoanalytic Association, 34*, 763–798.

Vitz, P. C. (1990). The use of stories in moral development: New psychological reasons for an old educational method. *American Psychologist, 45*, 709–720.

White, H. (1980). The value of narrativity in the representation of reality. *Critical Inquiry, 7*, 5–27.

Woolfolk, R. L., Sass, L. A., & Messer, S. B. (1988). Introduction to hermeneutics. In S. B. Messer, L. A. Sass, & R. L. Woolfolk (Eds.), *Hermeneutics and psychological theory: Interpretive perspectives on personality, psychotherapy, and psychopathology* (pp. 2–26). New Brunswick, NJ: Rutgers University Press.

CHAPTER 10

The Benefits to the Clinician of Psychotherapy Research: A Clinician-Researcher's View

Lester Luborsky

I AM ENTHUSIASTIC about taking part in this exchange between researchers and clinicians for four good reasons: (1) to get better acquainted with Greenberg's (this volume) views; (2) to correct stereotypes about clinicians and about researchers and about their collaborative coexistence; (3) to help the poor clinician analyst, Dr. A, in Greenberg's case example, who must be confused about the conflicting consultations; and (4) to respond to Greenberg's view that "the gap between psychotherapy researchers and clinicians resists closure and threatens to widen."

I will begin by trying to correct stereotypes about clinicians and researchers because they apply to me as well. I have been practicing psychoanalysis and psychoanalytic psychotherapy for 45 years and was a member of the Topeka Psychoanalytic Association and am currently a member of the Philadelphia Association for Psychoanalysis. So you would think that I would qualify as a clinician. That is often not the way life is. Clinicians who also have research competence have role problems. I was once asked to take part in a program with Morton Reiser on a topic of special interest to me: early traumatic scenes and their carryover in later life. A few weeks before the program the chairman of the program committee phoned me to ask for

Some of this paper was part of a debate with Jay Greenberg at the American Psychological Association Division 39 annual meeting in Philadelphia, April 4, 1992. The work on this paper was partially supported by a National Institute of Mental Health Research Scientist Award MH 40710–22 and National Institute on Drug Abuse Award #DA 0785-23 (to Lester Luborsky); partially supported by the Center for Psychotherapy Research, University of Pennsylvania Grant P 50 MH 45178 (to Paul Crits-Christoph); and by the editorial expertise of Margaret Morris.

further advice, saying, "The program is fine with you two on it, but we also need a clinician!" I tried to reassure him: "You already have two clinicians." But I wondered what his stereotyped thinking represented. I concluded that the clinician who does research risks being stereotyped as having a deficiency in clinical skill.

Greenberg's Case Example

Greenberg has provided us with a fascinating case example of different formulations among different analytic consultants about the same case. In his case example the analyst, Dr. A, listens to his patient, understands the patient, and accordingly makes a cogent interpretation. The supervisor of Dr. A then listens to the account by Dr. A and has a different view of the correct assessment of the patient and the interaction with the analyst. Finally, a consultant is drawn in who listens to the supervisor's account and offers yet another view.

Greenberg concludes that each of the three observers has a unique theory and that each attends to a unique set of data that supports his preferred formulation. But Greenberg himself is really a fourth consultant, whose view is that the others disagree. Greenberg's view itself raises a research question: How do we know they really disagree? A well-known research technique, such as paired comparisons, could help with this question. As presented, the four verdicts are like those in a story that I'm sure some of you know: A sexton overhears a rabbi counseling a couple. He hears the woman say, "The problem is XYZ," and the rabbi say, "You're right, it is XYZ." Then the man says, "The problem is ABC," and the rabbi says, "You're right, it is ABC." Afterward, the eavesdropping sexton protests to the rabbi, "How can they both be right?" And the rabbi responds, "You're right." And, in fact, the four views in the Greenberg series may differ in their rightness, or all may be right about different aspects of the case.

The series of observer formulations of Dr. A's case continues: Greenberg's case was then shown to me (I would be consultant number 5), and what do I say? I say, "You're right, they do appear to disagree in part." Clearly, agreement about accuracy of interpretation is a difficult task. Greenberg's case example illustrates that such different accounts of the same event about the patient and of the patient–therapist interaction can and do occur.

But how often does such disagreement among clinicians actually occur in the making of dynamic formulations? Here research has helped to answer the question as it is raised in the case example provided by Dr. Greenberg. Answer: it does usually happen. Witness the research reported by Seitz (1966), an analyst from the Chicago Psychoanalytic Institute who spent several years with his research group examining agreement on formulations from psychoanalytic sessions. This same study was repeated more systematically by DeWitt, Kaltreider, Weiss, and Horowitz (1983) in San Francisco with the same finding: analysts, in the way they usually function, often have a hard time agreeing with each other about formulations on the central concepts, such as the transference, they routinely use.

Suggestions on How to Improve Formulations and Interpretations

Can anything be done, either by clinicians or by researchers, to assist clinical practice in dynamic formulations and in accurate interpretations? My answer takes into account the fact that differences among clinicians stem from at least two major sources:

First, individual clinicians typically attend to different data within a case presentation, as Greenberg points out. An obvious remedy may be tried, that is, giving them exactly the same primary data, either a transcript or, preferably, a video tape. In some centers such innovations are already being tried. Paulina Kernberg (personal communication, 1991) has told me of the use of videotapes at the Westchester branch of Cornell Medical Center.

Second, clinicians use different ways of formulating that are based on different principles of conceptualization. The remedy here too is simple enough: ask clinicians to use the same guiding principles for drawing inferences from the same primary data as I exemplify below with the Core Conflictual Relationship Theme method. These guiding principles are not unusual or unclinical and their effect is to help the clinicians use the same guiding principles to a larger extent than they do.

In sum, the two sources of inter-clinician differences can be easily remedied by uniform instructions. For example, to the "clinicians" in the age-old fable of the blind men and the elephant, one would offer the advice to, first, always examine the trunk and, second, report on its size and function.

In the next section I present a clinical example that makes use of pre-agreed-upon principles for guiding inferences about transference. The principles specify the parts of the session to be given special attention and the components to be used in formulations of transference. As expected, guided measures of almost any concept tend to show more agreement among judges than do unguided measures (Holt, 1978). A method that provides such common guiding principles is the "core conflictual relationship theme" (CCRT) method (Luborsky & Crits-Christoph, 1990). (You can easily try this method by following the directions in that book.) The CCRT method represents a breakthrough in providing a clinically sound procedure for inferring a transference-related pattern. The CCRT method came about through self-conscious observations of my clinical processes in inferring a general relationship pattern from psychotherapy sessions. I noticed (1) that I attended especially to the parts of the session containing narratives about the patient's interactions with the therapist and with other people and (2) that I was especially impressed by parts of the narratives that were recurrent across sessions. I noticed that within each narrative three components were prominent: what the patient wanted from other people, how the other people reacted, and how the patient reacted to their reactions. The CCRT is in part, therefore, an interactional pattern between the patient and others, including the therapist, that focuses on this sequence:

$W \to RO \to RS$ (where W is wish, RO is response from others, and RS is response of self).

A Clinical Case Example to Illustrate the CCRT Method and Its Benefits

I cannot use much of Greenberg's case as an example because his description does not give enough clinical material. Yet there are two vignettes in the case treated by Dr. A that give just a glimpse of the probable CCRT. The wish of this female patient may be to get strength, knowledge, and affirmation from a man (the analyst); the response she expects from the other person is to be put down and tied down; her response is to feel helpless and passive. The analyst could include some of this formulation in his interpretations. The patient may get some understanding of the pattern but also may continue to interpret the analyst's responses as put downs; but the analyst can continue to explore the expectations she has of him.

My more complete example is of Mr. Alton (a pseudonym), who was diagnosed (using the American Psychiatric Association's 1987 standards, *DSM-III-R*) as having a social phobia. He was treated in psychodynamic psychotherapy for 24 once-weekly sessions with a highly experienced psychoanalyst, Dr. B. The form of therapy was similar to the time-limited supportive-expressive psychotherapy described in Luborsky (1984).

Mr. Alton was the middle child between an older brother and a younger sister. His parents were professionals. At the beginning of therapy Mr. Alton was in his early thirties and had been married for 3 years. His wife worked with him as a partner in their small design firm.

Mr. Alton hoped through therapy to overcome the moderately severe agoraphobic symptoms that were markedly and increasingly interfering with his work and marriage. He was anxious and phobically restricted from engaging in air and highway travel and from visiting unfamiliar restaurants and other public places. These symptoms had started when he was in college, while he was in conflict with his fiancée, with whom he later broke off the relationship.

The patient's father was persistently frustrated with his own professional

Table 10.1   Précis of First Five Relationship Episodes (REs) in Session 17 of the Therapy of Mr. Alton

The other person in the relationship episode	*Narrative*
RE 1: Wife	I didn't go on the trip with wife and partner. Feel I've failed. I couldn't push myself to go, so I blame myself. Also I'm using my fear as a weapon.
RE 2: Therapist	I was uncomfortable since we spoke last session. We spoke of developing my own pace. But then the session ended at 60 minutes! I felt a quick temper and suspiciousness of you for ending it then.
RE 3: Father	I relied on father's interpretation of what to do, but sometimes he didn't know what he was talking about. He said to succeed, wear suits and ties. I was angry and confronted him. I didn't feel bad about what I said to him.
RE 4: Fiancée	The girl I almost married in college had a distinct concept of the role I was supposed to play in her life. It was the reason our relationship fell apart and I got out of it. It was the time in my life when I started feeling ill in restaurants, so I stopped going. My work was a constant battle about what I was supposed to do.
RE 5: Father	I was living out what father taught us about success and careers. It is hard to rebel against father. The idea of "rebellion and trying to prove to him I can succeed" is a hard idea to hold on to. I'm scared of saying "I don't believe what you said"—it would be hurting him. He'd feel he'd failed because I'm in treatment.

career. Yet Mr. Alton often compared himself unfavorably with his father in terms of relative success; he also compared himself in the same way with his older brother.

The data, transcripts of the time-limited (24 once-weekly sessions) psychoanalytic psychotherapy, were based on videotapes of Sessions 4 and 17. To give you more of a sample, I have included in table 10.1, a précis of the first five relationship episodes in Session 17. I will describe here the results of the CCRT method, first with tailor-made clinical categories and then also with standard categories (more detail on these methods can be found in Luborsky & Crits-Christoph, 1990).

Table 10.2 Tailor-Made Categories Used by Three Judges for Ten Relationship Episodes (REs) in Sessions 4 and 17 of Therapy of PATIENT A

CCRT category	Judge L		Judge M		Judge P	
	Tailor-made category	No. of REs[a]	Tailor-made category	No. of REs[a]	Tailor-made category	No. of REs[a]
Wish						
	To carry on in my own way; to oppose pressures from those I am close to	7	To do what I want without giving in to the wishes of the other person	8	To stand up for what I want with others; to not go along with wishes of others	9
	To please and not hurt the other	4	To not hurt the other, so I try to live up to their expectations for me	4	To be close to others; to communicate and share	6
Negative Response from Other (NRO)						
	Controls me, pressures me, expects me to conform to their ideas	6	Constrains me, cuts me off	4	Unreceptive	3
			Expects me to do things his way	3	Doesn't understand me	3
					Leaves me	3
Negative Response from Self (NRS)						
	Feel helpless	5	Angry, frustrated, resentful	7	Not able to assert self; goes along with others	6
	Phobic symptoms (anxiety, etc.)	4				
	Self-blame	4	Nervous, upset, anxious	5	Anxious	5
Positive Response from Other (PRO)						
	Supportive and reassuring	5	Accepting, nonjudgmental	2	Understands me	1
					Likes me	1
					Receptive	1
Positive Response from Self (PRS)						
	Assertive, fight others' ideas	4	In control, not anxious	3	Do something about what I want (assert self)	4

[a]The number of REs that show the CCRT category

Table 10.3 Use of Standard CCRT Categories by Three Judges for Ten Relationship Episodes (REs) in Sessions 4 and 17 of the Therapy of Mr. Alton

		Judges		
		L #RE[a]	M #RE[a]	P #RE[a]
Wish (W)				
W 1	To assert my independence and autonomy	7	7	10
W 1A	To overcome other's domination; To be free of obligations imposed by others; To not be put down by others	7	7	9
W 1B	To achieve, be competent, be successful	5	4	4
W 2	To please the other person; To avoid hurting the other person	4	4	2
W 3	To get help, care, protection, and guidance from the other person	4	3	5
Negative Response From Other (NRO)	Dominating, controlling, interfering, intimidating, intruding	6	5	3
Negative Response From Self (NRS)	Anxious, tense, upset	5	7	10
	Helpless, less confident, ineffectual ("I do not know how to do things")	5	5	8
	Frustrated	2	6	4
	Angry, resentful, hating	2	5	5
Positive Response From Other (PRO)	Accepting, approving	3	2	2
Positive Response From Self (PRS)	Assertive, express self assertively, gain control	4	5	6
	Gain self-esteem, feel affirmed, self-confident	3	4	4

[a]The number of REs that show the CCRT category.
A = assertive, independent wishes; B = submissive, dependent wishes.

RESULTS OF CCRT TAILOR-MADE CLINICAL CATEGORIES

The usual CCRT scoring system is considered to be tailor-made because the judge uses his or her own words for the best-fitting formulation for a particular patient. For the CCRT analysis of Mr. Alton, three independent clinical judges scored the relationship episodes of two sessions (the results are given in table 10.2). The examples of each interaction type are listed in order of frequency, from most to least. For example, for Judge L the patient's wish, need, or intention is formulated as follows: "To carry on in my own way; to oppose pressures from those to whom I am close." This wish appears in seven of the ten relationship episodes found in the two sessions. For Judge M, the wish is "To do what I want without giving in to the wishes of the other person"; for Judge P the wish is "To stand up for what I want with others; to not go along with wishes of others." We see, by inspection alone, that the judges have made similar inferences.

But we can be more precise: we can use a paired comparisons method to examine the degree of agreement in the tailor-made clinical results (following a system by Levine & Luborsky, 1981). This method gives information on the difference in level of similarity of a sample of tailor-made categories from same-case pairs versus a sample of categories from different cases (mismatched pairs). We have shown by this method that, as expected, clinical judges agree with each other significantly more when categories are compared with those made by other judges on the *same* case than when they are from *different* cases.

RESULTS OF CCRT STANDARD CATEGORIES

Standard categories are a great improvement over tailor-made categories, for they simplify studies of reliability. But because standard categories restrict the range of clinical inference to some extent, the use of both tailor-made and standard category systems is recommended.

The results with standard categories are based on Luborsky's Edition 1 (6-10-85) list (Barber, Crits-Christoph, & Luborsky (1990). The system works in this way: for each relationship episode in a session, the clinical judge first makes tailor-made inferences and then translates these into their best-fitting standard categories. For the case of Mr. Alton, we found that the judges tended to agree in their selection of standard categories (table 10.3). For the wish category, all three judges chose two wishes about equally and at a higher frequency than for the other wishes. Closely related in meaning, these two wishes are as follows: (1) "To assert one's independence and autonomy" and (2) "To overcome other's domination and to be free of obligations imposed by others." The other wishes (see table 10.3) were chosen at a slightly lower frequency by all three judges. Two judges selected as most frequent the same Negative Response From Other (NRO): "Dominating, controlling, interfering, intimidating, intruding." For Positive Response From Other (PRO), all three judges most frequently selected "Accepting, approving." For the Negative Response From Self (NRS), "Anxious, tense, upset" was selected most frequently by all three judges. For the Positive Response From Self (PRS) category, the response "Assertive, express self assertively, gain control" was selected most frequently by all three judges. Inspection of the results shows much similarity between these standard categories and the tailor-made ones.

The results of these analyses using the CCRT show that clinicians can agree in case formulation and that they can go about it in a similar way. In contrast, what Greenberg has shown is only that when clinicians go about it in their own way, they do not agree, as has already been demonstrated by research studies.

Guided Versus Free Clinician Inferences

We come now to this basic question: Does clinical judgment based on agreed-upon principles distort the clinical process? To put it another way: Is there a serious danger in imposing any guided system on the process of making a clinical inference? The question involves the more fundamental issue of whether any guided method results in a transference formulation that misses what is essential for a particular patient. My conclusion at this point is that the danger is minimal and the gain is maximal (as the example of Mr. Alton suggests). Each clinician's usual judgments are not really unguided, they just follow different guides. They may derive these judgment systems from a combination of their reading of Freud (1912) and other expert clinicians with their own interests and styles. As compared with the guidance of the CCRT method, the unguided systems differ considerably from clinician to clinician. The CCRT method only offers a set of guiding principles *to be shared by all clinicians,* and that is what permits a greater degree of agreement. And the capacity to agree on transference formulations is a desirable asset both for clinicians and for researchers.

Do the uniform guidance principles in the CCRT method permit it to be considered a measure of the clinical concept of transference? An obstacle to coming to a firm conclusion on this form of the question is the absence of a systematic study of clinicians' unguided transference formulations versus CCRT formulations on the same sessions. We plan on doing such a study, but so far we have only a few cases on which we have both unguided and guided transference formulations. One of these cases is Mr. Alton; another is Ms. Cunningham, described in Luborsky and Crits-Christoph (1990, chapter 4). The clinical formulations of these cases showed relatively poor agreement while the CCRT formulations showed moderately good agreement.

This same validity question may also be presented in terms of the issue of salience versus frequency. Salient behaviors are those that are crucially or uniquely meaningful. The criticism is that the CCRT is inferred from the *high frequency* of behaviors but clinical formulations are inferred from *single salient* behaviors (for example, Bond & Shevrin, 1986). Our thesis is that clinicians actually use more than salience, in its restricted sense. Clinicians' reliance on salience is only apparent; in fact, the behaviors they focus on are associated with recurrent themes and therefore would be reflected in the

CCRT. Our thesis is easily illustrated in tables 10.2 and 10.3 and in Mr. Alton's five narratives from Session 17. A clinician might understand Mr. Alton's argument with his fiancée in Narrative 4 as a salient behavior, because after his fiancée told him how he should act to become successful, the patient not only became angry but also developed his phobia. We can see that each of the other narratives contains a similar salient behavior, illustrating what we mean by our thesis that salience is likely to be associated with high frequency.

We conclude with what seems to be a paradox in terms of acceptance of more exact methods of formulating the transference. Clinicians generally should search harder for improvements in their method of making such formulations. One obvious reason for their lack of urgency about making improvements must be their unawareness of the limits of their formulations and of their differences with each other. Also, they generally have confidence that they already know how to do this kind of formulation and that if they do not see the transference at the moment, they need only be patient and continue listening to the patient. And there is an even more basic reason for some clinicians' caution about the more exact methods of formulation: they are concerned about tampering with the conventional method of formulation. They fear any formal system will diminish or distort their natural clinical sensitivity. But we have not found such a reduction. Instead, after experience with the new methods clinicians have felt reassured, for they come to see that the methods offer a common language and a common conceptual domain for their formulations and do not reduce their sensitivity. So, we have come to believe that the clinician's sensitivity is still of high quality even after it has been guided by the focus offered by the CCRT method's more reliably recognized components that are the same for each clinician.

How to Choose Among Interpretations

We come now to our aim of helping the poor clinician, Dr. A, in Greenberg's case example, choose among interpretations. Each clinician and researcher has to have a way of deciding about alternative formulations; fortunately, in practice we do decide. But Greenberg ends by concluding that each of the clinician's views represents an alternative approach and that "the debate over which is the most useful will go on forever." His idea is that we cannot choose between the alternative explanations. He appears to be taking a view like that of the now very popular reader response position espoused by many literary critics, for example, Stanley Fish. The position is that we all have our own interpretations, that these interpretations are all equal, and that no one is privileged by special access to the best or the only interpretation.

Actually, there *are* ways to choose among interpretations. Even Greenberg almost suggests one way to choose between them when he mentions "the most useful" view; that is, he points to a utility criterion. Another major criterion for choosing among alternative formulations is the degree to which each one fits the material of the session. In fact, I have proposed this kind of criterion (Auerbach & Luborsky, 1968); my measure was the degree of convergence of each interpretation with the essence of the patient's main communications in the session. A version of this criterion—the degree of convergence between the interpretation and the CCRT—was used in Crits-Christoph and Luborsky (1988) and Crits-Christoph, Cooper, and Luborsky (1988) and was found to be correlated with the patient's benefit from the psychotherapy. In conclusion, the analyst in Greenberg's case example, Dr. A, would find this convergence criterion a useful guide in choosing among the many possible interpretations.

The Applications of Research to Other Clinical Topics

Some topics in dynamic psychotherapy are more easily examined by research than others. The topic that Greenberg illustrates in his example, the accuracy of formulations and interpretations, is one of the toughest. His example is of such complexity that any clinicians or researchers who might try to solve it might themselves need further therapy! The following are a few of the easier psychotherapy research questions, together with answers that both clinicians and clinical researchers may find valuable:

Which diagnosis is the least effectively treated by psychotherapy? Answer: antisocial personality (Woody, McLellan, Luborsky, & O'Brien, 1985).

Which diagnoses can be most effectively treated by psychotherapy? Answer: it is not the category of diagnosis but the severity of the diagnosis that is more predictive of outcome (Luborsky, Crits-Christoph, Mintz, & Auerbach, 1988).

Which forms of psychotherapy are considered to be more effective than dynamic psychotherapy in the treatment of drug addiction disorders? Answer: probably none; results showing nonsignificant differences among outcomes of different treatments are the rule (Woody et al., 1983).

To what extent can clinicians agree about formulations of transference? Answer: when clinicians follow their own individual styles, as Greenberg points out in his example, they do not agree. In the examples I used from the case of Mr. Alton I reconfirmed that conclusion by giving two expert psychoanalysts a transcript of Session 4 (Dr. Stewart Wolfe and Dr. Barbara Wolfe of Philadelphia). Their formulations were in agreement to some extent, but the CCRT formulations showed much more agreement among clinicians who applied it to that same session.

Are there specific qualities of sessions that can be more reliably judged than others? Answer: a reasonable consensus can be found in the descriptions of some aspects of psychotherapy sessions. Good agreement was found (Mintz, Auerbach, Luborsky, & Johnson, 1973) across all views (patients, therapists, and researchers) in descriptions of the patient's emotional state, such as distress, affection, and anger. But poor agreement was consistently found—a kind of Rashomon experience—in the evaluation of the quality of the therapist's relationship with the patient and of the overall quality of the session itself. In judging the quality of a session, therefore, it does matter whom one asks—the patient, the therapist, or an external observer.

To what extent can an early, mostly positive therapeutic alliance foretell the outcomes of psychotherapy? Answer: an early positive alliance can achieve predictive correlations of around .3 to .4; the negative alliance is close to zero (Luborsky, Crits-Christoph, Alexander, Margolis, & Cohen, 1983).

These and other factors in dynamic therapies have been reviewed in Luborsky et al. (1988), Miller, Luborsky, Barber, & Docherty (1993) and, Luborsky, Barber, & Crits-Christoph, (1992), which have direct answers to the questions we are discussing today.

A Reconciliation of the Views of Clinicians and Researchers

There is a gap in the usual style of the clinician and the researcher, and some of it is inevitable. On that Greenberg (this volume) and I agree. But it is not widening; on that we disagree. My explanation for the gap is much like Edelson's (1992): the researcher and the clinician have different requirements; therefore, the gap can never be closed. The therapist needs a formulation about a patient's dynamic conflicts at a particular moment in order to base interpretations on it. The interpretations have to fit the individual requirements of the patient at that moment in the treatment. To make the formulation and interpretation the therapist has to draw on his or her own clinical capacities and knowledge. Researchers tend to offer general principles that are comparable in their usefulness to the general principles from clinical lore. In that sense the clinical wisdom principles and the research principles can each be used from time to time. To be helpful a principle must aid the therapist with a formulation that fits the individual patient and even assists in deciding which part of the formulation is most relevant for interpretative intervention at a particular moment.

REFERENCES

American Psychiatric Association. (1987). *Diagnostic and statistical manual of mental disorders* (3rd ed., rev.). Washington, DC: Author.

Auerbach, A. H., & Luborsky, L. (1968). Accuracy of judgments of psychotherapy and the nature of the "good hour." In J. Shlien, H. F. Hunt, J. P. Matarazzo, & C. Savage (Eds.), *Research in psychotherapy, 3* (pp. 155–168). Washington, DC: American Psychological Association.

Barber, J., Crits-Christoph, P., & Luborsky, L. (1990). A guide to CCRT standard categories and their classification. In Luborsky, L. & Crits-Christoph, P. *Understanding transference—The CCRT method* (pp. 37–50). New York: Basic Books.

Bond, J., & Shevrin, H. (1986). *The clinical evaluation team method.* Unpublished manuscript.

Crits-Christoph, P., Cooper, A., & Luborsky, L. (1988). The accuracy of therapists' interpretations and the outcome of dynamic psychotherapy. *Journal of Consulting and Clinical Psychology, 56,* 490–495.

Crits-Christoph, P., & Luborsky, L. (1988). Application of the CCRT: A measure of adequacy of therapist's interpretation and a measure of patient's self-understanding. In University of Ulm, H. Dahl, H. Kachele, H. Thomae (Eds.), *Psychoanalytic Process Research Strategies* (pp. 117–128). New York: Springer.

DeWitt, K. N., Kaltreider, N., Weiss, D. S., & Horowitz, M. J. (1983). Judging change in psychotherapy: Reliability of clinical formulations. *Archives of General Psychiatry, 40,* 1121–1128.

Edelson, M. (1992). Can psychotherapy research answer this psychotherapist's questions? *Contemporary Psychoanalysis, 28,* 118–151.

Freud, S. (1958). The dynamics of the transference. In J. Strachey (Ed. & Trans.), *The standard edition of the complete psychological works of Sigmund Freud* (Vol. 12, pp. 99–108). London: Hogarth Press. (Original work published 1912).

Holt, R. R. (1978). *Methods in clinical psychology: Vol. 2. Prediction and research.* New York: Plenum.

Levine, F. J., & Luborsky, L. (1981). The core conflictual relationship theme method: A demonstration of reliable clinical inferences by the method of mismatched cases. In S. Tuttman, C. Kaye, & M. Zimmerman (Eds.), *Object and self: A developmental approach* (pp. 501–526). New York: International Universities Press.

Luborsky, L. (1973). Forgetting and remembering (momentary forgetting) during psychotherapy: A new sample. In M. Mayman (Ed.), Psychoanalytic research: Three approaches to the experimental study of subliminal processes. *Psychological Issues, 8* (No. 2), Monograph 30, 29–55.

Luborsky, L. (1984). *Principles of psychoanalytic psychotherapy: A manual for supportive-expressive (SE) treatment.* New York: Basic Books.

Luborsky, L., Barber, J., Crits-Christoph, P. (1992). Testing psychoanalytic propositions about personality change in psychotherapy. In J. Barron, M. Eagle, & D. Wolitsky (Eds.) *Interface of psychoanalysis and psychology.* Washington, DC: American Psychological Association.

Luborsky, L., & Crits-Christoph, P. (1988). Measures of psychoanalytic concepts: The last decade of research from "The Penn Studies." *International Journal of Psycho-Analysis, 69,* 75–86.

Luborsky, L., Crits-Christoph, P. (1990). *Understanding transference: The CCRT method (the core conflictual relationship theme).* New York: Basic Books.

Luborsky, L., Crits-Christoph, P., Alexander, L., Margolis, M., & Cohen, M. (1983). Two helping alliance methods for predicting outcomes of psychotherapy: A counting signs versus a global rating method. *Journal of Nervous and Mental Disease, 171,* 480–492.

Luborsky, L., Crits-Christoph, P., Mintz, J., Auerbach, A. (1988). *Who will benefit from psychotherapy? Predicting therapeutic outcomes.* New York: Basic Books.

Miller, N., Luborsky, L., Barber, J., Docherty, J. (1993). *Psychodynamic treatment research—A handbook for clinical practice.* New York: Basic Books.

Mintz, J., Auerbach, A., Luborsky, L., & Johnson, M. (1973). Patient's, therapist's, and observers' views of psychotherapy: A "Rashomon" experience or a reasonable consensus? *British Journal of Medical Psychology, 46,* 83–89.

Seitz, P. (1966). The consensus problem in psychoanalytic research. In L. Gottschalk & A. Auerbach (Eds.), *Methods of research in psychotherapy* (pp. 209–225). New York: Appleton-Century-Crofts.

Woody, G., Luborsky, L., McLellan, A. T., O'Brien, C., Beck, A. T., Blaine, J., Herman, I., & Hole, A. V. (1983). Psychotherapy for opiate addicts: Does it help? *Archives of General Psychiatry, 40,* 639–645.

Woody, G., McLellan, A. T., Luborsky, L., & O'Brien, C. (1985). Sociopathy and psychotherapy outcome. *Archives of General Psychiatry, 42,* 1081–1086.

CHAPTER 11

Spence and Havens: Examples of Practitioner Contributions to Bridging the Chasm

Karla Moras

A Researcher's Response to Spence's "The Failure to Ask the Hard Questions"

Since reading Spence's (1982) book *Narrative Truth and Historical Truth*, I have admired his efforts to put psychoanalysis on firmer conceptual ground. Such efforts foster clinically relevant and scientifically sound studies of psychoanalysis. Thus, I welcome the opportunity to respond to his critique of existing research on psychoanalysis.[1]

To organize and focus my response, I first identified points both that were prominent in Spence's chapter and that could be addressed by extant knowledge in the field of psychotherapy research. The remarks herein focus on four of Spence's points that meet the preceding criteria:

1) A major obstacle to obtaining research findings that are clinically relevant for psychoanalysis has been researchers' failure to "ask the hard questions."

2) Many facts about the psychoanalytic process remain unknown, even after 100 years of practice.

The helpful comments of Drs. Enrico Jones, Lester Luborsky, David Mark, and Norman D. Schaffer on sections of this chapter are gratefully acknowledged. However, they are not responsible for nor do they necessarily endorse the points made herein.

3) It is difficult to know what findings from psychoanalytic case studies are generalizable, because the studies typically are based on data (observations) that cannot be subjected to systematic scrutiny and verification by others, (that is, cannot be replicated in the scientific sense).

4) Experimental paradigms modeled after those used in mother–infant interaction research might usefully be adapted to examine central questions about psychoanalysis.

Each of the foregoing four points are discussed in the sections that follow.

RESEARCHERS' FAILURE TO ASK THE HARD QUESTIONS

Addressing the central topic of this volume, the gap between clinical practice and research findings, Spence observes: "One of the major obstacles to translating research findings into clinical practice stems from the researchers' failure to ask the hard questions that strike at the heart of our basic assumptions" (p. 22). Three of the hard questions Spence identifies are the following: Is there a dynamic unconscious? Can the dynamic unconscious be accessed via free association? Do mutative interpretations bring about structural alterations in the unconscious?

The experiences of several committed investigators who wanted to examine basic tenets of psychoanalysis suggest two major reasons why research progress has been inadequate on questions like those identified by Spence: (1) historically, investigators who had both the scientific expertise and the creative intellect required to design studies to test the highly abstract constructs that characterize psychoanalytic theory often were not rewarded by the psychoanalytic community for their efforts—and sometimes were harshly criticized—and (2) psychoanalytic concepts are often used metaphorically, as Spence points out, which makes them difficult to operationalize in ways that their developers and proponents find satisfactory (valid).

The Analytic Community's Reactions to Committed Investigators

Over the years, I became aware of the experiences of several investigators in the United States[1] who wanted to study psychoanalysis by using accepted scientific methods. Efforts of investigators who had the ability to conduct studies that could either confirm or suggest modifications of psychoanalytic theory often were negatively received by the psychoanalytic community. Historically, it was not unusual for critics to impugn an investigator's competence and intelligence by citing the inadequacy of his or her attempts to op-

---

[1] The observations herein apply only to research on psychoanalysis in the United States. The experience of European investigators might be different.

erationalize highly abstract constructs such as the dynamic unconscious. Such critics sometimes justify their remarks by noting that the "richness" of the constructs are not captured in the operationalization. Also psychoanalyst/investigators who reached conclusions that deviated from the "given theory" (Spence's term), such as Merton Gill (Gill & Hoffman, 1982), often experienced some degree of social opprobrium and were rarely if ever elevated by the analytic community. Gill, for example, seemed often to be treading a fine line; he risked being ejected from the analytic community as a heretic if some of his conclusions were not consistent with the accepted theory or, alternatively, being labeled a maverick, a term that indicated he had not been banished but also was not fully accepted.

The negative experiences of some investigators[2] who were willing to ask hard questions and provide hard answers, if necessary, seem sadly analogous to the current fate of analysts who believe that less than four sessions per week is acceptable. Spence notes that they are now barred from membership in the International Psychoanalytic Association. This fact itself is evidence against the flexibility and openness to scrutiny that are required for recognition and incorporation of the information on psychoanalysis that could be generated by accepted scientific methods.

In summary, historically the analytic community often provided more disincentives than incentives to investigators who had the intellect, expertise, and integrity needed to examine the basic tenets of psychoanalysis. Hence, many investigators focused their research elsewhere. Happily, however, signs of a shift have become increasingly evident over the last 8 to 10 years: Notably, for example, editorial support for research articles by the *Journal of the American Psychoanalytic Association*, and increasing recognition of research efforts at psychoanalytic meetings. Ideally, analytic institutes and the associations will continue to create incentives for investigators who can and will ask the hard questions, as well as collegial support for them when they produce hard answers.

Operationalization of Constructs

One of the most difficult aspects of research on psychotherapies is developing valid operational definitions of relevant theoretical constructs. The difficulty of operationally defining constructs can vary depending upon the level of abstraction at which a theory is written. Thus, for example, behavior theory is written at a low level of abstraction in that the constructs are directly linked to observables (for example, procedures and behaviors). In contrast psychoanalytic theory, with constructs like the dynamic unconscious and in-

[2]Exceptions to these observations, such as Hartvig Dahl, can of course be noted. However, such exceptions do not controvert the basic point that many skilled, bright investigators have been discouraged from their pursuits at least in part for the reasons described herein.

trapsychic structure, is written at a very high level of abstraction. This, in itself, would not create problems if psychoanalytic writings usually included attempts to link such constructs to observables and thereby provided some direction to those who seek to operationalize the constructs for research purposes. However, as Spence points out with his example of the construct "analytic surface," analytic writers generally avoid linking their central constructs to specific observables. Moreover, as Spence also points out, psychoanalytic constructs are often used as metaphors. The psychoanalytic community seems to endorse this practice, perhaps because the ambiguity associated with metaphorical constructs often is not as obvious in clinical discourse as it is in research discourse.

A closely related point is relevant. Usually, the first step toward operational definition of a construct is to define it with words. Even this basic step can be difficult with psychoanalytic constructs. This is because constructs are often used without definition. The attempt to remedy this problem by trying to deduce definitions of constructs by carefully studying their apparent referents in different contexts (as linguists do when they try to create dictionaries for languages) can be frustrating because the constructs often are used in many different ways in analytic writings (that is, have somewhat different meanings or referents depending upon the context and the writer).

In any event, the status of most of the central psychoanalytic constructs creates a difficult and risky situation for investigators. One danger is that no matter how intelligent and comprehensive an investigator's efforts to define and operationally define constructs are, the definitions are likely to be found inadequate and flawed by practicing and well-read psychoanalysts. The attempts will be found wanting largely because the definitions cannot simultaneously incorporate the various meanings that many analytic constructs have. In addition, once a construct is operationally defined, it can lose some of its aura or added meaning ("richness"). When an idea is grounded in observables and measurables, some analysts might experience disappointment. This phenomenon also might contribute to the rejection of investigators' painstaking efforts.

One way to ameliorate the situation would be for a segment of the analytic community to develop definitions of central constructs for use by investigators. Advantages would accrue to including experienced investigators in such a definitional effort. An analogy to this suggestion is the *DSM-III* Task Force (American Psychiatric Association, 1980), which was charged to create definitions of disorders largely to provide a foundation for psychiatric research.

Evidence exists that the situation is hopeful, however. For example, the therapeutic alliance is a construct that originated in psychoanalytic theory and that has been successfully operationalized many times (for example, Hartley & Strupp, 1983; Horvath & Greenberg, 1986; Luborsky, Crits-

Cristoph, Alexander, Margolis, & Cohen, 1983; Marziali, Marmar, & Krupnick, 1981). Moreover, findings consistently have been obtained that support Freud's tenet that a positive therapeutic alliance contributes to beneficial treatment outcome (for example, Horvath & Symonds, 1991).

Many Facts About the Psychoanalytic Process Remain Unknown

Spence notes that many basic aspects of the psychoanalytic process have not been investigated, including such fundamental questions as the following: "How does a reasonably good interpretation gain its effect? . . . How does the nature of the transference sometimes magnify and sometimes diminish the lexical content of an interpretation? . . . To what extent are analysts aware of the nonverbal dimension of their interventions?" (p. 23) In addition, Spence notes that almost nothing is known about the "average patient's experience of the analytic situation in its various phases" and that "dose–response effects are largely unstudied."

Spence attributes the lack of information on basic aspects of the psychoanalytic process to "investigative complacency." As I have implied by my observations in the preceding section, I of course would suggest that negative reactions to, and failure to reward and value, many who have seriously tried to conduct studies and who would provide hard answers when they are found has contributed to the complacency that Spence observes. Serious investigators might have been excluded and/or criticized into complacency.

In any event, information exists within the field of psychotherapy research that might be helpful to psychoanalysts, like Spence, who want more systematically based knowledge on psychoanalysis. Studies on psychotherapeutic processes of the type that Spence targets have been done on psychodynamic psychotherapy and on other forms of treatment. Thus, although the findings of existing studies might not be directly applicable to psychoanalysis, the methods used in the studies are likely to be. A few examples of such studies will be provided in the paragraphs that follow. It is suggested that psychoanalysts review the large body of psychotherapy process and process–outcome research (for example, Lambert & Hill, 1993; Orlinsky, Grawe, & Parks, 1994; Orlinsky & Howard, 1986) that has developed over the years, often conducted by psychodynamically oriented researchers, such as Strupp, Henry, and colleagues; Luborsky, Crits-Christoph, and colleagues; Silberschatz, Curtis, and colleagues of the Mt. Zion Psychotherapy Research Group (Silberschatz, Fretter, & Curtis 1986; Weiss & Sampson, 1986); William Piper and colleagues (Piper, Azim, McCallum, & Joyce, 1990; Piper et al., 1991); and Enrico Jones and colleagues (Jones, Cumming, & Pulos, 1993). Psychotherapy researchers who are not psychodynamically oriented also have contributed findings that are relevant to psychoanalytic constructs (for example, interpretation; see Hill, 1989).

The sections that follow give examples of studies that are relevant to Spence's questions about the psychoanalytic process.

How Does a Reasonably Good Interpretation Gain Its Effect?

Crits-Christoph, Cooper, and Luborsky (1988) addressed an aspect of this question in a study of 43 patients who received psychodynamic psychotherapy (lasting from 21 to 149 weeks). The study also illustrates the steps needed to answer the question raised by Spence. First, these investigators developed a method, accuracy of interpretation, to reliably identify a "reasonably good interpretation." They found that the accuracy of interpretations about certain aspects of patients' relationship themes related positively to outcome. However, they found that, contrary to one of their hypotheses, accurate interpretations did not have the most impact when delivered in the context of a positive alliance. The latter finding is relevant to another question that Spence raises about the psychoanalytic process, namely, How much is the effect of a reasonably good interpretation constrained by the state of the transference?

How Does the Nature of the Transference Sometimes Magnify and Sometimes Diminish the Lexical Content of an Interpretation?

The system of "configurational analysis" that Horowitz first published in 1979 provides at least one part of a method that seems readily adaptable to answering questions about the effect of the transference on the lexical content of an interpretation. Configurational analysis could be used to determine what transference state a patient is in when an interpretation is made.[3] Other methods used in psychotherapy research, such as "interpersonal process recall" (Elliott, 1986; Hill, 1989), could then be applied to determine the affective impact of and meaning attributed to interpretations when patients are in different transference states.

To What Extent Are Analysts Aware of the Nonverbal Dimension of Their Interventions?

Analysts' awareness of the interpersonal impact of their interventions and related demeanor can be readily examined with existing methods.

---

[3]One premise of configurational analysis is that patients have several different "states of mind" that are each defined by particular transferential self–other images (for example, adoring student [self] and benign, omnipotent mentor [other]). Furthermore, configurational analysis includes the premise that patients shift between states during treatment sessions and that the different states are observable and distinguished by for example, affect, body movements, and voice qualities. Thus, the system provides a

Benjamin's (1986) "structural analysis of social behavior" (SASB) can be applied to videotapes (preferably) or audiotapes of therapy sessions. The method reliably quantifies aspects of the interpersonal impact of interactions. Broadly, qualities of an individual's manner of relating to another are coded on four quadrants of interpersonal relatedness: dominance, submission, friendliness, and hostility. The quadrants are based on Leary's (1957) "interpersonal circumplex," a psychometrically sound dimensional structure for interpersonal relations. To address Spence's question, SASB codes of analysts' interventions could be compared with the analysts' own impressions of the probable interpersonal impact of their interventions.

The SASB method also could be used to address other questions raised by Spence, such as the impact of stating interpretations in different ways, for example, tentatively versus authoritatively. (The latter approach is discussed by Spence as having the potential to make patients feel that their mind is being read.)

What Is the Average Patient's Experience of the Analytic Situation in Its Various Phases?

One consistent and important focus of psychotherapy research over the past 25 years has been patients' perspectives on and perceptions of their treatment experience (for example, Gurman, 1977; Strupp, Fox, & Lessler, 1969). Reviews of this body of psychotherapy research provide excellent bibliographies of questions addressed and methods used to study the patient's perspective on treatment (Garfield, 1978, 1986). Hill's (1989) recent set of eight intensive case studies of patients' reactions to various types of therapist interventions, using the methodology of interpersonal process recall, might be a particularly useful model for examination of patients' experience in psychoanalysis. The interpersonal process recall method (Elliott, 1986) can be modified to be either more or less time-consuming and intrusive in the treatment process.

Dose–response Effects Are Largely Unstudied

Howard and colleagues (Howard, Kopta, Krause, & Orlinsky, 1986; McNeilly & Howard, 1991) have done pioneering research on dose–response effects in psychotherapy. For example, they reviewed data from different sources on 2,400 patients. A probit analysis indicated that about 50% of patients were improved by 8 sessions and about 75% were improved by 26 sessions. Their analyses also pointed to differential responsiveness depending

---

conceptual framework, as well as a measurement approach, that can be used to determine what transference state a patient is in when an interpretation is made.

upon the patient's diagnosis and the outcome criterion used (Howard et al., 1986). These studies provide models of how to examine the dose–response question that Spence raises about psychoanalysis.

THE SCIENTIFIC VALUE OF PSYCHOANALYTIC CASE STUDIES

Spence questions the value of psychoanalytic case studies that lack accompanying objective data, like audio- or videotapes of sessions, that are needed to allow an author's conclusions to be verified by others. However, Spence also seems hopeful that some part of the corpus of such case studies can be saved. He proposes, for example, that knowledge about memory be used to "immunize the case report against more obvious sources of infection" (p.25). He also suggests that procedures be used that can retrospectively separate the wheat (for example, the kinds of phenomena that can be accurately observed and recalled) from the chaff (phenomena that are generally subject to distortion by the observer) in case studies. Specifically, Spence calls for "a set of paradigmatic studies that would tell us, on the average, how much of a given phenomena is captured by the usual kind of anecdotal case report" (p. 25). Such studies, he says, would "begin to tell us how much of the traditional literature should be believed. Even if critical details are forgotten, can the clinical gist be trusted? Or, to take the opposite point of view, are anecdotal memories largely unreliable and therefore misleading, and apt to lead to a set of reports that is more wishful than descriptive. In that event, case studies do not deserve to be treated as data" (p. 25).

Several sources of information converge on the conclusion that the studies that Spence suggests are not needed and that the effort required to conduct them would be more profitably used conducting new, experimentally sound case studies that employ experimental case study methodology (Barlow & Hersen, 1984; Hilliard, 1993; Kazdin, 1982) or other research. First, the nature of the uncontrolled case study method precludes the conclusions of such studies being accepted as generalizable, established principles. The studies can, however, be used heuristically, as sources of clinically relevant hypotheses to test.

Secondly, as Gill and Hoffman (1982) discuss, anyone who has worked with colleagues on actual therapy session data (like audiotapes) is acutely aware that almost all of the phenomena presented are subject to several alternative perceptions and interpretations.[4] Moreover, observer consensus

---

[4]A report by Seitz (1966) provides a valuable perspective on problems associated with findings from traditional psychoanalytic case studies. Seitz describes the observations and conclusions of a group of eminent analysts (including George Pollock and Thomas French) who obtained a federal grant to study the consensus problem in psychoanalytic research, that is, "the difficulty that clinicians have in agreeing upon the interpretation of the same set of (interview) data" (p. 209).

seems more difficult to achieve the more abstract the variable of interest, for example, length of silence versus transference wish (Moras & Hill, 1991). Even apparently concrete variables like facial expressions can be surprisingly difficult to code reliably (Duncan & Fiske, 1977). These points are relevant because in psychoanalytic case studies the phenomena (variables or constructs) being observed generally are quite abstract. Furthermore, the interobserver reliability problem is compounded in the psychoanalytic case study method because the observer is also a participant in the process.

One recommendation is that psychoanalysts who want to continue to use the case study method review experimental case study designs (Barlow & Hersen, 1984; Chassan, 1979; Hilliard, 1993; Kazdin, 1982) to determine which designs might be suited to their questions. While experimental case study methodology has been used almost exclusively by behaviorally oriented clinical investigators, recent examples can be found of the application of this methodology to nonbehavioral treatments (for example, Moras, Telfer, & Barlow, 1993). Spence and colleagues (Spence, Dahl, & Jones, 1993) provide a recent example of how nonexperimental case study data can be combined with psychotherapy process research methods to test psychoanalytic hypotheses.

EXPERIMENTAL PARADIGMS LIKE THOSE USED IN MOTHER–INFANT INTERACTION RESEARCH MIGHT BE USEFUL FOR PSYCHOANALYTIC RESEARCH

Spence offers several specific suggestions about how psychoanalytic phenomena can be studied by using experimental methods that would allow replication of findings by other investigators. Most treatment researchers would, I believe, endorse his suggestions. In fact, one procedure that he suggests, namely, interrupting a session after certain types of interventions are made in order to ask the analysand what his or her reaction was to the intervention, is a variation of the aforementioned method of interpersonal process recall (Elliott, 1986).

Spence's own relevant research using audiotapes of psychoanalytic sessions (Spence et al., 1993) is noteworthy. Historically, the psychoanalytic community has rejected even audiotaping of sessions as an overly intrusive procedure that will necessarily and fundamentally change the very phenomenon to be studied (Gill & Hoffman, 1982).[5] An additional recommendation

---

[5]The observation that the method used to study a phenomenon is likely to change the phenomenon in some way is incontrovertible. Social psychologists, for example, have observed and bemoaned this situation. However, introducing methods to study a phenomenon does not necessarily mean that the aspects of the phenomenon that are the focus of study will be changed in a way that will invalidate conclusions. In any event, the psychoanalytic community faces a dilemma: if scientific methods are introduced into sessions, the process conceivably might be changed in a fundamental way, but if scientific methods continue to be ignored, psychoanalysis risks further criticism and marginal acceptance by the nonpsychoanalytic mental health community.

is that psychoanalyst/investigators review the psychotherapy process (for example, Greenberg & Pinsof, 1986; Kiesler, 1973; Russell, 1987) and process–outcome literature (for example, Hill, 1991; Lambert & Hill, 1993; Orlinsky, Grawe, & Parks, 1993; Orlinsky & Howard, 1986) with a focus on methods. There, relatively unobtrusive methods (like audiotaping sessions) can be found that are designed to both maximally preserve the natural phenomenon and study it. Furthermore, the existing methods and measures seem to readily lend themselves to the study of the psychoanalytic process.

CONCLUDING STATEMENT

I fully agree with Spence that research using currently accepted scientific methods is needed on psychoanalysis. From a nonanalyst's perspective, research is needed for two basic reasons: to keep the enterprise credible to outsiders and to enhance the effectiveness of psychoanalytic treatment. As a psychotherapy researcher, I see no inherent reason for research on psychoanalysis to lack clinical relevance. However, I am also aware of the difficulty, frustration, and effort that is associated with trying to ask the hard questions about any form of psychotherapy. Methods have their limitations, just as therapists do (for example, Gill & Hoffman, 1982). Moreover, the accumulation of research findings to support a single principle can take years, because of the need for replication. On the other hand, the field of psychoanalysis has experienced effects that can be associated with failure to accept the scientific method and its limitations. In contrast, more recent treatment approaches, like cognitive therapy (Beck, Rush, Shaw, & Emery, 1979; Hawton, Salkovskis, Kirk, & Clark, 1989), that have been subjected to considerable controlled study are enjoying widespread and enthusiastic acceptance by mental health professionals in all disciplines, including psychiatry.

A Researcher's Response to Havens's "Suggestions for Making Research More Applicable to Clinical Practice"

Dr. Havens's chapter provides several examples of excellent, research-ready (testable) material for studies that can have direct implications for clinical practice at the intervention-by-intervention level. Readers who are interested in investigating the effectiveness of the interventions that Havens proposes for paranoid developments, marked self-deprecatory trends, and other clinically common phenonomena are referred to writings by Laura Rice and Leslie Greenberg (Greenberg, 1984; Rice & Greenberg, 1984; Rice & Saperia, 1984). These two highly experienced psychotherapy researchers describe and illustrate research methods that are well suited to evaluate and refine interventions of the type Havens describes, that is, interventions that are designed to treat commonly observed clinical problems like the "impasses" Havens identifies.

My comments are focused on features of Havens's presentation that make his clinical ideas research-friendly, that is, eminently translatable into suitable research designs. I highlight features of Havens's work that make it an excellent model of how clinical observations and recommended interventions can be articulated in testable ways. Havens describes seven potential targets (or impasses, as he calls them) of therapeutic interventions. The first of the seven impasses he mentions, paranoid states, is used to illustrate the features of his descriptions that make his clinical observations readily testable.

DEFINITION OF THE CLINICAL PHENOMENA OF INTEREST: HOW TO IDENTIFY THE PATIENT SAMPLE

Havens starts by listing observable signs (criteria) that identify the clinical condition about which he is writing. In this case his interest is paranoid states, and he provides several defining features of such states, for example, "sustained attacks on therapist or others" and "evidence of externalization of blame or responsibility." Ideally, the signs that Havens identifies would be further elaborated upon and illustrated with specific examples. For example, a minimum period of time would be given in which the signs need to be observed to qualify as sustained, such as "manifested in treatment sessions for at least 3 weeks." In addition, several examples of each criterion would be given that could be observed in therapy session material. That is, examples of "attacks on the therapist" would be provided, such as "patient tells therapist that he or she is knowingly taking patient's money without providing adequate benefit."

DESCRIPTION OF RECOMMENDED INTERVENTIONS

The interventions that Havens proffers to resolve (change) paranoid states are described in a way that is specific enough for research purposes. Moreover, Havens's descriptions of interventions are particularly well suited for testing because they include three dimensions that all interventions necessarily have: posture (nonverbal), verbal content, and affective tone. Thus, Havens provides an unusually complete description of the interventions he advocates. Moreover, his description of each dimension is at a very concrete (observable) level. For example, for the postural dimension, he describes the specific seating arrangement that he believes is an important determinant of the effect of the intervention. Regarding content, Havens once again specifically describes the interventions that he advocates, noting, for example, that first-person pronouns should be replaced by third-person pronouns.

ASSUMPTIONS UNDERLYING RECOMMENDED INTERVENTIONS

The fact that Havens articulates the assumptions that support his recommended interventions is useful for research. The more complete the explication of the theoretical underpinning of recommended therapeutic interventions, the more likely it is that a researcher can design a study and procedures that provide a valid test of theoretically derived hypotheses about the impact and/or mechanisms of action of interventions.

OUTCOME MEASURES

Finally, Havens states what he regards as a valid measure of the effectiveness of the interventions. In essence, the measure he recommends is low frequency of the signs that he initially uses to define the clinical phenomenon his techniques are designed to affect. What Havens does here is consistent with procedures standardly used in treatment research based on group comparison designs. For example, when the efficacy of pharmacological and psychotherapeutic treatments for depression is examined, the major outcome measure typically is an index of depressive symptomatology.

CONCLUDING REMARKS

In my view, several of the impasses and their treatment that Dr. Havens describes are elegant examples of the conciseness that can be associated with clear thinking about clearly defined, observable phenomena. Moreover, several of his descriptions of clinical impasses and recommended interventions for them illustrate a way to think and write about clinical material that is readily translatable into clinically relevant studies. Thus, his work provides an excellent example of one way to bridge the gap between clinical practice and research that many clinicians experience.

REFERENCES

American Psychiatric Association. (1980). *Diagnostic and statistical manual of mental disorders* (3rd ed.). Washington, DC: American Psychiatric Press.

Barlow, D. H., & Hersen, M. (1984). *Single case experimental designs: Strategies for studying behavior change* (2nd ed.). New York: Pergamon Press.

Beck, A. T., Rush, A. J., Shaw, B. F., & Emery, G. (1979). *Cognitive therapy of depression.* New York: Guilford Press.

Benjamin, L. S. (1986). Breaking the family code: Analysis of videotapes of family interactions by structural analysis of social behavior (SASB). In L. S. Greenberg & W. M. Pinsof (Eds.), *The psychotherapeutic process: A research handbook* (pp. 391–438). New York: Guilford Press.

Chassan, J. B. (1979). *Research design in clinical psychology and psychiatry* (2nd ed.). New York: Wiley.

Crits-Christoph, P., Cooper, A., & Luborsky, L. (1988). The accuracy of therapists' interpretations and the outcome of dynamic psychotherapy. *Journal of Consulting and Clinical Psychology, 56,* 490–495.

Duncan, S., & Fiske, D. W. (1977). *Face-to-face interaction: Research, methods, and theory.* Hillsdale, NJ: Erlbaum.

Elliott, R. (1986). Interpersonal process recall (IPR) as a psychotherapy process research method. In L. S. Greenberg & W. M. Pinsof (Eds.), *The psychotherapeutic process: A research handbook* (pp. 503–527). New York: Guilford Press.

Garfield, S. L. (1978). Research on client variables in psychotherapy. In S. L. Garfield & A. E. Bergin (Eds.), *Handbook of psychotherapy and behavior change: An empirical analysis.* (2nd ed., pp. 191–232). New York: Wiley.

Garfield, S. L. (1986). Research on client variables in psychotherapy. In S. L. Garfield & A. E. Bergin (Eds.), *Handbook of psychotherapy and behavior change* (3rd ed., pp. 213–256). New York: Wiley.

Gill, M. M., & Hoffman, I. Z. (1982). *Analysis of transference: Vol. II. Studies of nine audio-recorded psychoanalytic sessions.* New York: International Universities Press.

Greenberg, L. S. (1984). Task analysis: The general approach. In L. N. Rice & L. S. Greenberg (Eds.), *Patterns of change: Intensive analysis of psychotherapy process* (pp. 124–148). New York: Guilford Press.

Greenberg, L. S., & Pinsof, W. (1986). *The psychotherapeutic process: A research handbook.* New York: Guilford Press.

Gurman, A. S. (1977). The patient's perception of the therapeutic relationship. In A. S. Gurman & A. M. Razin (Eds.), *Effective psychotherapy: A handbook of research* (pp. 503–543). New York: Pergamon Press.

Hartley, D. E., & Strupp, H. H. (1983). The therapeutic alliance: Its relationship to outcome in brief psychotherapy. In J. Masling (Ed.), *Empirical studies of psychoanalytical theories* (Vol. 1, pp. 1–37). Hillsdale, NJ: Erlbaum.

Hawton, K., Salkovskis, P. M., Kirk, J., & Clark, D. M. (Eds.). (1989). *Cognitive behaviour therapy for psychiatric problems: A practical guide.* Oxford: Oxford University Press.

Hill, C. E. (1989). *Therapist techniques and client outcomes: Eight cases of brief psychotherapy.* Newbury Park, CA: Sage.

Hill, C. E. (1991). Almost everything you ever wanted to know about how to do process research on counseling and psychotherapy but didn't know who to ask. In C. E. Watkins & L. J. Schneider (Eds.), *Research in counseling* (pp. 85–118). Hillsdale, NJ: Erlbaum.

Hilliard, R. B. (1993). Single-case methodology in psychotherapy process and outcome research. *Journal of Consulting and Clinical Psychology, 61* (3), 373–380.

Horowitz, M. J. (1979). *States of mind: Analysis of change in psychotherapy.* New York: Plenum.

Horvath, A. O., & Greenberg, L. S. (1986). The development of the working alliance inventory. In L. S. Greenberg & W. M. Pinsoff (Eds.), *The psychotherapeutic process: A research handbook* (pp. 529–556). New York: Guilford Press.

Horvath, A. O., & Symonds, B. D. (1991). Relation between working alliance and outcome in psychotherapy: A meta-analysis. *Journal of Consulting Psychology, 38,* 139–149.

Howard, K. I., Kopta, S. M., Krause, M. S., & Orlinsky, D. E. (1986). The dose-effect relationship in psychotherapy. *American Psychologist, 41,* 159–164.

Jones, E. E., Cumming, J. D., & Pulos, S. M. (1994). Tracing clinical themes across phases of treatment by a Q-set. In N. Miller, L. Luborsky, J. Barber, & J. Docherty (Eds.), *Psychodynamic treatment research: A handbook for clinical practice* (pp. 14–36). New York: Basic Books.

Kazdin, A. E. (1982). *Single-case research designs: Methods for clinical and applied settings.* New York: Oxford University Press.

Kiesler, D. J. (1973). *The process of psychotherapy.* Chicago: Aldine.

Lambert, M. J., & Hill, C. E. (1993). Assessing psychotherapy outcomes and processes. In A. E. Bergin & S. L. Garfield (Eds.), *Handbook of psychotherapy and behavior change* (4th ed., pp. 72–113). New York: Wiley.

Leary, T. (1957). *Interpersonal diagnosis of personality: A functional theory and methodology for personality evaluation.* New York: Ronald Press.

Luborsky, L., Crits-Cristoph, P., Alexander, L., Margolis, M., & Cohen, J. (1983). Two helping alliance methods for predicting outcomes of psychotherapy: A counting signs vs. a global rating method. *Journal of Nervous and Mental Disease, 171,* 480–491.

McNeilly, C. L., & Howard, K. I. (1991). The effects of psychotherapy: A reevaluation based on dosage. *Psychotherapy Research, 1,* 74–78.

Marziali, E., Marmar, E., & Krupnick, J. (1981). Therapeutic alliance scales: Development and relationship to psychotherapy outcome. *American Journal of Psychiatry, 138,* 361–364.

Moras, K., & Hill, C. E. (1991). Rater selection for psychotherapy process research: An evaluation of the state of the art. *Psychotherapy Research, 2,* 113–123.

Moras, K., Telfer, L. A., & Barlow, D. H. (1993). Efficacy and specific effects data on new treatments: A case study strategy with mixed anxiety-depression. *Journal of Consulting and Clinical Psychology, 61,* 412–420.

Orlinsky, D. E., & Howard, K. I. (1986). Process and outcome in psychotherapy. In S. L. Garfield & A. E. Bergin (Eds.), *Handbook of psychotherapy and behavior change* (3rd ed., pp. 311–381). New York: Wiley.

Orlinsky, D. E., Grawe, K., & Parks, B. K. (1993). Process and outcome in psychotherapy-noch einmal. In A. E. Bergin & S. L. Garfield (Eds.), *Handbook of psychotherapy and behavior change* (4th ed., pp. 270–376). New York: Wiley.

Piper, W. E., Azim, H. F. A., McCallum, M., & Joyce, A. S. (1990). Patient suitability and outcome in short-term individual psychotherapy. *Journal of Consulting and Clinical Psychology, 58,* 475–481.

Piper, W. E., Azim, H. F. A., Joyce, A. S., McCallum, M., Nixon, G. W. H., & Segal, P. S. (1991). Quality of object relations versus interpersonal functioning as predictors of therapeutic alliance and psychotherapy outcome. *Journal of Nervous and Mental Disease, 179,* 432–438.

Rice, L. N., & Greenberg, L. S. (1984). The new research paradigm. In L. N. Rice & L. S. Greenberg (Eds.), *Patterns of change: Intensive analysis of psychotherapy process* (pp. 7–25). New York: Guilford Press.

Rice, L. N., & Saperia, E. P. (1984). Task analysis and the resolution of problematic reactions. In L. N. Rice & L. S. Greenberg (Eds.), *Patterns of change: Intensive analysis of psychotherapy process* (pp. 29–65). New York: Guilford Press.

Russell, R. L. (Ed.). (1987). *Language of psychotherapy: Strategies of discovery.* New York: Plenum.

Seitz, P. F. D. (1966). The consensus problem in psychoanalytic research. In L. A. Gottschalk & A. H. Auerbach (Eds.), *Methods of research in psychotherapy* (pp. 209–225). New York: Appleton-Century-Crofts.

Silberschatz, G., Fretter, P. B., & Curtis, J. T. (1986). How do interpretations influence the process of psychotherapy? *Journal of Consulting and Clinical Psychology, 54,* 646–652.

Spence, D. P. (1982). *Narrative truth and historical truth: Meaning and interpretation in psychoanalysis.* New York: Norton.

Spence, D. P., Dahl, H., Jones, E. E. (1993). Impact of interpretation on associative freedom. *Journal of Consulting and Clinical Psychology, 61,* 395–402.

Strupp, H. H., Fox, R. E., & Lessler, K. (1969). *Patients view their psychotherapy.* Baltimore: Johns Hopkins Press.

Weiss, J., & Sampson, H. (1986). *The psychoanalytic process: Theory, clinical observation and empirical research.* New York: Guilford Press.

CHAPTER 12

Psychotherapy Research and the Views of Clinicians

Mardi J. Horowitz

PSYCHOTHERAPY RESEARCH has become more of an influence on the field of psychotherapy than many clinicians believe. The reason lies in modern economics: only effective treatments will be covered by insurance. We are on this train for better or worse, and we can make it better by using research to revitalize theories of how to formulate cases and choose appropriate psychotherapy techniques. Considering such goals, I comment first on the chapter by Greenberg and then on that by Spence.

Response to "Psychotherapy Research: A Clinician's View" by Jay Greenberg

Greenberg concludes that psychotherapy researchers and clinicians take diverse approaches. I am both researcher and clinician, and I agree that this has been the case. As a clinician, I act on the basis of both my intuition and my conscious plan, which in turn is based on a configurational formulation developed between hours of contact with the patient. My information processing during sessions moves along swiftly and combines observation and empathy. As a researcher, I can take much more time to form my inferences. I seek to check those inferences, which are just part of a formulation, against those drawn by other parties. One goal of research is just such checking of one's own views for agreement with other observers. In the future we can alter intuition by training based increasingly on research that is "clinician friendly" in that it helps with diagnosis, formulation, prognosis, and treatment planning.

The most clinician-friendly research is that which provides qualitative results that describe aspects of how one might formulate a case at multiple levels of inter-causation and use that formulation to plan for change to be facilitated by psychotherapy. Seeking consensus in research does not always involve quantitative methodology (other than some checks on reliability). Qualitative research can consist of a repeated review of material. The aim is a sober and objective pursuit of pattern recognition leading to descriptive and then explanatory models. This type of approach in research is not unlike the clinician's tasks of objective case formulation and planning how change processes may occur, but it is often more time-consuming.

As it happens, Greenberg takes such additional time, concluding that he is doing research by his self-conducted analysis. Like all self-analysis, it is interminable. Were he to record a monologue during his self-analysis so that other researchers could join in analyzing him, the process would come closer to the issues of reliability in clinical psychotherapy research.

The relevant issue is not whether these researchers would arrive at the same pattern recognition Greenberg does. There are always objective-to-subjective differences. Concerns regarding reliability and consensus have to do with whether the researchers would agree with each other.

Consensus in research depends upon operationally defining theoretical constructs, finding these constructs independently in the same materials, and modeling how the variables so measured may interact. Researchers might work to agree upon which themes or self-concepts are repetitive in Greenberg's self-analysis. They might all use the same format for recording their observations. Studying Greenberg's countertransferences, they might use role-relationship models of Greenberg's view of self, of patient, and of transactions. They might show a configuration of different self schemes and role-relationship models built from Greenberg's description of his countertransferences. They might do the same for the patient's transferences. Their agreement could then be checked.

A format used in configurational formulation for recording such inferences about internalized schematizations of self and relationship(s) is shown in figure 12.1. Groups of such role-relationship models can be put into a configuration of organizing views for several states of mind as shown in figure 12.2. This role-relationship model configuration is a qualitative format that can be used reliably (Horowitz & Eells, 1993; Horowitz, Eells, Singer, and Salovy, 1993; Eells, Horowitz, et al., 1993) and that has shown convergent validity with other formulation methods that use interpersonal models such as a precursor to the RRMC, Lester Luborsky's Core Conflictual Relationship Theme (Horowitz, 1989; Horowitz, Luborsky, & Popp, 1991; Horowitz, Merluzzi, et al., 1991).

Using this approach to states and person schemes one could conduct an analysis of recurrent themes of self and object representations and of sequences and layers of interpersonal beliefs within the mind of a subject (therapist or patient). Such a research effort would be quite relevant to the example presented by Greenberg and, more importantly, to the day-to-day work of therapy. Greenberg describes three points of view, those presented by the treating clinician, the supervising clinician, and the consultant to the supervisor. While not in full agreement, a pattern of self-and-other views was nonetheless repeated. Roles of self and other were sometimes reversed.

Figure 12.1. A Role-Relationship. The actions and traits depicted are a mental schema of what form real events *might* take. The patterned expected sequence of the events is labeled with successive numbers. Actions include emotional expressions and conscious experiences. Self-estimation may include pride, guilt, bolstering of self, and attacks on self.

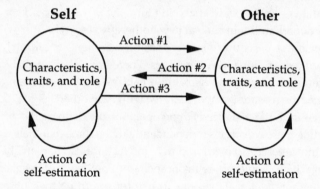

Figure 12.2. A Role-Relationship Models Cofiguration (RRMC) Format Characteristics of self and other in each state of mind are written in the circles. Transactional scripts can stem from ① an expression from the self, leading to ② a response from other, and to ③ reactions of the self to that expected response.

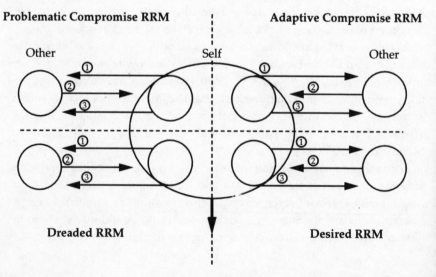

The reports were not competitive but, rather, additive, with each report enlarging the frame of understanding. Recording the transactive schemas in a systematic way provides the results of research to readers.

To unpack this, let us simplify the three frames of reference reported by Greenberg in an example. The analyst defines for the patient a repetitive intrapsychic schematization that he has inferred from his detection of repeated patterns and stories the patient tells about herself in relation to others. The therapist also sees reenacted in the transference a pattern that has to do with past memories and future expectations as well as the current enactment in the therapy context. This recurrent pattern is one in which the patient sees herself as being the passive and helpless object of interest to a powerful but somewhat out of control male who wants to force her into doing things that are both dangerous and exciting.

The supervisor then widens the frame a notch: he points out that the therapist, by giving an interpretation to a patient who has claimed she is unclear about what is going on, has enacted the powerful male person, once again forcing ideas that are dangerous but exciting upon the patient. The consultant then further widens the frame by noting that the supervisor has done the same thing to the treating clinician, forcing upon him an exciting and dangerous idea (in this instance, the idea that things are going on that have not been fully, consciously recognized).

What would a researcher do with such a record? He or she would have the recorded transaction transcribed and get judges to apply themselves to a repeated review of these materials. A format would allow the judges to put all their inferences into a common form in order to permit better comparisons.

Suppose a Role Relationship Models Configuration such as shown in figure 12.2 were used by the inference-making judges. New agreement-rating judges might then evaluate the overall goodness of fit of these role-relationship models to one another and to contrasting models from other patients. This can lead to significant findings of agreement. In a relevant study, Horowitz and Eells (1993) found that judges were able to relate RRMCs as construed by experts back to the original clinical material from which inferences were drawn in a manner beyond chance probabilities. In a study yet to be published, Horowitz, Eells, Singer, and Salovey (1993) found that five early therapy hours predicted RRMC from transference at therapy hours 60-plus and 120-plus.

The central point is this: a single clinician can make wonderful discoveries. These must be checked before they are taught to new clinicians. Such checks reduce the risk of bias present in research done by clinicians working alone on patient material and making authoritative assertions. Certainly, an audience would be pleased to have a reported agreement beyond the insights of a single clinician.

Some systematic approaches might turn out to be better than others in terms of yielding agreement on the same material and encompassing clinical richness. We might eventually find systematic routes to better case formulation. We might find out that persons trained in systematic procedures are able to make better formulations and, therefore, better treatment plans, which in turn achieve superior outcomes. With such systematic gains we might help the young therapist in supervision to recognize different states of transference and countertransference in each individual patient. We can teach our trainees to become "wiser" faster. That is, a systematic approach such as configurational formulation (Horowitz, 1987) could help a trainee understand patients a little more quickly and with less experience than would otherwise be the case.

Response to "The Failure to Ask the Hard Questions" by Donald Spence

Spence emphasizes what needs to be known, and I agree with him as he asserts the need to overhaul psychoanalytic theory. That revitalization will require new theory, excisions of some prior constructs about motives, a change in language, and an effort to establish linkages to other domains. As that effort proceeds, one will find that there are many areas of ambiguity.

One of the questions Spence poses has to do with a patient's memory for specific events. How does it change over time? Interpretations may affect inhibitions that have obstructed the recollection of major life episodes. Important reschematization can occur as memories are integrated with other knowledge structures, deepening an understanding of the motives and intentions of people who had roles in the recalled events.

As it happens, one area of research within our group at the University of California, San Francisco, has concerned the mourning process, in which recollection (including intrusive memories) is prominent. Both the memories of the relationship long before the death as well as the memories of the event surrounding the death are important for mourners to reconsider and difficult for them to review. That is one reason a mourning process takes place over many months. Only then does the person gradually reschematize his or her view of self in relation to the deceased; this is a modification of the structure of internalized knowledge. Until then, discrete perceptual memories, for example, of deathbed or illness scenes, may occur as intrusive images. Equally significant are inhibitions of memory during mourning. A person may be unable to remember the deceased, perhaps for months be unable to visualize the face or hear the voice. Later on, voluntary recollection in images is once again possible, because in the interim a working-through process has occurred. These apparent deflections of memory can be quantified.

Instruments such as the Impact of Event Scale (Horowitz, Wilner, & Alvarez, 1979) and the Stress Response Rating Scale (Horowitz, 1986; Weiss, Horowitz, & Wilner, 1984) give information about hypermemory or hyperattentiveness (intrusions) and hypomemory or hypoattentiveness (avoidances).

Change in intrusions or avoidances can be graphed over time showing a process of integration (Horowitz, 1986; Horowitz, Marmar, Weiss, Kaltreider, & Wilner, 1986). By recording psychotherapy discourse and by segmenting that discourse in terms of the topics under contemplation, one can examine the kind of verbal and nonverbal dimensions that Spence addresses in his article. In our program, analyses so far have focused on the patient's discourse, but equivalent measures are taken and can be assessed on therapist's discourse.

Such studies are currently under way and suggest that it is possible to show empirical evidence for psychoanalytic propositions about the coupling of heightened recollection and emotional display with defensive inhibitions to stifle emotion. For example, in a woman who received 28 hours of psychodynamically oriented psychotherapy for a pathological grief reaction, Horowitz, Milbrath, Jordan, and colleagues (in press) converged various verbal and nonverbal measures on issues having to do with the memory of the relationship with the deceased as compared with other topics of discourse. The results offer empirical support for theoretical models of conflict, because memories of the deceased were associated with both heightened emotionality and heightened signs of both verbal and nonverbal warding off. These quantitative results, using reliable measures of defensiveness and expression, were found in other intensively studied cases (Horowitz, Stinson, et al., in press).

In our research we used nonverbal warding-off behaviors, states of mind, and dyselaboration as independent measures. Dyselaboration is the assembly of several categories of verbal signs of defensive control processes: it includes obscurations, disavowels, jittering across the surface of topics, short-circuiting switches between topics, and deliberate use of low-meaning fillers. All of these were reliably judged (for example, Horowitz, Milbrath, Reidbord, & Stinson, 1993). The definitions used in these measures of defensive control can be useful in training clinicians to make better observations, as shown, for example, in table 12.1 for assessing "dyselaborations" during verbal communication.

Such research efforts indicate that it is possible both to incorporate clinical concerns into research practice and to infuse research methods with clinical wisdom. We have reached an era in which we can go beyond authoritative statements by clinicians, including opinions of committees of clinicians, as in the construction of *DSM-III* (American Psychiatric Association, 1980.). We can move toward greater precision of clinical description and therefore, clinical explanation.

Table 12.1   Categories of Dyselaboration

Level	Category	Definition of category
Level 0	No dyselaboration	
Level 1	Filler and hedging	Filler: Words that produce hesitation in the smooth flow of speech without adding content to the discourse, including repetitions of utterances that are not words (e.g., "eh," "er," "uhmm," and "mm") and phrases, such as "you know," "I mean," and "well," that do not function meaningfully in the sentence. More than one repetition of any word can be scored as filler if it does not serve to add or emphasize information in the discourse (e.g., "And, uh, but I . . . I actually . . . I . . . I . . . I felt as I . . . I as . . . was on the threshold of being anxious, but I . . . I . . . I wasn't").
		Hedging: Words that blunt, minimize, or dampen the original intent of a statement. Stalling by paraphrasing to avoid advancing a topic is also scored as hedging (e.g., "I was *a little bit* guilty about being there").
Level 2	Moving away from emotional concepts by peripheral statements or jittering	Peripheral statements: Moving from the meaningful heart of a topic to ideas that have less to do with the topic, i.e., redirecting the flow of ideas away from significant ones and toward less significant ones is scored under this category (e.g., "Um, I don't know, if it was after my brother died that I began to have these problems *but I* attribute it to my age. I mean, as I get older it is more difficult; I mean, it's okay but it's not like it was in my twenties"
		Jittering: Presentation of information that jumps in a disorderly fashion from perspective to perspective or alternates between process- and content-oriented comments (e.g., "No, I don't think that you know. But I think that, you know, I've thought about it a lot. Of course, I've wondered why this happens and in what connection and stuff. And I kept thinking that if it wasn't manipulative, in other words, that you weren't going to try to get me to think a different way about it, that it wasn't going to work. But it still seems manipulative")

Table 12.1 (*Continued*)

Level	Category	Definition of category
Level 3	Disavowal, misattribution, and deliberate misunderstandings	Disavowals that distort significance: A direct negation of a previously expressed wish, emotion, or feeling that the subject most likely does have (e.g., "I was very angry at my brother. Well, no, actually, I was not angry")
		Misattributions: Misleading the other by falsely ascribing wishes, actions, or emotions to someone other than the self or by falsely identifying the object of wishes, actions, and feelings; also scored in this category are shifts from the self as an active agent to the self as a passive recipient of actions, feelings, or wishes of others (e.g., "Some folks just get angry")
		Deliberate misunderstandings: These are scored when the speaker's response ignores or misconstrues clearly presented comments of the other speaker, while staying on the larger topic (e.g., if the therapist asks, "If I inquire about something, do you have the sense that I don't trust you?" and the patient says, "Like what other things have you inquired about that I hadn't trusted you with?")
Level 4	Shifting prematurely	Shifting to another topic at a point when the former topic is still clearly under discussion (distinguished from moving peripheral, which stays within the same topic): Patient: My daughter misses having a father, and I'm not quite ready to give her another one. Uh, but when I am, you know, it's going to be a battle. Therapist: It's not so simple to give her another one, either. It isn't just the matter of plugging in a new replacement. Patient: Mm-hm. Absolutely. Yeah, and I have not been able to sit down and do any of the paperwork I need to do, you know, just to keep my life in order. God, it's just this mountain, keeps growing.

It is important to note that a research effort can stitch back and forth between clinical work and empirical findings. Publications that do both teach new clinicians to use research data. For example, we reported outcome results in a book on how to do brief therapy—*Personality Styles and Brief Psychotherapy* (Horowitz et al., 1984)—and received informal feedback on how trainees found this useful.

The book *Stress Response Syndromes* (Horowitz, 1986) has case histories and data on the outcome of brief therapy as well as instructions on how to formulate a case and conduct the treatment. The task of research forces clear operational definitions, and reliability studies check whether these operational definitions are sufficiently clear and valid. The useful definitions can then be taught to training clinicians. In this way greater precision of language should revitalize psychotherapy theory in general.

Part of this combined approach, a convergence between psychodynamics and cognitive science, means a better language. There is greater precision of language used in cognitive theory simply because it has stemmed from more empirical research than has the clinical wisdom in psychodynamics. What about the long-standing fear that there will be a loss of poetics, hermeneutics, clinical richness, and emotional evocation when one uses a more precise language? This will not happen if we maintain a focus on the clinical phenomena of interest in psychodynamics: the richly emotional and conflictual texture of interpersonal relationships and personal identity over the life cycle.

It does not seem to me that this is too big a task; indeed, we are already moving toward it. This will be an exciting time, with important contributions to be made both by clinicians who do not do research and by researchers who understand the clinical enterprise.

REFERENCES

American Psychiatric Association. (1980). *Diagnostic and statistical manual of mental disorders* (3rd ed.). Washington, DC: American Psychiatric Press.

Horowitz, M. J. (1986). *Stress response syndromes* (2nd ed.). Northvale, NJ: Aronson.

Horowitz, M. J. (1987) *States of Mind: Configurational Analysis of Individual Personality.* New York: Plenum.

Horowitz, M. J. (1989). Relationship schema formulation: Role-relationship models and intrapsychic conflict. *Psychiatry, 52,* 260–274.

Horowitz, M. J. (Ed.). (1991). *Person schemas and maladaptive interpersonal patterns.* Chicago: University of Chicago Press.

Horowitz, M. J., & Eells, T. D. (1993). Role-relationship model configurations: A method of psychotherapy case formulation. *Psychotherapy Research, 3,* 56–68.

Horowitz, M. J., Luborsky, L., & Popp, C. (1991). A comparison of the role-relationship models configuration and the core conflictual relationship theme. In M. J. Horowitz (Ed.), *Person schemas and maladaptive interpersonal patterns* (pp. 197–212). Chicago: University of Chicago Press.

Horowitz, M. J., Marmar, C., Krupnick, J., Wilner, N., Kaltreider, N., & Wallerstein, R. S. (1984). *Personality styles and brief psychotherapy*. New York: Basic Books.

Horowitz, M. J., Marmar, C., Weiss, D., Kaltreider, N., & Wilner, N. (1986). Comprehensive analysis of change after brief dynamic psychotherapy. *American Journal of Psychiatry, 143,* 582–590.

Horowitz, M. J., Merluzzi, T. V., Ewert, M., Ghannam, J. H., Hartley, D., & Stinson, C. H. (1991). Role-relationship models configuration (RRMC). In M. J. Horowitz (Ed.), *Person schemas and maladaptive interpersonal patterns* (pp. 115–146). Chicago: University of Chicago Press.

Horowitz, M. J., Milbrath, C., Jordan, D., Stinson, C., Ewert, M., Redington, D. J., Fridhandler, B., Reidbord, S., & Hartley, D. (in press). Expressive and defensive behavior during discourse on unresolved topics: A single case study. *Journal of Personality.*

Horowitz, M. J., Milbrath, C., Reidbord, S., & Stinson, C. H. (1993). Elaboration and dyselaboration: Measures of expression and defense in discourse. *Psychotherapy Research.*

Horowitz, M. J., Stinson, C. H., Curtis, D., Ewert, M., Redington, D. J., Singer, J. L., Bucci, W., Mergenthaler, E., Milbrath, C., & Hartley, D. (1993). Topics and signs: Defensive control of emotional expression. *Journal of Consulting and Clinical Psychology.* 61:431–430

Horowitz, M. J., Wilner, N. & Alvarez, W. (1979). Impact of Events Scale: A measure of subjective stress. *Psychosomatic Mdicine, 41,* 209–218.

Luborsky, L., & Crits-Christoph, P. (Eds.). (1990). *Understanding transference: The CCRT method.* New York: Basic Books.

Weiss, D. S., Horowitz, M. J., & Wilner, N. (1984). Stress Response Rating Scale: A clinician's measure. *British Journal of Clinical Psychology, 23,* 202–215.

CHAPTER 13

Toward a Working Alliance Between Research and Practice

Jeremy D. Safran and J. Christopher Muran

The challenge of conducting research that is clinically meaningful has been a persistent nemesis in the psychotherapy field. Like an unsettled spirit, which sometimes slumbers but is never completely at peace, it continues to haunt researchers. The chapters by Edelson and by Kernberg and Clarkin in this volume have done a good job of articulating a number of the reasons for the limited impact of many of the research findings on practicing clinicians. As Edelson points out, psychotherapy research often fails to produce findings relevant to the here-and-now particularities of specific cases. Information about what general type of approach is useful for different patient populations does not provide the type of idiographic, context-sensitive information that is most relevant to clinicians. A related issue, raised in both chapters, is that psychotherapy research often fails to provide the type of novel findings that can truly inform the clinician. Instead, there is a tendency to simply recycle old clinical wisdoms in an impoverished form. While these are serious concerns, it is also important not to overlook the fact that many psychotherapy researchers have struggled with these concerns over the years and continue to do so. In recent years a number of developments have taken place in an attempt to make psychotherapy research more responsive to the needs of practicing clinicians. Many of the authors of the chapters in this volume have been major contributors to this "new look" in psychotherapy research. In this chapter we briefly describe some of the characteristics, as well as provide some examples, of this emerging paradigm shift.

The New Look in Psychotherapy Research

INTENSIVE ANALYSIS

There is a growing realization that the traditional clinical trial group comparison study has serious limitations as an exclusive approach to psychotherapy research. As Edelson suggests, the finding that a particular brand of therapy is effective for the average patient is of little value to practicing clinicians who are confronted with the question of how to proceed with the specific patient who is at this moment in front of them. Skilled clinicians are constantly adjusting their interventions in response to moment-to-moment changes in their patients (Rice & Greenberg, 1984). Group designs allow us to make general observations about the way in which the average patient responds to a general therapeutic approach. This global level of analysis, however, does not allow the exploration of the more subtle nuances of patient–therapist interactional patterns, which therapists need to understand to be effective. Intensive analysis of individual patients within sessions and over the course of therapy allows researchers to examine this type of intrasubject variability and therapist response (Safran, Rice, & Greenberg, 1988).

It is striking to note that over two decades ago the consensus of a group of leading psychotherapy researchers interviewed by Bergin and Strupp (1972) was that an overemphasis on large-scale clinical outcome studies would seriously limit the value of psychotherapy research to the practicing clinician and that there was an important need for the more intensive analysis of single cases in order to yield clinically useful information. Admittedly, the field has been slow to address the type of criticism spelled out in Bergin and Strupp's (1972) prescient survey and made by many of the authors in this volume. How can we account for this lag? At least part of the problem can no doubt be attributed to a self-conscious tendency among social science researchers to emulate what are taken to be the strategies of so-called hard sciences, such as physics and chemistry. Another reason has been the absence of clear-cut alternatives or guidelines for methodologically rigorous intensive analysis in psychotherapy research. Researchers have often tended to equate intensive analytic research with the uncontrolled case study. The situation, however, is changing, and a number of different approaches to intensive analysis are emerging. Examples include Rice and Greenberg's (1984) task analysis strategy; Horowitz's (1987) configurational analysis approach; McCullough's (1984) stage-process model approach; and Weiss, Sampson, and the Mount Zion Psychotherapy Research Group's (1987) plan formulation approach. Since a number of authors describe their approaches in detail elsewhere in this book, we will not go into greater detail here.

SENSITIVITY TO CONTEXT

The second characteristic of the new research paradigm consists of an increased sensitivity to the context in which interventions are administered and various change processes take place. Rather than asking the more traditional research question, What general treatment approach is effective for the average patient belonging to a particular population? a number of investigators are asking the question, What specific intervention is helpful in this specific context? For example, Greenberg (1984) has compared the relative effectiveness of the Gestalt two-chair intervention to empathic reflection in the context of what he terms a split, that is, a conflict between two partial tendencies of the self. Rice and Sapeira (1984) have compared the relative efficacy of an intervention termed "systematic evocative unfolding" to standard empathic reflection in the context of a particular client state considered an adverse reaction, that is, a state of distressing and puzzling confusion that a client experiences in response to a particular encounter. Weiss et al. (1987) have evaluated the hypothesis that specific types of therapist intervention will be more therapeutic in the context of specific plan formulations. Research of this type moves beyond the investigation of simple treatment-by-patient interactions to a level of specificity that is much closer to the level at which actual clinical decision making takes place. We agree with Edelson when he points out that clinicians do not as a rule ask the question, What general type of treatment strategy is appropriate for this general type of patient? but, rather, What specific response will be most facilitative in this specific moment with this specific patient?

DISCOVERY-ORIENTED AND QUALITATIVE RESEARCH

Various researchers have attempted to address both Edelson's concern that research should offer new insights and intuitions and Kernberg and Clarkin's criticism that much of the published psychotherapy research is trivial by advocating that the traditional emphasis on hypothesis testing in psychotherapy research be augmented with a discovery-oriented approach. Mahrer (1988) has been a persuasive spokesman for the importance of discovery-oriented research and has articulated a number of methodological guidelines. Similarly, a number of researchers are emphasizing the importance of supplementing the traditional emphasis on hypothesis testing and quantitative analysis with analyses that are more qualitative in nature. They argue that an exclusive preoccupation with quantification restricts the researcher's attention to relatively gross phenomena that are easily measured and to simple hypotheses that are easily tested. As a result, many of the more subtle phenomena that are of real interest to the clinician are ignored. Stiles (1991) has recently presented a useful paper that articulates a number of criteria for evaluating the methodological soundness of research that is more qualitative in nature. Many of the researchers already cited and in this volume use one or another form of discovery-oriented or qualitative analysis in varying degrees in their research programs. Some noteworthy examples include Rennie (1992), who has adapted the approach of grounded research from sociology in an attempt to discover patient deferential behavior in therapy and Elliott (1984), who has explored the nature of the patient's subjective experience during moments of insight in psychotherapy by using the interpersonal process recall approach. The attempt to discover underlying processes of change also plays an important role in Rice and Greenberg's (1984) task analysis strategy. One of the problems with psychology research in general and psychotherapy research in particular is that there is a tendency to neglect the importance of observation, since the phenomenon of interest is much closer to home than is the case in the physical sciences. This in turn has led to a tendency to test hypotheses before there are hypotheses worth testing (Meehl, 1978; Safran et al., 1988). As Weimer (1979) asserts, "Scientific hypotheses, if they are good informative ones, are highly novel, bold conjectures that are as logically improbable as probable. . . . The aim of science is to learn new things—not to enshrine reality" (p. 38).

FOCUS ON UNDERLYING MECHANISMS

After the initial heyday of psychotherapy process research with Carl Rogers and his colleagues, the attempt to elucidate the underlying mechanisms through which change takes place took a back seat to psychotherapy outcome research, which focuses on the evaluation of therapeutic efficacy. The traditional criticism of process research has centered around a concern about practical relevance of psychotherapy research of a more theoretical nature. The rejection of psychotherapy process research as having a rightful place in a scientific discipline stems in part from a misunderstanding of how progress takes place in the hard sciences and from the assumption that science should be exclusively concerned with prediction and control and that explanation does not play an important role (Safran et al., 1988). We believe that the increasing acceptance by the research mainstream of the potential relevance of research that attempts to explicate the underlying mechanisms of change has been an important factor increasing the relevance of research to the clinician in recent years.

IDENTIFICATION OF CHANGE EVENTS

An important contribution to the new research paradigm had been the investigation of specific psychotherapy change events, that is, recurring patterns of psychotherapy process that consistently lead to change. Examples of this approach have already been cited, such as Greenberg's (1984) research on the two-chair intervention, Rice and Sapeira's (1984) research on systematic evocative unfolding events, and Elliott's (1984) research on insight. Research of this type incorporates a number of the features already described. Delineating a circumscribed, well-defined change event of practical and theoretical significance increases the context sensitivity of current research. Moreover, such research usually entails some attempt to explicate the underlying mechanisms through which the change takes place. And the researcher typically incorporates discovery-oriented, qualitative, and intensive analytic strategies as part of the research program. One of the central features of the change-events paradigm that increases the potential relevance of psychotherapy research to the clinician is its attempt to find some middle ground between traditional research strategies that buy generalizability at the cost of clinical meaningfulness and case study approaches, which capture the richness of the clinical situation at the expense of generalizability. By narrowing the range of investigation to a specific but generalizable change process, the researcher is able to focus intensively on some of the more subtle nuances of patient, therapist, and patient–therapist interactional processes that the clinician needs to understand. Since a change event is, however, by definition a recurring pattern of therapeutic process leading to change, generalizations can be made.

Models of Patient States and Patterns of Change

Another important contribution that also incorporates many of the features already discussed and increases the relevance of psychotherapy research to the clinician is the attempt to develop models to capture regularities in the sequencing of characteristic patient states, patient performance patterns, and patient–therapist interactional patterns that are associated with change. Process models of this type are clinically instructive because they can sensitize clinicians to subtleties of therapeutic process that might otherwise remain elusive. The key thing about them is that they are based on rigorous, intensive observation of single cases that can reveal patterns that can be more difficult to detect in observational efforts subscribing to an exclusively extensive analysis. Because they are based on systematic observation, they can function as a valuable adjunct to one of the most important tools clinicians have at their disposal, namely, their own pattern recognition abilities. A knowledge of the different states through which the patient travels or progresses during the resolution process can provide clinicians with benchmarks to indicate when the therapeutic process is on task and when it is off task. The different stages of the resolution model can thus function as indices of progress, providing the therapist with information about how things are proceeding on a moment-by-moment basis. For example, Horowitz's (1987) configurational analysis approach can sensitize the clinician to regularities in the manner in which a particular patient cycles between different states of mind, that is, different characteristic ways of processing, reacting to, and defending against difficult or painful affective experiences. This in turn can help the therapist become aware of the therapist–patient interactional factors that mediate the transition between different states. Greenberg's (1984) task analysis of the two-chair intervention can sensitize clinicians to the types of shifts in patient performance that suggest that the patient is progressing along the pathway to resolution. McCullough's (1984) stage-process model approach maps out the different stages that one can expect over the course of therapy in the treatment of specific disorders (for example, dysthymic disorder).

An Application of the New Research Paradigm to the Study of the Therapeutic Alliance

In order to illustrate the new research developments we have just described, we present in this section our ongoing research program designed to clarify the role of therapeutic alliance in the psychotherapeutic process.[1]

BACKGROUND AND SIGNIFICANCE

From Freud's (1912/1958) early theoretical papers on transference to the present, the therapeutic relationship has been an important focus of concern in the psychotherapy literature (for example, Frank, 1961; Strupp, 1989). It has received particular attention from the interpersonal and object relations traditions, where psychological and psychopathological development has been couched in a relational context (see Greenberg & Mitchell, 1983, for a review). In addition, it has even begun to attract the interest of cognitive (for example, Guidano, 1991; Safran & Segal, 1990) and behavioral theorists (for example, Kohlenberg & Tsai, 1991). The therapeutic relationship has recently been described as the "quintessential integrative variable," because its importance does not seem to lie within one school of thought (Wolfe & Goldfried, 1988). This growing consensus regarding the importance of the therapeutic relationship has been influenced by two robust findings from the literature on psychotherapy research. The first is that while psychotherapy

[1]The program was initiated in the mid-eighties at the Clarke Institute of Psychiatry in Toronto by the first author and is currently under the auspices of the Derner Institute at Adelphi University and the Brief Psychotherapy Research Project at Beth Israel Medical Center in New York, where it is supported in part by a grant from the National Institute of Mental Health (Safran, Muran, & Winston, 1992).

has been shown to be effective, no particular treatment has been shown to be consistently more effective than any other (for example, Smith & Glass, 1977). The second is that the best predictor of outcome in psychotherapy is the quality of the therapeutic alliance, as measured in different ways and from different perspectives (for example, Hartley, 1985; Horvath & Symonds, 1991; Luborsky & Auerbach, 1985; Strupp, 1989). In fact, Lambert, Shapiro, and Bergin (1986) concluded that while only 15% of the outcome variance is attributable to specific factors, such as treatment intervention, up to 45% of the variance is attributable to nonspecific factors, such as patient expectation that therapy will help and the therapeutic alliance.

While empirical evidence has been consistent in implicating the therapeutic relationship as a critical variable mediating treatment outcome, the research has had less to say about factors mediating the establishment of a good therapeutic alliance or about the resolution of problems in the therapeutic alliance. It is precisely this area, however, that is critical to clarify in order to improve our understanding of how to work with patients who are not benefiting from psychotherapy. In one attempt to address this issue, Foreman and Marmar (1985) examined differences in therapist interventions with poor therapeutic alliance cases that improved over the course of therapy versus those that remained unchanged or deteriorated further. This study was preliminary, however, in that it coded therapist interventions at a fairly global level rather than attempt to capture more subtle patterns of change in patient–therapist interactions associated with shifts in the quality of the therapeutic alliance.

The objective of our ongoing research efforts has been to explore the processes involved in resolving ruptures in the therapeutic alliance (Safran, Crocker, McMain, & Murray, 1990; Safran, Muran, & Samstag, 1993, in press). The rationale for this focus is that improving our understanding of these processes will provide important information relevant to avoiding potential treatment failures. Moreover, the mending of a tear in the patient–therapist relationship, or what Kohut (1984) has referred to as an empathic failure, can constitute an important corrective emotional experience that modifies the patient's interpersonal schema or generalized representation of self–other interactions (Safran, 1990a, 1990b, 1993a, 1993b). We have been attempting to develop a model of the patterns of patient–therapist transactional sequences associated with improvements in the therapeutic alliance (Safran et al., 1990, 1993, 1994). Our assumption is that this type of fine-grained change process model has the potential to provide clinicians with information about the subtleties of dynamic interactional sequences that can have a substantial impact on their clinical practice. The development of a finely detailed model of recurrent patterns can sensitize clinicians to some of the nuances of the clinical process that are typically relegated to the domain of intuitive clinical wisdom rather than explicated and tested empirically.

In this respect, our approach has been guided by the task analysis paradigm for psychotherapy research (Greenberg, 1986; Rice & Greenberg, 1984; Safran, Rice, & Greenberg, 1988). It has also been influenced by the states of mind perspective articulated by Horowitz (1987) and the stage-process model proposed by McCullough (1984). These approaches share the intuition that psychotherapy process can be seen as a sequence of recurring states that take place in identifiable patterns. By identifying these recurring states and modeling patterns of transition between them, it is thus possible to develop a road map that will sensitize the clinician to sequential patterns that are likely to occur. The idea here is not to develop an intervention manual that is rigidly prescriptive in nature but, rather, to broaden the range of options available to clinicians by providing a map that sensitizes them to a range of process states (either patient, therapist, or interactional) that may occur in a particular context as well as identifies interventions that may mediate the transition between different states.

MODELING THE RESOLUTION OF ALLIANCE RUPTURES

In a systematic attempt to clarify the processes involved in the resolution of therapeutic alliance ruptures, we have developed a preliminary stage-process model that captures the patterns of patient–therapist transactions associated with rupture resolution (Safran, 1993a, 1993b; Safran et al., 1990, 1993, 1994). This model has thus far developed from intensive observation of several cases, and some evidence has been obtained regarding the ability of the model to distinguish between therapy sessions in which alliance ruptures were resolved and those in which they remained unresolved. Our study of the resolution process incorporates a number of the most recent research developments, described earlier, and to date has included the following stages: (1) the identification of ruptures and rupture resolution sessions with postsession questionnaires completed by both patient and therapist; (2) the development of a preliminary model of rupture resolution from the intensive observations of 28 identified sessions; (3) the operationalization of the components of the model with preexisting process measures, such as the Structural Analysis of Social Behavior (Benjamin, 1974), Experiencing Scales (Klein, Mathieu-Coughlan, & Kiesler, 1986), and the client vocal quality scale (Rice & Kerr, 1986); (4) the development of a rupture resolution coding system, including criteria based on the aforementioned process measures plus semantic definitions; and (5) the preliminary verification of the model.

The model, consisting of five patient states and three therapist interventions, both of which were predicted to occur in a particular sequence, was submitted to a preliminary test in two ways. First, a series of pairwise comparisons was conducted between four resolution sessions (that is, those in which problems in the alliance had been resolved) and four nonresolution sessions (that is, those in which alliance problems remained unresolved) in order to assess the relative frequency of the model components in the two types of sessions. All eight sessions involved the same therapist, and the resolution sessions were matched with the nonresolution sessions by patient. Then a series of comfirmatory sequential analyses were conducted to compare resolution versus nonresolution sessions with regard to the sequential patterning of model components. The results were by and large consistent with the hypothesized model and suggest that a disciplined and consistent focus on the here and now of the therapeutic relationship and the willingness of therapists to explore and acknowledge their own contribution to the interaction facilitate patients' ability to deal with the alliance rupture in a direct, self-assertive fashion and to acquire an experientially grounded insight into their own contribution to the alliance rupture.

Process–Outcome Research and Treatment Development

Currently, we are conducting a pilot study funded by the National Institute of Mental Health (NIMH) at Beth Israel Medical Center that is designed to test the efficacy of a treatment whose development has been influenced by the process research that we have just described and to further refine our model of the processes involved in resolving alliance ruptures. This project constitutes an important link between the research process and treatment development. It employs an innovative methodology designed to overcome an important obstacle to finding differences in treatment efficacy and to be maximally sensitive to any real treatment effects that occur. The hypothesis guiding our proposed research strategy is that a major obstacle to finding treatment differences is a lack of contextual specificity (Beutler, 1991; Gendlin, 1986; Greenberg, 1986). In the standard clinical trial study, clustering patients together on the basis of a standard diagnostic criterion and then administering a general therapeutic approach commits the error of subscribing to the uniformity assumption described by Kiesler (1973) two decades ago. In this type of treatment design, the patient group is sufficiently heterogeneous with respect to important characteristics so that some will always benefit while others will not, regardless of the particular treatment approach, thereby washing out treatment differences.

To the extent, however, that patients can be grouped together on the basis of a variable that in theory is particularly relevant to a specific intervention, the possibility of finding treatment differences should be increased (Beutler, 1991). Following this line of reasoning, we hypothesize that selecting patients for treatment with whom therapists are having difficulties establishing a therapeutic alliance, should increase the possibility that an intervention designed specifically to resolve problems or ruptures in the alliance will have more impact than one that is not (Safran, 1990b; Safran & Segal, 1990). This type of patient selection strategy goes beyond the more traditional factorial design of clustering patients on the basis of a static or dispositional characteristic (for example, diagnostic category) by selecting on the basis of a relevant in-session performance variable (that is, ability or failure to establish an adequate therapeutic alliance). This should increase the power of the design by reducing the slippage resulting from selection on the basis of the type of trait variable that has been shown to have limited predictive validity (Beutler, 1991; Mischel, 1968).

In brief, the study attempts to target those patients in Beth Israel's Brief Psychotherapy Research Project undergoing traditional cognitive-behavioral or psychodynamic psychotherapies who are having difficulty forming a good alliance with their therapists and who are, therefore, at risk of having a poor outcome or dropping out of therapy. This is determined early in treatment based on selection criteria derived from both patient and therapist postsession ratings and from third-party observer ratings of the quality and nature of the therapeutic relationship.[2] These patients are offered the option of transferring to another treatment condition. Those who choose to transfer are then randomly assigned to one of two alternatives: (1) an experimental treatment based on principles emerging from our rupture resolution research and from relevant clinical and theoretical literature or (2) a control treatment that is different from the one they currently are in (that is, cognitive-behavioral or psychodynamic). The experimental treatment involves maintaining a sharp focus on therapeutic interactions in the here and now. Therapists selectively self-disclose their feelings or counter-transference reactions for purposes of helping patients develop an awareness of their impact on others and are encouraged to become aware of and acknowledge their own contributions to the interactions with patients.

All sessions are videotaped and serve as a source of data for evaluating the outcome as well as the process that accounts for the outcome. Outcome, both intermediate and ultimate, is also assessed by therapist and patient self-report measures, which are completed at intake, midphase, and termination of therapy, as well as after every session. These measures include idiographic (Muran, Samstag, Segal, & Winston, 1992) and nomothetic (Safran & Hill, 1989) strategies that we have developed to assess patient cognitive-interpersonal cycles. One goal of the study is to evaluate the hypothesis that patients reassigned to the experimental treatment will show greater improvement than those reassigned to the other treatments. Other goals include developing a treatment manual and adherence scale for the treatment being developed, as well as refining criteria for determining potential treat-

---

[2]See the following for relevant preliminary research regarding these selection criteria: Muran & Safran, 1990; Muran, Segal, Samstag, & Schumann, in press; 1992; Safran & Wallner, 1991; Safran et al., 1987; Winston et al., 1992.

ment failures and extending our preliminary findings regarding the validity of a model representing the processes involved in resolving problems in the therapeutic alliance. The implementation of this study demonstrates the way in which there can be an integration of psychotherapy research, incorporating the features described in the first part of this chapter, with both the development and evaluation of new treatment strategies. New findings emerging from the data collected in this study will in turn inform further refinements in our understanding of the change process in an ongoing cycle of process analysis, treatment development, and treatment evaluation, followed by another round of process analysis.

Why the Chasm and How to Bridge It

We were struck by the fact that although many of the concerns that Edelson and Kernberg and Clarkin raise about clinical research are important, these authors are apparently unfamiliar with the various developments outlined in this and other chapters that were the result of efforts to address these concerns. Our intent here is not simply to defend the value of psychotherapy research but also to raise the questions of why clinical theorists like Edelson, Kernberg, and Clarkin may be unaware of recent developments in psychotherapy research and of what can be done to increase the dialogue between clinicians and researchers. In this respect, we believe that while some aspects of this split are the result of real limitations of psychotherapy research as a possible source of guidance for clinicians, other aspects of this split are attributable to psychological and sociological factors. Both clinicians and researchers have epistemological biases that are associated with fundamental worldviews that are not easily modified. These worldviews are intertwined with one's personal sense of identity and are further consolidated and maintained by the need to establish and maintain one's personal identity by defining the self in opposition to the other. Nonempirically oriented clinicians have a bias toward discounting the potential instructiveness of information derived from research whereas researchers tend to have less faith in clinical opinion as the ultimate authority.

While it is easy enough to theorize about the underlying causes of the problem and to propose solutions, it is more difficult to implement those solutions. Regardless of the daunting nature of the task, however, it seems clear that the first step has to be the initiation of some type of dialogue. The current volume is an important step in the right direction, and we hope that this is the beginning of a trend. In addition, there are number of other steps that can be taken in terms of training at the graduate school level. For example, greater emphasis should be placed on teaching students to think about the contributions and limitations of conventional psychotherapy research, and to explore the role of research in knowledge development from the perspectives of the philosophy and sociology of science. The failure to do so has a number of negative repercussions. First, many students who do become interested in a research career have a naive perspective on methodology that leads them to understand things from the perspective of the letter rather than the spirit of the law. This discourages the development of more innovative research studies and designs and encourages the type of trivial research studies to which Kernberg and Clarkin allude. Second, some gifted students who might potentially become creative researchers are discouraged from pursuing that path because they dismiss or discount the possibility of research contributing to knowledge in any substantial way. The underlying theme here is that it would be useful for students to be trained in a fashion that encourages a stance of methodological pluralism and creativity.

It also seems to be particularly appropriate for students training in fields where they are going to be consumers and possibly producers of psychologically oriented research to develop an understanding of the sociological and psychological factors that inevitably play a role in the development of the field. For example, our understanding of various phenomena is not shaped in an unmediated fashion by empirical results. As Weimer (1979) points out, research is one tool in a rhetorical transaction between members of a scientific community. As Kuhn (1962) argued long ago, there are a variety of different sociological forces eventuating in the ultimate acceptance of a given theoretical perspective by a scientific community. These forces shape the type of research funded and conducted, the publication policies of journals, and the way in which data emerging from research are interpreted. Many graduate students have at least some passing familiarity with contemporary developments in the philosophy of science that challenge the received view or the logical empiricist perspective on science (for example, Feyerabend, 1975; Lakatos, 1978; Polanyi, 1958; Toulmin, 1986). The implications of these developments for conducting psychotherapy research are, however, rarely grappled with in a systematic way in graduate training or integrated into students' clinical and research training. An educational shift in this direction can increase the ability of students to become not only discriminating consumers but also self-aware, reflective producers of psychotherapy research. A failure to explore these kinds of issues can lead to an overidealized image of the way science actually works and, ultimately, to cynicism about the field of research when the discrepancy between the received view and reality becomes apparent. This cynicism can lead practitioners to throw out the baby with the bathwater.

Another way to resolve the rupture between research and practice involves reorienting our clinical training programs so that students who do not become researchers become more interested in the findings of psychotherapy research and students who do become psychotherapy researchers become more sensitive to the real-world concerns of the practicing clinician. At the present time most training programs in clinical psychology teach research methodology and data analysis as if students were going to become active researchers. Students are thus taught how to design, conduct, and analyze studies, but little emphasis is placed on explicitly examining how relevant various forms of research are to clinicians or on how to increase the relevance of research to the clinician and how to extract clinically relevant information from published research. As a rule, greater emphasis is placed on considerations of internal validity than external validity. The issues of external validity or clinical relevance may be explored in passing but only as asides or concerns of secondary importance. More time should be spent helping students to recognize and formulate for themselves the characteristics of research that is relevant. A useful assignment would be, for example, to have students search the literature for examples of clinically relevant research. Another assignment might consist of having students start with published research studies that have limited clinical relevance, for one reason or another, and suggest ways in which the studies could be modified in order to increase their clinical relevance.

Emphasis should be placed on helping students to develop not only a critical intelligence that focuses on identifying methodological inadequacies but also a constructive intelligence that focuses on the informed and thoughtful consumption of existing research findings and the exploration of creative ways of moving the field forward. When exclusive emphasis is placed on developing a critical intelligence, there is a danger that students will develop an unrealistic and idealized perspective that can lead to a wholesale dismissal of the entire field rather than to attempt to glean what can be extracted from the field in a discriminating fashion and to engage in constructive efforts to refine their own research in order to make it more relevant clinically.

It is important for students to be exposed to multiple alternative research paradigms. In addition to the standard group design of experimental research, which is most conventionally accepted in psychology, students should be exposed to the newer developments in psychotherapy research such as those described in this volume. They should also be exposed to alternative research paradigms from other fields, such as sociology and anthropology. Emphasis should be placed on exploring the relative strengths and weaknesses of alternative research paradigms rather than simply learning them in a rote fashion. These can be explored by discussing questions such as the following: What can be learned from clinical trial outcome studies? What can be learned from traditional psychoanalytic case studies? What can be learned from behavioral single-case studies? What can be learned from other intensive analysis approaches?

Process Is Product: The Clinical By-Products of Research

We believe that there are a number of less tangible benefits or by-products of the research process that can have a valuable clinical impact on those involved in the research process—and ultimately on the culture of psychotherapy as a whole. By examining the nature of these by-products, it should be possible to intentionally increase the positive impact of this indirect process on those who are directly involved in the research process and, through a combination of training and dissemination practices, on the nonresearcher clinician as well.

THE EMPIRICAL ATTITUDE

One of the most important potential by-products of conducting psychotherapy research for those practicing clinicians directly involved in the research process is the development of an empirical attitude, that is, a commitment to evaluate one's theories in light of observed phenomena rather than selectively attend to events in order to support one's theory. Most clinicians would agree that the willingness and ability to modify our theories to fit our patients, rather than the other way around, is one of the most important attributes of a good therapist. Yet we all know that this, like many things, is easier said than done. Being actively involved in the psychotherapy research process is, of course, no guarantee that this type of empirical attitude will generalize to one's practice as a clinician—nor even that one will develop a true empirical attitude as a researcher. Nor is the practice of conducting psychotherapy research the only way to develop this type of empirical attitude. It is, however, one way of cultivating it and to the extent that we are consciously aware of the importance of this attitude and understand it to be the essence of what psychotherapy research is all about, we increase the possibility of attaining this potential by-product. The cultivation of an empirical attitude should not be equated with a narrow-minded and naive positivist outlook that declines to accept the possible reality of phenomena that cannot be easily measured or the possible usefulness of theories that cannot be easily tested. The enemy is ideological fanaticism, whether it comes in the form of an antiempirical attitude that fails to recognize the potential contributions of empirical research of any kind or a scientistic approach that involves a rigid and superficial understanding of the way in which science really operates.

CONCEPTUAL CLARITY

There is something about the practice of operationalizing one's concepts for research purposes and articulating what would constitute evidence for and against a given hypothesis that also constitutes good training for a clinician. In clinical practice muddleheadedness and dogmatic certainty make dangerous bedmates. We are not demeaning the value of clinical intuition, nor are we arguing that only those phenomena that can be clearly understood exist. The point we are making is that concepts should reveal, not conceal. The logic associated with the process of construct development and validation in the context of empirical research is a useful tool for facilitating clear thinking in all enterprises.

Making the Implicit Explicit

Another by-product of the type of operationalization necessary for doing research is that it helps to make the implicit explicit. The best way to learn is to teach, as the well-known maxim puts it; in the same way, the activity of thinking about a phenomenon in a researchable way requires one to explicate aspects of that phenomenon that are normally taken for granted. For example, in our research program on the therapeutic alliance, it has been necessary to develop methods for clearly identifying when different kinds of ruptures in the alliance have taken place and have been resolved. This forces us to go beyond our intuitive sense of when there is a rupture in relatedness with a patient and when such ruptures are worked through in a constructive therapeutic fashion. How do we know when the quality of patient–therapist relatedness shifts? What are the cues? How can we discriminate between those situations in which such ruptures are resolved in a constructive therapeutic fashion and those in which they are simply avoided or dealt with in a superficial fashion? These are methodological questions that have to be tackled in order to investigate the processes that lead to the resolution of therapeutic alliance ruptures, yet what may at first glance appear to be rather straightforward and perhaps dry methodological questions emerge as important catalysts in their own right for enriching our clinical understanding.

In order to develop valid and reliable ways of measuring therapeutic alliance ruptures and their resolution, an ongoing cycling back and forth between implicit theory and observation of the relevant phenomena must take place. When we are required to articulate in operational terms the clues on which our intuitions are based, we are compelled to observe the relevant clinical phenomena in a more rigorous fashion *and* to examine our own implicit theories more carefully. Operationalizing terms thus reduces the gap between theory and phenomenon. This simple process of measurement development thus emerges as a type of bootstrapping activity in which construct development and validation occur simultaneously in a mutually enhancing fashion (for example, Rice & Sapeira, 1984; Safran et al., 1988). This process in and of itself contributes to our understanding of clinical phenomena.

Another example, which is discussed by Kernberg and Clarkin, consists of the activity of developing manuals for different forms of psychotherapy. This process, in and of itself, contributes to a clearer articulation of what the therapist actually does in therapy. Of course, the development of treatment manuals is not without its drawbacks. The Vanderbilt II Study (Henry & Strupp, 1991), for example, found that those therapists who demonstrated greater adherence to a manual also demonstrated more negative therapeutic process with their patients. This, however, is not an insoluble problem. The problem arises when we fail to recognize that the specific techniques articulated in a manual do not necessarily capture the essence of the approach and that one can apply these techniques and "miss the boat" in some fundamental way. The fact that it is possible to mistake the finger pointing at the moon for the moon, however, does not diminish the value of pointing at the moon. A good jazz musician knows that the essence of a creative performance can never be fully articulated in advance, but he also knows that a lot of painstaking rote learning and practice has to take place before such creativity is possible. Kernberg and Clarkin's practice of exposing trainees to different senior clinicians administering the same approach in their own distinctive ways seems to be one useful approach to remedying the problem. It may also be important to think through this problem in a more thorough way and to begin to develop a second generation of therapy manuals and associated training techniques that are intentionally designed not only to help therapists acquire a working knowledge of the basics of the approach but at the same time to nurture the development of their own unique, creative styles, which are related to their own personalities. We do not, however, believe that the development of a flexible and creative approach to psychotherapy is incompatible with learning to administer protocol-consistent interventions, any more than playing jazz is inconsistent with practicing musical scales.

ACCOUNTABILITY AND DEMYSTIFICATION

Those who argue against the usefulness of psychotherapy research and the development of manuals for different forms of psychotherapy will sometimes argue that such activities are intrinsically antithetical to the practice of psychotherapy because they fail to take into account the mysterious, ineffable, and artistic aspects of the enterprise. We have some empathy for this position because we fully believe that therapy is a mysterious process that in essence is fundamentally ineffable in many ways. It is important, however, to distinguish between mystery and mystification. The attempt to think clearly about psychotherapy, to investigate it empirically and to demand a certain amount of accountability, does not have to blind one to the mystery that lies at the heart of the process. On the other hand, the insistence that psychotherapy cannot or should not be empirically investigated is often associated with a type of arrogance and unwillingness to engage in self-examination that in the long run can only be harmful to the field and to our patients.

Regardless of the particular tangible product that may come out of a particular psychotherapy study, the process of documenting more carefully what actually takes place in therapy is in and of itself a tremendous mark of progress in the field. One of the greatest obstacles to development in our field is that we very rarely learn in public forums what actually goes on in therapy sessions. Clinical case conferences and the majority of clinical/theoretical books and articles typically provide the audience with the clinician's narrative of what took place in psychotherapy. Recently, one of us attended a psychotherapy conference at which the focus of one of the panels was "How do patients shape their therapists?" The panel members, who were all well-respected senior clinicians, responded to the question with various theoretical treatises—on the interpersonal and intrapsychic mechanisms through which therapists and patients influence one another, healthy versus unhealthy types of influence, and so on. At the end of the presentations one of the audience members asked the panel members if they could provide actual examples of situations in which they had learned from their patients. The panel members struggled with this apparently simple question as if they had been asked the most complex and obscure theoretical question. To the dismay of the audience, one of the more august senior clinicians responded to the question with another complex theoretical treatise. It was as if she was unable to distinguish between her theory and the object of her theory. It was difficult not to wonder what it would feel like to be a patient sitting in a room with her. Would one feel heard or seen?

Case presentations and theoretical formulations vary considerably with respect to how high their level of abstraction is and how remote they are from the clinical phenomena on which they are actually based. Even those case descriptions, however, that minimize the degree of abstraction as much as possible are nevertheless filtered through the clinician's narrative lens. As a result, we are rarely in a position of being able to see what actually went on in a therapy session. Two clinicians may sound highly similar in theory but look very different in practice. To the extent that our theoretical writings fail to correspond to what actually takes place in therapy, it is difficult for our theories to develop in a way that will have a positive impact on practice. For this reason, anything that increases the degree of correspondence between theory and practice stands to benefit the field of psychotherapy. The type of accountability that research requires can thus play an important role in this process.

Concluding Comments

The challenge of conducting psychotherapy research that impacts upon practice in a clinically meaningful way is a daunting one. The tension between art and science in psychology in general and the field of psychotherapy in particular is a perennial one, and any claims to have resolved this tension in a definitive way would be trivializing a profoundly difficult issue. There are times when we ourselves, like many in the field of psychotherapy research, have doubts about the ultimate payoff of the field. Freud (1937/1964) once spoke of psychoanalysis as an "impossible profession." Psychotherapy research, with all its complexities and ambiguities, seems to us to be no less impossible. The challenge is to continue to try to do clinically meaningful research in full awareness of these complexities and ambiguities, using whatever doubts arise to spur us on to greater efforts and to deeper levels of understanding.

REFERENCES

Benjamin, L. S. (1974). Structural analysis of social behavior. *Psychological Review, 81,* 392–425.

Bergin, A. E., & Strupp, H. H. (1972). *Changing frontiers in the science of psychotherapy.* Chicago: Aldine Atherton.

Beutler, L. E. (1991). Have all won and must all have prizes? Revisiting Luborsky et al.'s verdict. *Journal of Clinical and Consulting Psychology, 59,* 226–232.

Elliott, R. (1984). A discovery-oriented approach to significant change events: Interpersonal process recall and comprehensive process analysis. In L. N. Rice & L. S. Greenberg (Eds.), *Patterns of change: Intensive analysis of psychotherapy process* (pp. 249–286). New York: Guilford Press.

Feyerabend, P. (1975). *Against method: An outline of anarchistic theory of knowledge.* London: Verso.

Foreman, S. A., & Marmar, C. R. (1985). Therapist actions that address initially poor therapeutic alliances in psychotherapy. *American Journal of Psychiatry, 142,* 922–926.

Frank, J. (1961). *Persuasion and healing.* Baltimore: John Hopkins Press.

Freud, S. (1958). The dynamics of transference. In J. Strachey (Ed. & Trans.), *The standard edition of the complete psychological works of Sigmund Freud* (Vol. 12, pp. 97–108). London: Hogarth. (Original work published 1912)

Freud, S. (1964). Analysis terminable and interminable. In J. Strachey (Ed. & Trans.), *The standard edition of the complete psychological works of Sigmund Freud* (Vol. 23, pp. 216–253). London: Hogarth. (Original work published 1937).

Gendlin, E. T. (1986). What comes after traditional psychotherapy research? *American Psychologist, 41,* 131–136.

Greenberg, J., & Mitchell, S. (1983). *Object relations in psychoanalytic theory.* Cambridge, MA: Harvard University Press.

Greenberg, L. S. (1984). A task analysis of interpersonal conflict resolution. In L. N. Rice & L. S. Greenberg (Eds.), *Patterns of change: Intensive analysis of psychotherapy process* (pp. 67–123). New York: Guilford Press.

Greenberg, L. S. (1986). Change process research. *Journal of Consulting and Clinical Psychology, 54,* 4–9.

Guidano, V. (1991). *The self in process.* New York: Guilford Press.

Hartley, D. (1985). Research on the therapeutic alliance in psychotherapy. In American Psychiatric Association (Ed.), *Psychiatric update* (Vol. 4, pp. 532–549). Washington, DC: American Psychiatric Association Press.

Henry, W. P., & Strupp, H. H. (1991). Vanderbilt University: The Vanderbilt Center for Psychotherapy Research. In L. E. Beutler (Ed.), *Psychotherapy research* (pp. 166–174). Washington, DC: American Psychological Association.

Horowitz, M. J. (1987). *States of Mind* (2nd ed.). New York: Plenum.

Horvath, A. O., & Symonds, B. D. (1991). Relation between working alliance and outcome in psychotherapy: A meta-analysis. *Journal of Clinical and Consulting Psychology, 38,* 139–149.

Kiesler, D. J. (1973). *The process of psychotherapy: Empirical foundations and systems of analysis.* Chicago: Aldine.

Klein, M. H., Mathieu-Coughlan, P., & Kiesler, D. J. (1986). The Experiencing Scales. In L. S. Greenberg & W. M. Pinsoff (Eds.), *The psychotherapeutic process: A research handbook* (pp. 529–556). New York: Guilford Press.

Kohut, H. (1984). *How does analysis cure?* Chicago: University of Chicago Press.

Kuhn, T. (1962). *The structure of scientific revolutions.* Chicago: University of Chicago Press.

Lakatos, I. (1978). Falsification and the methodology of scientific research programs. In J. Worrall & G. Currie (Eds.), *The methodology of scientific research programs: Imre Lakatos philosophical papers* (Vol. 1, pp. 8–101). Cambridge, U.K.: Cambridge University Press.

Lambert, M., Shapiro, D., & Bergin, A. (1986). The effectiveness of psychotherapy. In S. Garfield & A. Bergin (Eds.), *Handbook of psychotherapy and behavior change* (pp. 157–212). New York: Wiley.

Luborsky, L., & Auerbach, A. (1985). The therapeutic relationship in psychodynamic psychotherapy: The research evidence and its meaning for practice. In R. Hales & A. Frances (Eds.), *Psychiatry update: American Psychiatric Association Annual Review* (Vol. 4).

McCullough, J. P. (1984). The need for a new single-case design structure in applied cognitive psychology. *Psychotherapy, 21,* 389–400.

Mahrer, A. (1988). Discovery-oriented psychotherapy research: Rationale, aims, and methods. *American Psychologist, 43,* 694–702.

Meehl, P. (1978). Theoretical risks and tabular asterisks: S. R. Karl, S. R. Ronald, and the slow progress of soft psychology. *Journal of Consulting and Clinical Psychology, 46,* 806–834.

Mischel, W. (1968). *Personality and assessment.* New York: Wiley.

Muran, J. C., & Safran, J. D. (1990). *Measuring session change and predicting outcome in cognitive therapy.* Poster presented at the annual convention of the Association for the Advancement of Behavior Therapy, San Francisco.

Muran, J. C., Samstag, L. W., Segal, Z. V., & Winston, A. (1992). *Procedural manual for interpersonal scenarios.* Pittsburgh, PA: Behavioral Measurement Database Services.

Muran, J. C., Segal, Z. V., Samstag, L. W., & Schumann, C. (in press). Patient pretreatment, interpersonal problems, and therapeutic alliance in short-term cognitive therapy. *Journal of Consulting and Clinical Psychology.*

Polanyi, M. (1958). *Personal knowledge: Toward a post-critical philosophy.* Chicago: University of Chicago Press.

Rennie, D. L. (1992). Qualitative analysis of the client's experience of psychotherapy: The unfolding of reflexivity. In S. G. Toukmanian & D. L. Rennie (Eds.), *Psychotherapy process research: Paradigmatic and narrative approaches* (pp. 211–233). Newbury Park, CA: Sage.

Rice, L. N., & Greenberg, L. S. (1984). *Patterns of change: Intensive analysis of psychotherapy process.* New York: Guilford Press.

Rice, L. N., & Kerr, G. P. (1986). Measures of client and therapist vocal quality. In L. S. Greenberg & W. M. Pinsoff (Eds.), *The psychotherapeutic process: A research handbook* (pp. 529–556). New York: Guilford Press.

Rice, L. N., & Sapeira, E. P. (1984). Task analysis and the resolution of problematic reactions. In L. N. Rice & L. S. Greenberg (Eds.), *Patterns of change: Intensive analysis of psychotherapy process* (pp. 29–66). New York: Guilford Press.

Safran, J. D. (1990a). Towards a refinement of cognitive therapy in light of interpersonal theory: 1. Theory. *Clinical Psychology Review, 10,* 87–105.

Safran, J. D. (1990b). Towards a refinement of cognitive therapy in light of interpersonal theory: 2. Practice. *Clinical Psychology Review, 10,* 107–122.

Safran, J. D. (1993a). Breaches in the therapeutic alliance: An arena for negotiating authentic relatedness. *Psychotherapy, 30,* 11–23.

Safran, J. D. (1993b). The therapeutic alliance rupture as a trans-theoretical phenomenon: Definitional and conceptual issues. *Journal of Psychotherapy Integration, 3,* 33–49.

Safran, J. D., Crocker, P., McMain, S., & Murray, P. (1990). Therapeutic alliance rupture as a therapy event for empirical investigation. *Psychotherapy, 27,* 154–165.

Safran, J. D., & Hill, C. (1989). *The Interpersonal Schema Questionnaire.* Unpublished scale, Clarke Institute of Psychiatry, Toronto, Canada.

Safran, J. D., Muran, J. C., & Samstag, L. W. (1993). *Modeling process patterns associated with the resolution of therapeutic alliance ruptures.* Manuscript submitted for publication.

Safran, J. D., Muran, J. C., Samstag, L. W. (1994). Resolving therapeutic alliance ruptures: A task analytic investigation. In A. O. Horvath & L. S. Greenberg (Eds.), *The working alliance: Theory, research and practice.* New York: Wiley.

Safran, J. D., Muran, J. C., & Winston, A. (1992, September). *Resolving problems in the therapeutic alliance.* A grant proposal 1R03MH50246-01 approved and funded by the National Institute of Mental Health, Washington, DC.

Safran, J. D., Rice, L. N., Greenberg, L. S. (1988). Integrating psychotherapy research and practice: Modeling the change process. *Psychotherapy, 25,* 1–17.

Safran, J. D., & Segal, Z. V. (1990). *Interpersonal process in cognitive therapy.* New York: Basic Books.

Safran, J. D., Vallis, T. M., Segal, Z. V., Shaw, B. F., Balong, W., & Epstein, L. (1987). Measuring session change in cognitive therapy. *Journal of Cognitive Psychotherapy: An International Quarterly, 1,* 117–128.

Safran, J. D., & Wallner, L. K. (1991). The relative predictive validity of two therapeutic alliance measures in cognitive therapy. *Psychological Asssessment, 3,* 188–195.

Smith, M. L., & Glass, G. V. (1977). Meta-analysis of psychotherapy outcome studies. *American Psychologist, 132,* 752–760.

Stiles, W. S. (1991, June). *Quality control in qualitative research.* Paper presented at the annual conference of the Society for Psychotherapy Research, Lyon, France.

Strupp, H. H. (1989). The nonspecific hypothesis of therapeutic effectiveness: A current assessment. *American Journal of Orthopsychiatry, 37,* 947–954.

Toulmin, S. (1986). *The place of reason in ethics.* Chicago: University of Chicago Press.

Weimer, W. B. (1979). *Notes on the methodology of scientific research.* Hillsdale, NJ: Erlbaum.

Weiss, J., Sampson, H., & the Mount Zion Psychotherapy Research Group. (1987). *The psychoanalytic process: Theory, clinical observations, and empirical research.* New York: Guilford Press.

Winston, A., McCullough, L., Pollack, J., Laikin, M., Pinsker, H., Nezu, A., Flegenheimer, W., & Sadow, J. (1989). The Beth Israel Psychotherapy Research Program: Toward an integration of theory and discovery. *Journal of Integrative and Eclectic Psychotherapy, 8,* 344–356.

Winston, A., Muran, J. C., Safran, J. D., Samstag, L. W., Twining, L., & Braverman, P. (1992, July). *Towards validation of patient and therapist self-report measures of suboutcome.* Paper presented at the annual conference of the Society for Psychotherapy Research, Berkeley, CA.

Wolfe, B. E., & Goldfried, M. R. (1988). Research on psychotherapy integration: Recommendations and conclusions from an NIMH workshop. *Journal of Consulting and Clinical Psychology, 56,* 448–451.

CHAPTER 14

Investigating the Process of Change: Clinical Applications of Process Research

Renee H. Rhodes and Leslie Greenberg

IN THIS CHAPTER we offer some general suggestions about how process research should be conducted to best serve the practicing clinician. We suggest a partnership between the clinician and the researcher to preserve the richness and complexity of the psychotherapeutic process as it unfolds over time. This collaboration involves breaking down complex therapies into meaningful episodes or events in order to discover the discrete patient–therapist performances that lead to change. Implicit in this approach is the belief that the process of psychotherapy can be examined in terms of a series of small in-session and postsession outcomes resulting from specific patient–therapist interactions.

The chapter consists of three sections. In the first section we spell out our process research perspective, respond to Edelson's concerns (this volume) about how to investigate the inherently subjective nature of the psychotherapeutic process, and elaborate on Havens's suggestions (this volume) on how to embrace a process research approach when studying the clinical interventions he has found helpful. In a general response to both Edelson and Havens we confront the challenges to and concerns about the limitations of process research in the study of the complex, subjective, internal change processes that presumably occur over time in psychotherapy. In the next section we suggest how a task analytic approach to the study of change events (Greenberg, 1984, 1986, 1991) provides one tool for overcoming the obstacles that clinicians see researchers encountering when they attempt to preserve theoretically sophisticated clinical notions about therapeutic change while producing results that are specific enough to be operationalized at a clinically meaningful level. In the last section we propose a new approach that combines the task analytic method (Greenberg, 1986) with qualitative research methods such as grounded theory (Rennie, 1992; Strauss & Corbin, 1990) and "comprehensive process analysis" (Elliott, 1989). This integrative process research approach provides a way to preserve the knowledge base in clinical theory and experience while also remaining open to discover new levels of the phenomenon we are investigating by directly asking the patients and therapists what *they* are experiencing. This new approach combines observable patient performances with subjective reports about covert patient-therapist experiences during these performances in order to build an event change model that is phenomenologically grounded. By doing so, the research has direct applicability to the practicing clinician and also keeps the investigation close to the edge of discovery during the preliminary model-building stages. Finally, we provide an example of how this new process research program works by briefly describing a study we are conducting at Yale University on the resolution of misunderstanding events.

Response to Edelson and Havens

The following overview of psychotherapy process research responds directly to Edelson's and Havens's concerns about the global answers psychotherapy research has provided to the specific challenges practicing clinicians face. Edelson provides his view of the gap between the psychotherapy researcher and the psychotherapist in the beginning of his chapter. He states that psychotherapy researchers are interested in the "big questions" of general personality theory, psychopathology, and psychotherapeutic process and in response to these questions focus their efforts on the "practical" questions of differential treatment efficacy and comparisons between psychotherapeutic interventions and other forms of treatment. He next contrasts the psychotherapy researcher's general interest to the psychotherapist's particular interests in particular patients. He suggests that the psychotherapy researcher's indifference to the concerns of the psychotherapist, that is, to the "here-and-now particulars" they encounter, is partly a function of methodological shortcomings. Underlying these shortcomings is what Edelson identifies as a "lack of generally agreed upon criteria for selecting what is to count as an observation and for selecting these observations." Edelson recommends that the criteria for choosing clinical phenomena to investigate and the method for determining how to study these phenomena should be guided by two basic principles: The first principle, relating to the development of criteria for observations, is to focus research investigations on real, practical concerns of clinicians. The second, relating to the development of methods of observation, is to stay discovery oriented. That is, psychotherapy researchers should include data that disconfirm "ideas we hold dear" and use measurements that "prevent us from describing our observations in a way that infects them with the very ideas we want to test." In response to charges against and suggestions for the psychotherapy researcher, the following overview suggests how psychotherapy process research has set out to tackle the challenges Edelson identifies.

Havens also voices his concerns about "the contrast between the global nature of research recommendations and the usually specific character of clinical dilemmas." An experienced clinician, he offers suggestions about how to close the gap between research and clinical practice and outlines a program using a significant event process research approach to investigate the resolution of clinical impasses. We have responded to Havens's clinical perspective on process research by highlighting the challenges that psychotherapy researchers face when they must operationalize complex clinical phenomena at a specific enough level to ensure that the results are directly applicable to clinical practice.

OVERVIEW OF PROCESS RESEARCH

As psychotherapy researchers interested in the process of change in psychotherapy, we ask ourselves three questions at the onset of each new study: What phenomena should we study to understand how therapeutic change takes place? How can we study the phenomenon of therapeutic change? How can we demonstrate that the therapeutic processes lead to change?

As discovery-oriented researchers, our project is not one of disproving or proving the theoretical assumptions underlying the major schools of therapy. In fact, we view research as highly discovery oriented and not as an endeavor designed to validate general theories that are stated in a manner that often cannot be disconfirmed. We are also not solely motivated to answer global outcome questions and prefer to avoid global differential treatment questions aimed at evaluating which treatment works best for which patient population. We are not unconcerned with these issues, but we are confident that our phenomenon-focused process research will yield valuable information about the mechanisms of change that produce in-session and postsession outcomes. We believe that understanding change at this level is necessary before we can understand treatment-wide change. We also are confident that the results of this type of change process research can be used both to clarify theory and to enhance outcome research concerning treatment efficacy.

As psychotherapy process researchers, we focus our sights on the palpable, observable, describable level of therapeutic phenomena to build a bottom-up view of how people change in psychotherapy. We do not, however, propose a mindless, theoretically ungrounded empirical investigation of phenomena. We believe it is important for investigators to use their original (theoretical) focus to ground their investigations. At the same time, they need to stay receptive to discovery through the compelling repeated particularities across sessions that are revealed through scrutiny of in-session performances between therapist and patient (Greenberg, 1986; Rice & Greenberg, 1984).

In our process research approach, theoretical views guide the selection and observation of change events. The goal is to look for the process patterns of change in the events. The description of patterns more closely approximates the actuality of the interior of clinical phenomena than do measures of fixed points in a therapy that are sampled at intervals and then averaged to determine a final outcome. To isolate key components that make up the patterns of change, attention needs to be focused on particular events that are hypothesized to be potential change moments in psychotherapy; the relationship between these change events and outcome is then traced (Greenberg, 1986, 1991). This focus bypasses the questions of how to match effective treatments with diagnostic categories; however, we are confident that this approach lays down the ground work for revealing mechanisms of change that can then be integrated back into the effort to answer differential treatment and global outcome questions (Greenberg, 1991).

THE ROLE OF THEORY AND CLINICAL WISDOM IN EVENT SELECTION

A critical step in psychotherapy process research is deciding which phenomenon to base a study on. The answer to this question of what to study is in some ways obvious. It makes sense to begin by studying the parts of therapy where people change (Greenberg, 1986). What constitutes change will be conceived differently from therapeutic modality to therapeutic modality. Therapists have various implicit and explicit objectives and definitions of what constitutes therapeutic gain. For some therapeutic schools, the patient's capacity to experience emotions rather than talk about them represents an important gain. For other schools, insights into defensive strategies or changes in irrational beliefs or collecting schema that are inconsistent with evidence are seen as essential ingredients of the therapeutic process. For yet other theoreticians, an important aspect of the psychotherapeutic change process entails the reconstruction of the self through the use of narration. All of these theoretically derived views of change could be operationalized into researchable moments that are defined and chosen on the basis of particular theoretical parameters.

There are certain common change processes that occur in a psychotherapy session regardless of whether the patient is diagnosed with bulimia nervosa, obsessive-compulsive disorder, depression, and borderline personality disorder. It is this notion that guides the research strategy of focusing the investigation of therapeutic change at the episodic or event level. For example, it has been established that in the treatment of all of the aforementioned groups there are variables that are not specific to any particular diagnostic category or treatment approach that impact outcome, such as the development and maintenance of a good working alliance. (Luborsky, Singer, & Luborsky, 1975). In our view, there are many components to the development and maintenance of a good therapeutic alliance; to understand them we need to do more than administer an occasional measurement of the alliance—or even repeated measurements of the alliance over time—and then compare it to ratings obtained at termination. Rather, psychotherapy researchers need to break down the processes involved in establishing and maintaining an alliance; they need to study the actual exchanges that are usually buried when data from measures of alliance are averaged across the session, the individual treatment, or the entire sample. By focusing on particular in-session performances of tasks related to the alliance, we are able to begin to understand what therapists and patients need to do to make treatment more collaborative and therefore effective when they are sitting across from each other. For example, through the use of patients' self-report about their experiences of and reactions to their therapists during specific events, the researcher can gain access to internal and covert patient processes that are often not shared with the therapist. In this regard our research findings are relevant to clinicians.

To embark on this type of research program the process researcher/clinician might pick recurring events related to the building and maintenance of the therapeutic alliance, such as the resolution of moments of misunderstanding, and investigate these events as they occur, in the sequence of therapist–patient exchanges (Rhodes, Geller, Greenberg, & Elliott, 1992).

In his chapter Edelson suggests self-narration as a possible important process variable. To investigate the transformational process as represented by changes in the patient's narrative, the researcher would isolate various dimensions of the narrative process and chart their change using a narrative event paradigm. This means targeting segments of the session where a patient is engaged in self-narrative and observing characteristics of the stories that might contribute to patient change. The researcher might ask, How does the story change and in what way? The researcher might speculate that stories change by becoming closed or open, that they vary in degree of rigidity or structure, that patients become more focused on specific agendas, that the basic themes change, and so forth. Each one of these shifts represents significant psychic processes that are part of the researchers' implicit clinical map of the change phenomenon. Having specified how narratives might be an agent of change, the researcher would then need to develop measures to capture these hypothesized change processes. Possibly, the transformation occurs by some as yet unguessed-at process in the patient, such as the initial posing of a question and then a reconsideration of that question, and such processes in the therapist as adopting an exploratory, inquiring stance.

As process researchers, we believe that it is necessary to concretely define abstract hypotheses about change at the level of therapeutic interaction and to study effects in in-session contexts rather than at the level of global treatment effects on the patient measured at termination. We intentionally constrain ourselves to a level of specificity that does not stray too far from the actual therapeutic phenomenon. By operationalizing our research questions on the level of actual sequences of observable patient performances and patient subjective reports of experiences during targeted events, we obtain answers, however finite, that are, we believe, highly relevant to clinicians.

For example, results from Rennie's (1985) research on patients' deference and preliminary results from our current investigation of the resolution process of misunderstanding events (Rhodes et al., 1992) indicate that patients frequently do not report to their therapist that they feel misunderstood. They justify keeping these experiences and reactions covert through various attributions about the nature of therapy, including (1) the belief that the therapist must know they feel misunderstood and that this must be part of the therapist's plan and (2) the fear that they would be out of place in asserting themselves or challenging their therapist, since it is they who have come for psychotherapy. Challenging the therapist when the therapist misunderstands them is, ironically, perceived by patients as obstructing the work of therapy. During our interviews with patients participating in the Misunderstanding Study, patients not only have verbalized such beliefs to us but have offered compensatory attributions about why their therapists do not understand them, and rarely hold the therapist accountable. While these patient experiences of deference have been reported in the literature (Rennie, 1985), it was so striking for the investigators, patients, and therapists to become aware of this deference that open discussions about it have had a direct impact on the therapists and patients in our project. It has promoted direct communication between therapists and patients and has encouraged patients to investigate their role in the therapy process.

TRANSLATING THEORETICAL HYPOTHESES ABOUT EPISODIC CHANGE INTO PROCESS RESEARCH DESIGNS

The procedure of operationalizing theoretical questions into preliminary models that can be tested by comparison to observable, discrete recurring sequences of interactions between therapist and patient is one of the most challenging aspects of process research design. We are sympathetic to Havens's warning against trivialization when investigation of therapeutic phenomena occurs at too general a level and concur with his concerns about the "global nature of research as opposed to the specific character of clinical dilemmas." Our response to this concern is to suggest that the most critical step in mapping out a clinical change event for purposes of investigation is to build a model that reflects what is observed and what is experienced by the participants and not resort to modeling abstract versions of internal dynamics. Therefore, during the design phase of the research, the process researcher/clinician is always working from the general theoretical level to the specific level of clinical observation. This movement from the theoretical to the observable and experiential and then back from the specific to the general is a circular process of model construction.

SPECIFICITY VERSUS COMPLEXITY: THE APPLICATION OF CLINICAL THEORY TO PROCESS RESEARCH DESIGN

The research philosophy introduced earlier could be applied, for example, to a change event that Havens suggests in his chapter. He proposes, on the basis of his clinical experience and theoretical perspective, that the "performative" intervention will produce change in response to a patient's self-deprecatory statement. A performative intervention, as Havens defines it, is the use of a positive declaration about the patient to the patient, when he or she is engaged in self-deprecatory exclamations. Havens explains that this intervention is aimed at contacting the internal critic within the patient, and he explains why he believes this contact promotes the development of a more self-accepting stance in the patient. To investigate the active ingredients of change as a result of this performative intervention, the model of change needs to be unpacked further and the event defined more specifically. This means constructing a hypothesized event model at the level of the moment-by-moment level of conversation that describes what the therapist and patient are doing and experiencing.

The first step for a process researcher using a recurring change event paradigm is to define adequately how to locate the onset of the event across patients by specifying an observable marker or a particular problem space. There are many levels of self-deprecatory remarks and behaviors in patients. Moreover, these experiences are caused by a multitude of interpersonal and intrapersonal stimuli. In describing the event to study, it is essential to be clear on the definitions of the marker of the event and the descriptions a researcher would use to identify and operationalize the sequences within the event. Is it necessary for patients to castigate themselves during the session? Should the event be restricted to self-deprecatory feelings being experienced in the session or could the definition of a self-deprecatory event be expanded to include patients' memories in the session of times when they have been critical of themselves? These are the types of definition issues that are raised when trying to arrive at an event marker. The marker of the change event denotes the patient's being in a particular state of mind and the belief that at this point certain therapeutic interventions will produce change. For example, Greenberg (1975, 1984) defines conflict splits and, more recently, self-evaluative splits

(Greenberg, Rice, & Elliott, 1993) as markers of opportunities for intervening with two-chair dialogue.

Once the researcher constructs the initial hypothetical model of how change occurs when performative interventions are made and the model is specified at the level of observation and experiential description, the self-deprecatory marker of an event needs to be reliably defined so that comparable data can then be collected across subjects or over time within the same subject's treatment. The next step in this research would be to study the immediate impact on the patient after the performative intervention. To do this, one might record, starting with the marker of the patient's self-deprecatory statement, the sequence of events at the level of the talk turn; the statements would then be transcribed and the outcome of the performative intervention analyzed using resolution criteria generated out of the original hypothesis.

DISCRETE AND COMPLEX CHANGE PROCESSES OVER TIME

Havens might be correct when he states, in reference to self-deprecatory remarks, that "the process of resolution is slow ... [and that] therefore counts of self-deprecatory comments need to be made at widely spaced intervals." The dilemma faced by process researchers is that to understand the process over time we need to first freeze-frame time in order to examine the components of process that add up to change. This is by no means a mechanistic approach, and we are not implying that the sum of the parts adds up to the whole. We recognize that the process of psychotherapeutic change itself changes as progress in the patient is made. One way to capture this process is to start by focusing on the actual processes of change from moment to moment, examining the observable performances and subjective experiences of the patient before, during, and after each performative intervention, to use Havens's example. These points are made to underscore the importance of specificity (that is, what people actually say and do, their manner, the timing, the nonverbal communication, and so forth) when defining and examining therapeutic events so that the results of investigating these events are useful for practicing clinicians. At the heart of the process researcher's dilemma is the problem of applying the maximum amount of specificity while taking into account the complexity of the internal change processes activated by the therapeutic encounter. Actual sequences of therapist–patient exchanges, multiple data perspectives using the therapist's reports, the patient's reports, and independent observer reports help ground the research in the clinical realm. To study the healing power in performative interventions Havens suggests, a strategy of taking "counts" of the patient's self-deprecatory remarks, presumably to monitor their diminishment. For process researchers an interesting question here is *how* the performative intervention helps the patient, not just *whether* it helps. In order to understand the gradual nature of improvement, for example, of patients whose therapist makes repeated use of a performative intervention following the self-deprecatory marker, the targeted event needs to be studied repeatedly so that a model can be constructed to explain the transmuting process in the patient over time.

THEORY VERIFICATION VERSUS DISCOVERY

Another major issue process researchers confront when choosing a potential therapeutic change moment for investigation is deciding how to balance theory verification with discovery. How can process researchers use the theoretical perspective that originally influenced their choice to investigate a potential change event as a preliminary guide for their observations in such a way that they are also open to learning something new and unexpected about their subject? This methodological challenge has its analogy on the clinical level. How do we listen to our client at the edge of what we know about them without presupposing that we know the truth while, at the same time, being guided by a framework that grounds, enriches, and organizes our observations? As researchers, how can we check out our hunches and test our theories while also being taught by our investigations? The dialectical process between theorizing and observation can produce discovery.

One way to achieve this balance is to employ a rational-empirical research strategy that initially accommodates our hypotheses but also assures that all data collected are not filtered solely through those hypotheses. This strategy can use the approaches developed for the task analytic procedure to build and test models of change (Greenberg, 1984, 1991; Rice & Greenberg, 1984); approaches developed for interpersonal process recall (IPR; Elliott, 1986), a tape-assisted interview to provide patients' subjective accounts to inform our models; and the grounded theory approach (Rennie, 1992; Strauss & Corbin, 1990) to explore selected phenomena in an open-ended spirit.

For example, if investigators using the aforementioned process tools want to study the active ingredients of change when patients tell a story about themselves, they might start by building a hypothetical model of steps in story telling events that they, on the basis of their clinical experience and theoretical views, believe lead to positive patient change. If this process is conceived of as taking place over time, it would be broken down into stages. A model would be constructed to describe the sequences of observable behaviors and patient-reported internal experiences that are evident in story telling events. To do this, a definition of the story telling event is necessary and criteria would need to be developed to identify these events. This means that either the therapist identifies a significant story event after a given session, the patient identifies it, or the researcher selects it. Given the importance of the subjective perspective in this event, the patient's self-report would be the natural choice for identifying the event. Since each person's story is different, the model's purpose is to capture what is comparable in the patterns across stories. In this way the uniqueness of each subject is preserved while the underlying process is explicated. This is what process researchers mean when they speak of patterns of change (Rice & Greenberg, 1984).

Or the strategy for our hypothetical research problem could be based on specifying and developing measures of the observable behaviors of in-session performances. To test this model beyond the observable patient and therapist behaviors, tape-assisted methods in IPR could be used to gather information in an open-ended way about patients' inner experience while they are telling the story. The IPR consultant could perform a postsession interview (after a session in which a significant story has been identified), during which a researcher plays a tape of the narrative event for the patient and asks open-ended questions. These data can then be used to check the original hypothesized model and amend it. This process is iterative and continues through several subjects until the model is saturated and the investigator no longer gains new information about how change occurs during the performance sequence of the story telling event. If the investigator is curious to open up the investigation beyond the preliminary model, she or he can perform a grounded theory analysis of the client's experience of the key narrative episode. This might entail sorting out the key meaning units within each story, forming categories from these meaning units, and then creating a structure using axial coding (Strauss & Corbin, 1990) to relate the categories sequentially to each other. Axial coding provides a way to link subcategories to a category in a set of relationships, for example, between background context, action-interaction strategies, and impact. The grounded theory analysis results could then be used to enhance the model derived from the rational-empirical task analysis.

Through this general introduction to the concerns and objectives of psychotherapy process researchers, we have attempted to respond to Edelson's critique of the schism between psychotherapy research and the subjective complexity of psychotherapy and to Havens's concerns about the "contrast between the global nature of research recommendations and the usually specific character of clinical dilemmas." We agree with them both regarding the all too general level of the enterprise of psychotherapy research to answer the very real and specific concerns of practitioners. We join with Havens, and are more hopeful than Edelson, in considering the possibilities of developing methodologies that will enable the clinician/researcher to investigate relevant clinical issues. We believe that we have developed a method of doing this by employing a rational-empirical approach, which entails the following sequence of steps: (1) using theoretical, clinical, and empirical sources to develop hypothetical (event level) change models; (2) examining the clinical phenomena in our chosen event from multiple perspectives (observer and participant); and (3) revising our models according to the examination of the actual in-therapy performances. Moreover, since client change is a complex developmental process, we are working on devising methodologies that not only penetrate into the momentary interior of change events as they occur but also investigate the ways in which the time between therapy sessions and the process over time are experienced by the patient. This essentially means that an enhanced appreciation for the immediate and background context surrounding an event provides greater understanding of the change mechanisms within the event. For example, we might find in our task analytic study about story telling events that change occurs over time, perhaps even several years. Events within therapy sessions and during the intervals between sessions have an impact on how patients tell stories about themselves. Comprehensive process analysis (CPA; Elliott, 1989) routinely includes questions that explore current life context along with those that investigate the in-therapy event.

Having responded to the chapters by Edelson and Havens in general, we now lay out more formally the steps of a task analytic research program to further indicate how an investigation might build a model of a change event.

Task Analysis of Therapeutic Change

As we have said, task analysis of therapeutic change relies on the identification and examination of recurring change events in therapy to provide a better understanding of clinical change processes in the contexts of clinically meaningful units. We believe that it is possible to divide the therapeutic encounter into a set of significant events that capture potent and effective aspects of therapy in producing change. An event was defined initially (Greenberg, 1975; Rice & Greenberg, 1984) as an interactional sequence between patient and therapist that consists of a clinical marker followed by a series of therapist interventions and an ensuing patient performance that, if successful, results in the patient achieving an effective resolution. The patient marker consists of a patient statement that indicates to the therapist that the patient is in a particular currently experienced problem space. For example, Rice (1984) identified an event in a client-centered therapy called "systematic evocative unfolding of problematic reactions." The event begins with a patient marker in which patients express a lack of comprehension about why they have reacted in a particular way and ends when patients understand their reaction in terms of how they perceived the situation that provoked the reaction. Greenberg (1984) identified an event from Gestalt therapy that is referred to as the two-chair dialogue for resolving splits. This event begins with a statement of conflict between two aspects of the self with a current sense of struggle.

There are two major phases within an event-based task analytic research program: first, the completion of a rational-empirical task analysis and, second, the verification of the model of change (Greenberg, 1984, 1991). The rational-empirical analysis involves the following six major steps:

1) Explication of the clinician's cognitive map of how change occurs
2) Description of the change task and specification of the task environment
3) Evaluation of the potency of the task environment (therapist intervention)
4) Rational task analysis of how change possibly occurs
5) Empirical analysis of how change actually occurs
6) Construction of a rational-empirical model

Initially, the task must be selected and described as clearly as possible. This involves delineating the precise behavioral components of the patient marker. An example of a marker would be when a patient reports feeling misunderstood or expresses a conflict between two aspects of self or expresses puzzlement at one of his or her reactions. Once the issue of defining the starting point (or affective problem that is to be resolved) has been achieved, the task environment must be specified. This is done by compiling a manual of suitable therapist interventions for facilitating task resolution. Once this manual of therapist interventions has been developed, therapist adherence to this can be checked. The patient's problem-solving performance can then be studied in what is regarded as a similar or controlled environment, that is, when the therapist uses an intervention from the manual while he or she is problem solving with the patient. This is a research simplification strategy (Bordin, 1979) that allows one to study patient performance while bracketing the therapist intervention that is regarded as similar across situations.

The third procedure involves testing to see that change of some type does in fact occur when the task is worked on in this environment. This is an opportunity for comparative or controlled studies of therapist interventions to confirm that something potent is occurring, that is, that problems are being resolved or progress is being made. This addresses to some extent the problem of not initially knowing what resolution looks like. One approximates resolution by studying events in which something important, according to the best existing measures of productive process and participants' and observers' reports, seems to be occurring.

The fourth procedure requires that investigators construct an idealized performance of the task by asking themselves how the task can be solved. This requirement distinguishes this approach from purely empirical task analyses to the extent that the investigator goes beyond performance analyses and the use of behavioral data culled from the subject's performance. The idealized performance model of possible resolution strategies makes explicit the therapist's implicit experiential knowledge and guides the investigator in her or his observations of how patients achieve resolution of their affective tasks. In addition, it provides an initial understanding of how patients perform, which can then be checked against actual performances.

In the fifth procedure, the empirical task analysis, the investigator describes an actual performance of a subject involved in the task and attempts to identify the sequence of steps involved. Ideally, these steps are then diagramed. The empirically generated analysis is then compared with the rational analysis to correct any mistakes in the latter. This procedure is followed by a number of performances, resulting in successive modifications of the initial performance diagram. Finally, a model of the patient's performance is developed.

The model may be of two types: a performance model or a model of more internal mental operations. The former consists of a detailed description of patient behavior whereas the latter describes the operation of the psychological system that would have generated the change performance (Greenberg, 1984). To date, performance models have been predominant in the area of psychotherapy research. The ultimate goal of task analysis as a therapeutic framework is, however, to develop a model of the underlying mental operations and competencies that produced the performance, a model that illustrates the internal processes by which patients change.

To perform a task analysis the research clinician intensively studies therapy transcripts to develop a model of a change event. The model describes the therapist and patient behaviors thought to be necessary to effect the changes that occur during the change event. For example, we are currently working on building models of the resolution of a misunderstanding between therapist and patient (Rhodes et al., 1992) and of resolving a lingering bad feeling toward a significant other (Greenberg, 1991). The initial models are subsequently compared to other in-therapy performances of the same event and subjected to revision. This procedure continues in an iterative fashion until the research clinician is satisfied that the model represents the process being studied.

VERIFICATION OF MODELS OF CHANGE

Although the major research effort in this investigation strategy is concentrated on inductive, discovery-oriented steps of cycling between hypothesized possible performances and observed actual performances, verification of models constructed by this method is viewed as essential. On the basis of the newly constructed models, hypotheses concerning patients' performances of the task are advanced for further examination or refutation. Two

major strategies are useful in this stage of the research program: (1) validation of models and (2) relating process to outcome.

In the validation step a group of resolution and nonresolution performances of a particular event are compared to validate the hypothesis that
specific components discriminate between successful and unsuccessful performances at a statistically significant level. In the first step patient process is
related to outcome. The advantage of relating process to outcome at this
stage of the research program is that one now has a complex model of how
change occurs, and this model, which acts as the hypothetical causal link between specified patient processes and outcome, provides increased control
of patient performance variance. The design essentially answers the question
of whether the patients who engage in the hypothesized in-therapy process
have better outcomes than those who don't.

Methodological Challenges of Staying at the Edge of Discovery: An Integrative Research Strategy

As stated earlier in the explanation of task analysis, discovery-oriented research involves a rational-empirical strategy, which incorporates both theory-generated hypothesis testing and discovery-oriented approaches.
Rennie (1992) makes a distinction between these two research strategies by
ascribing to those process researchers who use the theory-generated hypothesis testing approach a paradigmatic research philosophy and to those who
use the discovery-oriented approach a narrative research philosophy. In the
paradigmatic research philosophy the underlying assumption is that there
are realities that apply across patients and that we can devise models to explain behavior across patients. Task analysis, where change event models
are constructed and tested, represents this philosophy. At the other end of
the methodological spectrum—but, in our opinion, not in the opposing corner—is a narrative approach, which is similar to the therapeutic view held
by Edelson. This research strategy is informed by a constructivist view in
which no two patients' subjective experiences are exactly comparable.
Patient expressions are viewed as demonstrating intentionality rather than
explainable regularities. Therefore, some of those that ascribe to the narrative tradition assert that the single-case design is the only viable method of
investigation to capture the meaningfulness of the client's subjective experience in all of its particularity. Discovery-oriented methodologies, such as
comprehensive process analysis (Elliott, 1989) and interpersonal process recall (IPR; Elliott, 1986) can be seen as loosely falling within the narrative tradition, although their application is by no means limited to the single-case
design approach.

In its extreme form the question is, Must process researchers sacrifice practical clinical and theoretical wisdom (used to construct and test models in the rational-empirical tradition) in order to (1) honor the subjectivity and uniqueness of each clinical case and (2) discover elements outside of their hypothesized models? We are optimistic that it is not necessary to polarize the two process research strategies and force an either/or methodological choice. In an integrative process research strategy there is a ongoing dialogue between hypothesis testing and discovery-oriented grounded theory investigation as part of the research effort. By combining task analysis and grounded theory research strategies, initial clinical hunches and theoretical assumptions can be used to construct a change event model that is tested by using both participant- and observer-based information in the hope of capturing regularities across both patient performance and patient-reported experience.

The hypothesized model is then revised and developed as the researcher checks back and forth between model and single-case examples of the event. Concurrently, the same event is explored using narrative techniques. This can be done in two ways: First, investigators differentiate two tracks in their model of change events. The first is the observable performance track, which can be measured using standardized process instruments to establish observable regularities. The second track uses the participants' subjective reports, which are collected using the IPR method, where patients and therapists view the targeted event on videotape and provide their perspectives. This dual strategy is designed to generate two types of task analytic models: the performance model built from observable behavior and an internal mental operations model derived from subjective report. The observable and subjective levels of an in-therapy performance can also be analyzed using a grounded theory approach, which can then be used to challenge and further test the initial theoretical assumptions in the hypothesized model. In this way there is a constant feedback loop between hypothesis testing and grounded theory. We use theoretical notions and observations without letting either blind our research endeavor in a tautological way. In addition, we use patients' reports on their experience to keep us continually in contact with their inner experience and the meaning of events to them.

MISUNDERSTANDING EVENTS: MODELS OF SUBJECTIVE EXPERIENCE AND
OBSERVABLE PERFORMANCE

The first question raised at the beginning of this chapter was, What should psychotherapy process researchers study? We answered that it is important to start with fundamental questions about therapeutic change processes. We have recently begun studying an event that represents an intersection between a number of different theoretical modalities. The patient's experience of being understood and misunderstood in therapy has been the target of extensive theoretical attention (Bordin, 1979; Kohut, 1971; Rogers, 1975), and alliance ruptures have begun to be empirically investigated (Rhodes et al., 1992; Safran, McMain, Crocker, & Murray, 1990). Relational events clearly represent an important therapeutic change process. We are particularly interested in the type of change that occurs in the empathic understanding of the experience of being misunderstood (Geller, 1987; Kohut, 1971). One of the pathways to being understood entails the give-and-take process of the client expressing himself or herself and the therapist attempting to grasp the client's meaning. This inevitably results in misunderstandings, en route, with some ending in breakdowns in communication and others ending in resolution of the misunderstanding. The notion that a temporary misunderstanding between patient and therapist can be a constructive rather than destructive part of an interpersonal pattern (Kohut, 1971) serves as the basis for our study of the resolution of misunderstanding.

To understand the resolution process in this event we used multiple data sources to gain access both to performance and to the patient's subjective experience. This means that not only were the transcripts of client-reported misunderstanding events analyzed to build and test models of the resolution process but patient and therapists were also interviewed using tape-assisted IPR (Elliott, 1986) in order to obtain the patient's subjective account of the misunderstanding and the ensuing resolution process. This provided new information that our hypotheses had not anticipated. Our emphasis is thus on the patient's reported and observed experience in misunderstanding events. We rely on the patient's informing us when he or she feels misunderstood rather than attempting to locate this event through objective measures. This assures us of collecting a range of events, some of which might have been missed if collected by the use of a standardized measurement procedure. For example, we have found that some patients feel profoundly misunderstood when their therapist glances at his or her watch, others feel misunderstood by their therapist's active and engaged style, and still others feel comforted by an engaged, confrontative style and misunderstood when their therapist is more neutral.

Our design for this study represents the integration of what Rennie (1992) has called the paradigmatic and the narrative. We started with a hypothetical model derived from experiential and self-psychological principles about the change process involved in the resolution of misunderstanding and then marked our misunderstanding events using the patient as informant. We then collected data from three sources for each event: the actual transcript of the event, the patient's description of his or her internal experience during the event, and the therapist's description of his or her internal experience during the event. We first tested our hypotheses by means of our preliminary performance model of the event, using various process measures to compare the actual to the hypothesized interactional sequence between the therapist and patient. Secondly, we conducted a more open-ended analysis meant to generate hypotheses and used the tape-assisted recall information to do a comprehensive process analysis of the patient's subjective experience (Elliott, 1989). This second method adds depth and context to our observer-level data. This leaves us with both a performance track, derived from the transcripts, and a subjective tract, derived from the recall interviews.

Lastly, by studying multiple event instances of resolution of misunderstanding from the same subject over the course of the therapy, we can build both an actual in-session performance model of how the process of resolving misunderstandings benefits the patient and a model about the change process that occurs over time.

Conclusion

The approach we are proposing is consistent with an epistemology of practice that involves a context-specific body of procedural knowledge much more than a general declarative theory. This means that as clinicians we are interested in discovering how to intervene in a particular situation, not in codifying a general set of immutable facts. In clinical practice the chief source of knowledge on which experienced clinicians rely is their own experience. Practice involves the application and adaptation of general knowledge to the uniqueness of particular clinical situations.

Experts' knowledge is always dynamic and fosters context-dependent understanding by generating patterns, or schema, to understand covariations of complex sets of factors. Clinicians become expert by experiencing many variations of a given type of situation and by developing a repertoire of patterns to describe these situations. Therapists have the capacity to discern when the elements and relationships of a constructed pattern do not fit a particular situation to which the pattern has been applied. This then allows the therapist to refine, develop, and reorganize the pattern to more closely fit the specific situation. Patterns are thus refined and adjusted over time with experience and reflection. These patterns guide therapists in what to attend to and how to respond. The development of particularized contextual knowledge thus occurs by adapting and revising previously held models until they fit a particular situation.

We have proposed an approach to psychotherapy research that parallels the process of becoming a clinical expert and adds a means of making discerned patterns into explicit models. We also provide ways of measuring and testing for the presence of these patterns of change and their effects. We believe that this type of process research provides an approach to investigation that generates clinically useful knowledge born out of the combination of tacit knowledge and systematic investigation. This combination accelerates learning by harnessing the procedural knowledge of clinical experts and rendering explicit what has sometimes been obscured by theory and is therefore inaccessible to the inexperienced therapist. This type of approach has helped us bridge the practitioner–scientist gap, and we believe its development and application to a variety of therapeutic approaches and to the study of experts will help explicate how psychotherapy leads to change.

REFERENCES

Bordin, E. S. (1979). The generalizability of the psychoanalytic concept of the working alliance. *Psychotherapy: Theory, Research and Practice, 16,* 252–260.

Elliott, R. (1986). Interpersonal process recall (IPR) as a process research method. In L. Greenberg & W. Pinsof (Eds.), *The psychotherapeutic process* (pp. 503–529). New York: Guilford Press.

Elliott, R. (1989). Comprehensive process analysis: Understanding the change process in significant therapy events. In M. Packer & R. B. Addison (Eds.), *Entering the circle: Hermeneutic investigation in psychology* (pp. 165–184). Albany, NY: State University of New York Press.

Geller, J. D. (1987). The process of psychotherapy: Separation and the complex interplay among empathy, insight and internalization. In J. B. Feshbach and S. B. Feshbach (Eds.), *The psychology of separation and loss* (pp. 173–195). San Francisco: Jossey-Bass.

Greenberg, L. S. (1975). A task analytic approach to the study of psychotherapeutic events. *Dissertation Abstracts International, 37,* 4647B.

Greenberg, L. S. (1984). A task analysis of intrapersonal conflict resolution. In L. Rice & L. Greenberg (Eds.), *Patterns of change* (pp. 67–124). New York: Guilford Press.

Greenberg, L. S. (1986). Change process research. *Journal of Consulting and Clinical Psychology, 54,* 4–9.

Greenberg, L. S. (1991). Research in the process of change. *Psychotherapy Research, 1,* 14–24.

Greenberg, L., Rice, L., & Elliott, R. (1993). *Facilitating emotional change: The moment by moment process.* New York: Guilford Press.

Kohut, H. (1971). *The analysis of the self.* New York: International Universities Press.

Luborsky, L., Singer, B., & Luborsky, L. (1975). Comparative studies of psychotherapies: Is it true that "Everyone has won and all must have prizes"? *Archives of General Psychiatry, 32,* 995–1008.

Rennie, D. L. (1985, May). *Client deference in the psychotherapy relationship.* Paper presented at the meeting of the Society for Psychotherapeutic Research, Evanston, IL.

Rennie, D. L. (1992). Qualitative analysis of the client's experience of psychotherapy: The unfolding of reflexivity. In S. G. Toukmanian & D. L. Rennie (Eds.), *Psychotherapy process research: Paradigmatic and narrative approaches.* Newbury Park, CA: Sage.

Rhodes, R., Geller, J., Greenberg, L., Elliott, R. (1992, June 25). *Preliminary task analytic model of the resolution of misunderstanding events.* Panel presented at the meeting of the Society for Psychotherapy Research, Berkeley, CA.

Rice, L. N. (1984). *Manual for systematic evocative unfolding.* Unpublished manuscript, York University, Toronto, Canada.

Rice, L. N., & Greenberg, L. (Eds.). (1984). *Patterns of change.* New York: Guilford Press.

Rogers, C. R. (1975). Empathic: An unappreciated way of being. *Counseling Psychologist, 5*(2), 2–10.

Safran, J. D., McMain, S., Crocker, P., & Murray, P. (1990). Therapeutic alliance rupture as a therapy event for empirical investigation. *Psychotherapy, 27,* 154–164.

Strauss, A., & Corbin, J. (1990). *Basics of qualitative research: Grounded theory procedures and techniques.* Newbury Park, CA: Sage.

CHAPTER 15

From Research to Practice to Research to . . .

Michael S. Maling and Kenneth I. Howard

MANY PSYCHOTHERAPY researchers and practitioners have grappled with the difficult issues encountered in the effort to integrate these seemingly separate realms into a unified field of endeavor. One major difficulty has been in the attempt to apply aggregate statistical findings to the treatment of a specific patient. Findings are typically based on the average patient. Yet the mean is a statistical abstraction; it does not represent any actual person. Thus, generalizing from an observed sample mean to an individual patient is problematic. This is one manifestation of the problems endemic to making causal attributions based on an inductive line of reasoning. It is very likely that any characteristic that is "statistically" descriptive of a patient group, hypothetically representative of a larger population, is inaccurate when attributed to any one individual within that group. Further, the research process may have a disruptive impact on treatment, making generalizations based on research findings more problematic (Firth, Shapiro, & Parry, 1986).

Another problem is related to the instruments that researchers tend to select when assessing treatment. The variables that are commonly assessed in research endeavors usually entail change scores based on established psychometric methods. In clinical practice, however, change in test scores is not what is assessed. For psychotherapists, change in a patient is indicated by factors such as enhanced levels of insight; mollified and better integrated affective states; more adaptive cognitive and behavioral coping strategies; enrichment in interpersonal relationships, which are increasingly characterized

This work was partially supported by grants R01 MH42901 and K05 MH00924 from the National Institute of Mental Health.

by a spirit of mutuality; self-integration; and reduction of angst associated with perceptions of isolation from others. Standard measures for many of these constructs are not available, and clinicians seem reluctant to define these constructs in a way that would lead to operationalization and quantification.

With a paradigm shift in service delivery well under way, it seems prudent for psychotherapists to press vigilantly toward the ideal of integrating research with practice. A research-based practice would enhance the capacity of clinicians to respond with streamlined, effective treatments to the calls for cost-effectiveness emanating from those who manage the mental health care of patients. At the same time, the adoption of a utilitarian philosophy by psychotherapy researchers would stimulate projects that accommodate the pragmatic needs of clinicians while retaining an investment in the statistical standards of reliability and validity.

Psychotherapy Research

In the early days of the formal psychotherapy research endeavor very few clinicians or clinical investigators questioned the value of using randomized contrasting group designs to investigate psychotherapy. The reasons for this research strategy were clear when the dominant questions posed to the psychological community were general ones, typically related to the overall efficacy of psychotherapy. This research trend was stimulated by the need to respond to the challenge to the practice community to demonstrate the efficacy of psychotherapy in comparison to spontaneous remission (Eysenck, 1952). The results of meta-analyses of numerous contrasting group studies, generated in response to Eysenck's challenge, have indicated that psychotherapy is indeed a useful vehicle in the remediation of psychological distress (Howard, Lueger, Maling, & Martinovich, 1993; Lyons & Woods, 1991; Shapiro & Shapiro, 1982; Smith & Glass, 1977; Smith, Glass, & Miller, 1980; Weisz, Weiss, Alicke, & Klotz, 1987). Indeed, psychotherapy is the best-documented medical intervention in history!

The most salient finding of these meta-analytic studies is that there no longer exists a reason to investigate the general question of treatment efficacy. Psychotherapy works for the great majority of patients. Research questions today concern the influence of specific components on psychotherapy outcome and are summarized by the following query: "What treatment, by whom, is most effective for this individual with that specific problem, under which set of circumstances?" (Paul, 1967, p. 111). Since Paul reframed the research challenge, many psychotherapy process/outcome researchers have been investigating micro- and miniprocesses. These investigators have addressed what they feel is a certain arbitrariness in the process/outcome distinction. Novel methodologies have been developed to assess differentiating levels of effectiveness within treatment. In short, researchers have been investigating the treatment options that have been most beneficial (that is, that indicate clinical efficacy) in within-therapy situation-specific contexts. Greenberg and Pinsof (1986) refer to these suboutcomes as "little o," in contrast to the traditional "big O," which refers to an oversimplified understanding of outcome, namely, the entire course of psychotherapy as assessed by contrasting pre- and posttherapy patient measures.

The appropriate unit of observation to use in evaluating within-treatment processes and suboutcomes is a subject of active debate. Some researchers investigate psychotherapy at the level of the phoneme, the smallest unit of discernible speech. In contrast, other investigators suggest the use of much larger units of measurement; these are labeled therapeutic episodes and are defined by the thematic context, observation of which may last for several sessions (Rice & Greenberg, 1984; Safran, McMain, Crocker, & Murray, 1990). The definition of the ideal observational unit, however, may not require consensus. Different perspectives may yield valuable data. For example, in the many verbal and nonverbal interactions that occur within episodes certain therapist communications may be more effective than others in staying the course toward larger episodic goals or may be more affectively syncopated with the patient's current phenomenological experience. From the clinician's perspective, a significant unit of observation may be the single session (Friedlander, Thibodeau, & Ward, 1985; Orlinsky & Howard, 1967) or a within-session intervention delivered at a "good moment" in treatment (Mahrer, 1985, 1988; Mahrer & Nadler, 1986; Mahrer, White, Howard, Gagnon, & MacPhee, 1992). Clinical notes are most useful when data are organized across sessions. The resulting clinical descriptions are more like movies than snapshots. A productive research strategy based on this perspective would define the unit of observation as the combined total of several patient–therapist interactions; thus, the relational component of the therapeutic discourse could be tapped while a content analytic approach is used to understand psychotherapy suboutcomes. This methodology is underscored by Malan (1963, 1976a, 1976b), who uses triangular patient–therapist–genetic transference interpretations as a regular part of his psychotherapeutic work and as a tool to assess prospective patients' suitability for treatment.

Other researchers have taken a more molar approach to the question of psychotherapy suboutcomes by examining dyadic relationships (Beitman, 1987), perceptions of self-efficacy (Bandura, 1977), symptomatic relief (Uhlenhuth & Duncan, 1968), or entire courses of psychotherapy across patients and diagnoses (Cashdan, 1973; Howard et al., 1993; Whitehorn, 1959). Howard et al. demonstrated empirically that psychotherapy proceeds in identifiable phases; therapeutic movement was shown to proceed generally from the intra- to the interpersonal realms, with therapy impacting, in a reasonably sequential fashion, upon patients' subjective experience of well-being, their perceived level of symptomatic distress, and their general functioning. This work was a further development of an earlier study of the dose–effect relationship in psychotherapy (Howard, Kopta, Krause, & Orlinsky, 1986) in which a dose of eight sessions was found to be sufficient, in general, to significantly improve 50% of outpatients. Probit analyses revealed a log-linear relationship between normalized mean improvement (that is, positive outcome) and the log of session number. This meta-analysis indicated that psychotherapy seems to exert its most powerful impact very early in treatment. For those who remain in treatment, larger doses are required to enhance functioning in measurable, but incrementally smaller, units of progress. Overall, the data of these studies suggest, when juxtaposed with Eysenck's (1952) percent improvement estimates, that "psychotherapy accomplishes in 15 sessions what spontaneous remission takes two years to do" (McNeilly & Howard, 1991, p. 74). This is extremely meaningful to patients who are suffering from mental distress and who, quite understandably, desire the most rapid relief possible.

Research and Practice

As noted earlier, insofar as psychotherapy research uses the traditional methodology of group comparison, in contrast to the intensive study of prototypical single cases, research findings will have little direct impact on a therapist's treatment of a particular case. As Edelson (this volume) points out, practitioners respond to the uniqueness of the person they are treating and recognize that no two patients are alike. The treatment of patients is much too complex to allow for the uncritical use of any intervention without consideration of the total problem to be addressed. For example, physicians do not prescribe penicillin for every diagnosed bacterial infection, as another antibiotic may be more situationally efficacious; further, even if penicillin is the prevailing treatment of choice for a particular infection, the physician must ensure that the patient is not allergic to this medication.

Practitioners do believe, however, that their training and experience provide a knowledge base that is sufficient to the task of enabling generalizations of effective technique across patients. With these components providing the framework for their clinical perspective, practitioners generalize from personal clinical schemata of patient groups by delivering specific interventions for particular patients they are currently treating. The underlying assumption that clinicians make here is that there are classes or groups of patients who respond similarly to the same technical interventions.

The use of clinical (and life) experience in psychotherapy is, however, contextualized and general. As Edelson (this volume) points out, practicing therapists seldom make specific reference to a particular case or theory in treating an individual patient. In a similar vein, the use of psychotherapy research is contextual and general. All of this experience and research should influence therapists-in-training rather than those of us who have been in the field for many years.

We believe, in counterpoint, that it is important to learn the operational processes that facilitate construction of a "file of memories" (Edelson, this volume). It is felt that these memories accrue, are schematically organized, and result in the capacity to make sound clinical judgments. Only with an understanding of this process can we develop a knowledge base of dyadic interactions that is sufficient to make the training process of young psychotherapists a conceptually tight and empirically substantiated experience. The justification for an operational theoretical model of psychotherapy developed along these lines is that within-session predictive capacity could be enhanced for individual patients by utilizing appropriate schemata generated from the "file of memories." Such a model, therefore, would help organize the transactions that occur in the unique, yet puzzlingly collective, bipersonal field of individual psychotherapy. A comprehensive empirically derived operational theoretical model would create a stable base from which it would be justifiable for researchers as well as practitioners to make generalizations across and within persons. In this manner, making causal attributions of psychotherapy outcomes and suboutcomes based on a deductive line of reasoning could flow from an inductive line of reasoning without having to make a quantum leap.

We now turn our attention to Spence's chapter in this volume. Some of the questions Spence poses in his chapter—such as "How does a reasonably good interpretation gain its effect?"—are beyond any known empirical methodology and are probably unanswerable in principle. "How" questions have an infinite number of answers. However, if investigators have a hypothesis that leads them to ask, "Can a reasonably good interpretation gain its effect by being stated authoritatively rather than tentatively?" they need only find operationalizations for the concepts "authoritative," "tentative," "reasonably good interpretation," and "effect." Of course, this would require a good working alliance between clinical theorist (the person responsible for posing the question) and clinical researcher (the person responsible for providing a reasonably unequivocal answer to the question).

Given no responsibility for answering clinical questions, clinicians are free to ask unanswerable questions (and retain their current beliefs). Given no responsibility for asking clinically relevant questions, researchers are free to ask the kinds of questions that current scientific methodology allows them to answer (the "drunkard's search"). Without dialogue during the planning of a study, each party acts in its own perceived self-interest. For psychotherapy research to be clinically meaningful (applicable to practice), there must a feedback loop from researcher to practitioner to researcher to practitioner to . . .

Probably the best examples of good psychoanalytic research are the Alexander and French (Chicago Institute for Psychoanalysis) studies, the Menninger study, and the Penn studies (under Luborsky). These are all characterized by multidisciplinary teams consisting of researchers and practitioners with high respect for the ideas of each team member.

From our perspective, both the Spence and the Edelson chapters of this volume ignore the research literature. For example, Spence asks, "Is there any evidence that the number of sessions per week bears any relation to outcome?" There certainly is (see Orlinsky & Howard, 1986). Another question—"Is there any evidence that total number of hours of treatment is related to outcome?"—also has been answered (see Howard et al., 1986; Orlinsky & Howard, 1986).

One problem with psychoanalytic studies, as indicated by Spence, is that they are anecdotal. This stems from the fact that the training of analysts does not include much course work in the statistical and scientific methodology of the social sciences. If training programs included such course work and required the completion of an independent piece of research (analogous to the Ph.D. dissertation), we would find a quantum jump in the quality (and quantity) of research on psychoanalysis.

Because the influence of research on practice is indirect, it is likely to have its greatest relevance in the training of therapists and in the making of mental health policy. Almost all training programs have a clinical research component aimed at teaching critical thinking, encouraging systematic observation, and making the professional therapist an intelligent consumer of research findings. The result of this training, in terms of the way new therapists actually practice, has never been documented. Training, however, certainly influences the thinking of practitioners in some way and encourages them to use techniques that have been shown to be effective.

Perhaps the greatest role of psychotherapy research has been in the broad area of mental health policy. In the first place, the mere existence of such scientific research is a public statement that psychotherapy has a scientific base; it thus provides some defense against the general skepticism about this treatment and its practitioners. After all, palmists and astrologers claim that they are effective and that their clients are helped, but there is no scientific effort to support the validity or efficacy of their interventions.

Psychotherapy research has provided scientific confirmation for the practice of psychotherapy, both by its very existence and by the consistent findings of treatment efficacy. With the growing influence of third-party payers, there has been much reliance on the cumulative psychotherapy outcome research to justify the inclusion of psychotherapy in health insurance programs. Meta-analyses, particularly the one conducted by Smith, Glass, and Miller (1980) have been particularly important in settling this matter.

As managed care has grown, so has an interest in the quality of care provided by practitioners. What had been a cottage industry of individual practitioners, accountable only to themselves and to their patients, has now grown into a multibillion dollar industry that has come under the scrutiny of third-party payers. One new task for psychotherapy research is to provide these payers with a means for documenting treatment efficacy and guiding the allocation of scarce health dollars. It is the responsibility of both clinical scientists and practitioners to see that this is done in a clinically sensitive manner, one that is responsive to the needs of the patients we serve.

REFERENCES

Bandura, A. (1977). Self-efficacy: Toward a unifying theory of behavioral change. *Psychological Review, 84,* 191–215.

Beitman, B. D. (1987). *The structure of individual psychotherapy.* New York: Guilford Press.

Cashdan, S. (1973). *Interactional psychotherapy.* New York: Grune & Stratton.

Eysenck, H. J. (1952). The effects of psychotherapy: An evaluation. *Journal of Consulting Psychology, 16,* 319–324.

Firth, J., Shapiro, D. A., & Parry, G. (1986). The impact of research on the practice of psychotherapy. *British Journal of Psychotherapy, 2,* 169–179.

Friedlander, M. L., Thibodeau, J. R., & Ward, L. G. (1985). Discriminating the "good" from the "bad" therapy hour: A study of dyadic interaction. *Psychotherapy, 22,* 631–642.

Greenberg, L. S., & Pinsof, W. M. (1986). Process research: Current trends and future perspectives. In L. S. Greenberg & W. M. Pinsof (Eds.), *The psychotherapeutic process: A research handbook* (pp. 3–20). New York: Guilford Press.

Howard, K. I., Kopta, M. S., Krause, M. S., & Orlinsky, D. E. (1986). The dose-effect relationship in psychotherapy. *American Psychologist, 41,* 159–164.

Howard, K. I., Lueger, R. J., Maling, M. S., & Martinovich, Z. (1993). A phase model of psychotherapy outcome: Causal mediation of change. *Journal of Consulting and Clinical Psychology, 61,* 678–685.

Lyons, L. C., & Woods, P. J. (1991). The efficacy of rational-emotive therapy: A quantitative review of the outcome research. *Clinical Psychology Review, 11,* 357–369.

Mahrer, A. R. (1985). *Psychotherapeutic change: An alternative approach to meaning and measurement.* New York: Norton.

Mahrer, A. R. (1988). Research and clinical applications of "good moments" in psychotherapy. *Journal of Integrative and Eclectic Psychotherapy, 7,* 81–93.

Mahrer, A. R., & Nadler, W. P. (1986). Good moments in psychotherapy: A preliminary review, a list, and some promising research avenues. *Journal of Consulting and Clinical Psychology, 54,* 10–15.

Mahrer, A. R., White, M. V., Howard, M. T., Gagnon, R., & MacPhee, D. C. (1992). How to bring about some very good moments in psychotherapy sessions. *Psychotherapy Research, 2,* 252–265.

Malan, D. H. (1963). *A study of brief psychotherapy.* London: Tavistock.

Malan, D. H. (1976a). *The frontier of brief psychotherapy.* New York: Plenum.

Malan, D. H. (1976b). *Toward the validation of dynamic psychotherapy: A replication.* New York: Plenum.

McNeilly, C. L., & Howard, K. I. (1991). The effects of psychotherapy: A reevaluation based on dosage. *Psychotherapy Research, 1,* 74–78.

Orlinsky, D. E., & Howard K. I. (1967). The good therapy hour: Experiential correlates of patients' and therapists' evaluations of therapy sessions. *Archives of General Psychiatry, 16,* 621–632.

Orlinsky, D. E., & Howard, K. I. (1986). Process and outcome in psychotherapy. In S. L. Garfield & A. E. Bergin (Eds.), *Handbook of psychotherapy and behavior change* (3rd ed.; pp. 311–381). New York: Wiley.

Paul, G. L. (1967). Outcome research in psychotherapy. *Journal of Consulting Psychology, 31,* 109–118.

Rice, L. N., & Greenberg, L. S. (1984). *Patterns of change: Intensive analysis of psychotherapy process.* New York: Guilford Press.

Safran, J. D., McMain, S., Crocker, P., & Murray, P. (1990). Therapeutic alliance rupture as a therapy event for empirical investigation. *Psychotherapy, 27,* 154–165.

Shapiro, D. A., & Shapiro, D. (1982). Meta-analysis of comparative therapy outcome research: A critical appraisal. *Behavioral Psychotherapy, 10,* 4–25.

Smith, M. L., & Glass, G. V. (1977). Meta-analysis of psychotherapy outcome studies. *American Psychologist, 32,* 752–760.

Smith, M. L., Glass, G. V., & Miller, T. I. (1980). *The benefits of psychotherapy.* Baltimore, MD: Johns Hopkins University Press.

Uhlenhuth, E. H., & Duncan, D. B. (1968). Subjective change with medical student therapists: Some determinants of change in psychoneurotic outpatients. *Archives of General Psychiatry, 18,* 532–540.

Weisz, J. R., Weiss, B., Alicke, M. D., & Klotz, M. L. (1987). Effectiveness of psychotherapy with children and adolescents: A meta-analysis for clinicians. *Journal of Consulting and Clinical Psychology, 55,* 542–549.

Whitehorn, J. C. (1959). Goals of psychotherapy. In E. A. Rubinstein & M. B. Parloff (Eds.), *Research in psychotherapy.* Washington, DC: American Psychological Association.

CHAPTER 16

Conclusion

P. Forrest Talley, Hans H. Strupp, and Stephen F. Butler

IN REVIEWING the chapters of this book we looked for points of agreement among the contributors but found only a few. What stands out with the greatest clarity regarding the present relationship between research and practice is the clinicians' perspective that research is not significantly informative to the therapeutic enterprise and the researchers' view that clinicians have turned a deaf ear to meaningful empirical findings. We are not surprised that these two views have emerged, each held within opposing camps, for it was just these two views that prompted the development of this book.

Despite these differences about its current status, most of the authors agree that scientific inquiry at the very least offers the *promise* of becoming more clinically useful. What stands in the way of our ability to better fulfill this potential? Many of our contributors would argue that it is the frequently obscure meaning of clinical research findings. The scientific literature in psychotherapy is replete with articles about fascinating topics that leave one wondering what in the world they have to do with the actual practice of therapy.

We believe there are several reasons why psychotherapy research findings frequently appear to be inapplicable to practice, and when applicable are frequently ignored.[1] In this concluding chapter we briefly look at a few of these, limiting ourselves to the issues of research design, funding priorities, misapplication of research findings, and market forces in research and practice.

---

[1]We recognize that some psychotherapy research is not intended to have any direct applications to practice, and consequently we direct our comments throughout the chapter to those investigations that are so intended.

Research Design

Throughout this volume a single theme emerges again and again: to be clinically meaningful, research must provide a therapeutic context for its interpretation. This condition, however, is seldom met by traditional research investigations, which as a result, leave the practitioner with little practical guidance from the scientific camp. It is not, we would stress, that research provides no guidance at all to the practitioner. In fact, several authors in this volume have given clear examples of findings that are clinically important. Luborsky points out that antisocial personality disorder is the most difficult diagnosis to treat through psychotherapy, that the severity of diagnosis is strongly predictive of outcome, and that an early positive alliance between patient and therapist is highly correlated with outcome. Howard and Maling have supplied examples as well. They remind us that there is a significant relation between treatment outcome and total number of treatment hours and that the number of sessions per week is similarly related to therapeutic progress.

These are important findings, to be sure, and ones that should improve the quality of treatment. Yet they do not go far enough. When hearing such examples, the practitioner is right to request application guidelines and may well ask the following questions: If antisocial patients are the most difficult to treat, what do I do with a patient who has this diagnosis? Lower my goals? If a strong therapeutic alliance facilitates good outcomes, how do I build such an alliance, and do I take a different approach depending on specific patient qualities? If more sessions mean greater gains, this may be a general rule to follow, but does this apply to all my patients or just those who are most severely disturbed? How do I know if a patient needs fewer sessions?

In part, these questions of application arise because the clinical context provided with the research findings is insufficient. This raises the question of why the clinical context of research investigations is so frequently lost. After all, most psychotherapy researchers are also practicing clinicians, and in conversations with them about their research one is struck by the fact that the specific questions addressed in their studies are at least informed by, if not partially derived from, their clinical experiences. Therefore, a clinical context is implicit in the asking of the question.

We think that the clinical context in which most research questions are initially embedded is stripped away in the investigative process and that this outcome is largely due to methodological restrictions. Having long been the "poor relation" within the family of science and faced with a subject matter of enormous complexity and subtlety, psychological researchers have gained renown for their efforts to adhere to strict scientific canons of investigation. This labor is reflected in the methodologies that have been developed for research in psychotherapy and in the sometimes overwrought concerns that such methods are intended to address. A glance at any modern textbook on research design and analysis reveals a plethora of discussions about measurement error, reliability, confounding variables, demand versus expectancy effects, and so on. To deal with these and other concerns one finds a corresponding cornucopia of methods, including multigroup correlated-groups designs and factorial correlated-groups designs as well as designs involving matched groups, time series, interrupted time series, cross-lagged panels, within-subjects, and so on. Too often, it seems, the clinical meaning of research is sacrificed on the altar of methodological rigor. This is not worrisome when the purpose of the research is to investigate a theoretical issue, test the sensitivity of a particular research instrument, or investigate other matters similarly removed from clinical application. But there is a large body of research that is intended to have application to the practice of therapy, and we frequently find these efforts hampered by adherence to standards of methodological rigor that obscure the therapeutic context of their results.

This concern has been voiced by several contributors to this volume, who tend to single out group design methodology as the worst culprit when it comes to obscuring clinical context (although we can think of several statistical manipulations that are close runners-up). Group designs are criticized in this respect because they minimize individual differences, which is exactly what a researcher requires but what a clinician finds frustrating. Moreover, such studies often yield a glut of findings about an abstraction: an average patient in an average therapy with an average therapist about whom, on average, we know little.

The remedy for this problem is not to discard group methodologies, or other methods with similar shortcomings, for they clearly serve a valuable function for some investigative purposes. Instead, we suggest that alternative methodologies be employed as well and that their development be encouraged. Examples of the type of alternatives we have in mind are provided by the work of several contributors to this volume. Lester Luborsky's core conflictual relationship theme (CCRT) methodology readily comes to mind, as does Mardi Horowitz's configurational analysis. Each of these methods attempts to schematize, and thereby generalize, the interpersonal meaning and context of particular patients' dynamics and particular patient–therapist interactions. Still other methodologies that have recently been developed seem well suited for use as an adjunct to group design. The systematic case study approach of Elliott and Morrow-Bradley, for example, could be used for following up results derived from group research and for reestablishing a clinical context for their understanding. Although some of these methods are likely to sacrifice scientific rigor for greater clinical context, we are not concerned. As Kaplan (1964) has remarked, "It is less important to draw a fine line between what is 'scientific' and what is not than to cherish every opportunity for scientific growth. There is no need for behavioral science to tighten its immigration laws against subversive aliens. Scientific institutions are not so easily overthrown" (p. 28).

Funding

Many of the authors in this volume have endorsed process research as an approach that has the best chance of providing therapists with meaningful findings. This call for more process studies, as well as intensive small-sample investigations and case study analysis, has been present for several years now. And yet despite this sentiment among the research community, National Institute of Mental Health (NIMH) funding for these types of investigations fell dramatically between 1986 and 1991 (Wolfe, 1993a, 1993b). Those receiving the *least* financial support were investigators of therapist–patient interactions and their contributions to the therapeutic change process. During this same time period funding for other psychosocial research increased. It is ironic that precisely the kind of research recommended by many authors in this book is the kind of research that has not been financially supported by NIMH.[2]

Our impression is that this trend is partly due to the bias within NIMH toward funding studies with practical applications. For NIMH, however, practical investigations are marked by research designs that emulate those used in medicine. Within psychotherapy research this means those studies that use a group design (most often seen in clinical trials research). As we have argued earlier in this chapter, it is just this type of methodology that frequently fails to produce practical results for the clinician. The disjunction between goals and methods advocated by NIMH is somewhat ironic, and it does not further the goal of making research results more directly applicable to clinical practice.

Misapplication of Research Findings

Another troubling issue, often ignored but growing more pressing, is the use of research results by third-party payers in a manner that is detrimental to the interests of patients and therapists alike. Elliott and Morrow-Bradley make the point that managed-care institutions have justified questionable restrictions on patient care through the myopic selection of psychotherapy research findings.[3] The use of research by the managed care industry is marked

---

[2]There is some evidence that recent NIMH requests for applications reflect a more congenial attitude toward process research.

[3]It is worth noting as well that managed-care companies claim to have achieved in a few short years what scores of psychotherapists have been unable to accomplish over the course of several decades, namely, the goal of finding wide-ranging and specific applications for psychotherapy research.

by a blissful insensibility to limitations in applicability. For instance, the out-comes of studies using a narrow range of patient types are routinely general-ized to substance-abusing, suicidal, personality-disordered patients with multiple diagnoses and severe social deficits. Yet for purposes of research these kinds of patients with complicated diagnoses are generally avoided. In such instances, the failure of managed care corporations to appreciate the limitations of the data works against therapists and patients alike.

Consider, for example, the NIMH Collaborative Study for the Treatment of Depression (Elkin, Shea, Watkins, et al., 1989), whose results were repre-sented in the lay press as confirming the assertion that "depression can now be cured in 16 sessions." However, a follow-up study of depression (Frank, Kupfer, Perel, et al., 1990) has provided strong evidence that unipolar de-pression requires longer-term treatment in order to forestall a significant re-lapse rate. In that study, Frank et al. reported that even monthly sessions of interpersonal therapy significantly extended survival time, tripling the me-dian survival time from 21 weeks (medication clinic with placebo drugs) to 54 weeks (therapy alone) to 74 weeks (therapy plus placebo drugs). The best survival rates resulted from continued treatment involving either medica-tion clinic with imipramine, or interpersonal therapy plus imipramine. To conclude on the basis of one clinical trial that 16 weeks of treatment is all that is needed appears to be a gross and misleading overgeneralization.

Market Forces

Research and practice share the common purpose of seeking to explain the following kinds of questions: How has a patient's psychopathology devel-oped? In what way does it currently influence a patient's life? What accounts for the changes, good and bad, seen in a patient's state of well-being? So why is it that two enterprises sharing similar questions fail to reciprocally in-fluence one another more strongly? Part of the answer is that each enterprise speaks to a different audience—patients versus scientific colleagues.

Although each of these audiences may share a common concern—for ex-ample, how best to alleviate situational depression—each will also have dis-tinct preferences for how the question should be framed and investigated, how results should be evaluated, and what evidence should be accepted as valid. It follows that one's success in addressing the issue of depression will be judged by very different standards. Clinicians and researchers approach similar questions in different ways because of the distinct preferences and standards of acceptance held by the audience they serve.

This issue is most clearly seen in scientific psychology, where the very structure of research implies a shared set of values concerning the questions that can be meaningfully addressed, how they are to be conceptualized, the methods by which they are to be answered, and so on. Adherence to these norms is vital for individuals who hope to win credibility in their field, for without credibility a researcher's prospects for professional recognition, promotion, and extramural funding are dim.

Similar forces are at work in clinical practice. The audience to whom the clinician must answer is composed first and foremost of patients. They expect understanding, and in the light of that understanding they further expect to find solutions to their problems in living and relief from their suffering. Patient and therapist form an alliance, both committed to relieving the former's distress. In this endeavor both recognize the patient's privileged position of being the final arbiter of what is true or false, helpful or benign, pertinent or irrelevant. The patient's role in this process thereby affects the strategy of exploration, the way questions are framed, the evidence collected, and even the language used to describe the endeavor. The result is that this process differs markedly from that in which the researcher becomes engaged when struggling with a similar question. Not only do these differences exist, but the structure of psychotherapy demands that different rules of inquiry and explanation be exercised. If the standards of research were applied to answering questions within an individual therapy, very little would ever be said, for these standards are virtually impossible to meet in such a setting. If practitioners cannot speak to the patient's needs, it is unlikely that their services will be in demand. Consequently, it behooves the clinician to adhere to standards of inquiry and explanation that fulfill the patient's expectations, even if they are not compatible with standards applied in research settings.

In sum, the clinician's standards and methods of inquiry must be supportive of the successful practice of psychotherapy as judged by patients, just as the standards used by researchers must be supportive of successful research as judged by scientific colleagues. These "market forces" pull therapists and researchers to intellectually and behaviorally approach the solution to common problems in very different ways. These solutions, and the methods by which they are brought about, are frequently not compatible with one another, thereby adding to the gap between research and practice.

Future Directions

There are formidable barriers to a rapprochement between research and practice, and they require our attention. There are, however, strong indications for believing that interest in this impasse will quicken in the next few years, the chief motivating force being the growing financial dependence of the two factions. As mentioned earlier, within the clinical arena there is increasing pressure to provide empirical evidence to justify clinical decisions (for example, type of therapy provided, length of therapy, and frequency of sessions). This result derives both from the greater involvement of managed care companies and from the need for practitioners to protect themselves in an increasingly competitive and litigious society.

In a similar vein, researchers are increasingly expected to prove that tax-payers' money supporting their studies has been money well spent. In the case of psychotherapy researchers the question is, Have results of their efforts provided new information that can significantly improve the care of mental health patients? As contributors to this volume have pointed out, there are other potential benefits of psychotherapy research, but this question remains central and the answer one gives has profound implications.

The cost of not addressing the gap that separates practice and research is great, and it is becoming more fateful. Yet, to the great benefit of all, the field seems to be moving to confront the issue. In conclusion, we would like to add some suggestions for steps that might prove helpful.

1. The development of clear methods of constructing case studies and the explication of different conceptual strategies for their analyses is sorely needed. To be most helpful, case studies should be developed with the same conceptual rigor we expect of other psychological studies, albeit using different methods and constructs. Edelson's (1988) work is recommended for those interested in pursuing this topic (see especially chapters 9 and 11).[4] Edelson shows that the case study framework for inquiry does not preclude the formulation and testing of specific hypotheses. He also proposes criteria for judging the veracity of these hypotheses, including the vanquished-rival argument, the risky-prediction argument, the convergence argument, and so on. Most importantly, he notes the significance of specifying what observations would count as evidence against the hypotheses put forward (à la falsifiability). As frequently mentioned in this and other chapters, the analysis of an individual patient affords a perspective on treatment that is missing in other types of studies; because it is at the level of the individual case that practitioners learn most about therapy, it clearly behooves us to make more strenuous efforts to utilize this form of investigation.

2. When possible, research papers should include brief vignettes and case studies to illustrate the clinical import of a question being investigated or the possible application of a result.

---

[4]Some might think it preposterous to compare the academic worth of clinical observation and analysis to empirical study. It is therefore interesting to note that Paul Meehl (1978), one of the most rigorous dust bowl empiricists, is much more impressed with Freud's clinical observations than with the majority of statistics that embellish the pages of our scientific journals.

3. It is necessary to investigate what *types* of research are most helpful to clinicians and what makes them so. The possibilities are virtually endless—process research, outcome research, research by diagnostic category, and so on.

4. Efforts need to be made to better understand how to disseminate knowledge to clinicians in a way that is most readily accessible and understandable. It may be that the trend toward the creation of manuals to assist therapists will partially meet this need, and this trend can be further expanded.

5. Training programs should include instruction on how to make greater clinical use of research results. A complementary effort is required to teach young researchers how to conduct an investigation that has clinical applicability.

In sum, the marriage of research and practice is still more of a wish than a reality. Profound obstacles stand in the way of meaningfully linking these two enterprises. As a community of mental health professionals, however, we have been lax in our efforts to address this rift. This laxity stands as an anomaly within a professional group that prides itself on improving communication skills. Surely this intradisciplinary lacuna is worthy of our attention. The good news is that it is just this sort of problem that psychology is well equipped to solve.

REFERENCES

Edelson, M. (1988). *Psychoanalysis: A theory in crisis.* Chicago: University of Chicago Press.

Elkin, I., Shea, T., Watkins, J. T., Imber, S. D., Sotsky, S. M., Collins, J. F., Glass, D. R., Pilkonis, P. A., Leber, W. R., Docherty, J. R., Fiester, S. J., Parloff, M. B. (1989). National Institute of Mental Health Treatment of Depression Collaborative Research Program: General effectiveness of treatments. *Archives of General Psychiatry, 46,* 971–982.

Frank, E., Kupfer, D., Perel, J. M., Cornes, C., Jarrett, D. B., Mallinger, A. G., Thase, E. M., McEachran, A. B., Grochocinski, V. J. (1990). Three-year outcomes for maintenance therapies in recurrent depression. *Archives of General Psychiatry, 46,* 1093–1099.

Kaplan, A. (1964). *The conduct of inquiry.* San Francisco: Chandler.

Meehl, P. E. (1978). Theoretical risks and tabular asterisks: Sir Karl, Sir Ronald, and the slow progress of soft psychology. *Journal of Consulting and Clinical Psychology, 26,* 806–834.

Wolfe, B. (1993a). Psychotherapy research funding for fiscal years 1986–1990. *Psychotherapy and Rehabilitation Research Bulletin, 1,* 7–9.

Wolfe, B. (1993b). Psychosocial treatment and rehabilitation research funding for fiscal year 1991. *Psychotherapy and Rehabilitation Research Bulletin, 1,* 10–11.

Name Index

Subject Index

Acting out, in borderline personality disorder (BPD), 46, 50

Adjustment disorders, 126

Affect, in borderline personality disorder (BPD), 40, 42

Affective disorder, borderline personality disorder (BPD) as variant of, 41, 42

Anecdotal reports, in research, 24–28, 251

Anger in borderline personality disorder (BPD), 40, 41, 42

Anticonvulsant medications, in borderline personality disorder (BPD), 46

Antidepressant medications, in borderline personality disorder (BPD), 46

Antisocial personality disorder: borderline personality disorder (BPD) and, 43–44; psychotherapy treatment of, 177

Anxiety, Freud's theories of, 14–15

Associations, observational models of, 33–34

Audiotapes: analysis of interpretation using, 187, 189, 190; borderline personality disorder (BPD) treatment on, 51–52

Axis I disorders, with borderline personality disorder (BPD), 41, 44, 47

Axis II disorders, with borderline personality disorder (BPD), 43–44, 47

Behavioral therapies, research foundation for, 102

Benzodiazepines, in borderline personality disorder (BPD), 46

Borderline personality disorder (BPD): audiotaping and videotaping of therapists treating, 47–48, 51–52; Axis I comorbidity with, 41, 44, 47; Axis II comorbidity with, 41, 43–44, 47; borderline personality organization (BPO) and, 42–44; clinical research objectives for, 47–48; cognitive-behavioral approach to, 45; differences of therapist's personal style in approach to, 54; differential therapeutics of, 40–47; DSM–III–R criteria for, 40–41, 56; duration of treatment of, 46; factor analysis of criteria for, 41–42; format of treatment of, 45; goals of treatment of, 45–46; interest in research on, 126; interpretation in, 49–50; medications tried with, 46; psychodynamic